KARL BARTH, THE JEWS, AND JUDAISM

# Karl Barth, the Jews, and Judaism

*edited by*

George Hunsinger

WILLIAM B. EERDMANS PUBLISHING COMPANY
GRAND RAPIDS, MICHIGAN

Wm. B. Eerdmans Publishing Co.
4035 Park East Court SE, Grand Rapids, MI 49546
www.eerdmans.com

© 2018 George Hunsinger
All rights reserved

Hardcover edition 2018
Paperback edition 2019

ISBN 978-0-8028-7718-5

**Library of Congress Cataloging-in-Publication Data**

Names: Hunsinger, George, editor.
Title: Karl Barth, the Jews, and Judaism / edited by George Hunsinger.
Description: Grand Rapids : Eerdmans Publishing Co., 2018. | Includes bibliographical references and index.
Identifiers: LCCN 2017034285 | ISBN 9780802877185 (pbk. : alk. paper)
Subjects: LCSH: Barth, Karl, 1886-1968. | Christianity and other religions—Judaism. | Judaism—Relations—Christianity. | Judaism (Christian theology)
Classification: LCC BX4827.B3 K3825 2018 | DDC 261.2/6092—dc23
LC record available at https://lccn.loc.gov/2017034285

## Contents

*Preface* — vii

1. How Jewish Was Karl Barth?
   DAVID NOVAK — 1

2. Karl Barth and the Jews: The History of a Relationship
   EBERHARD BUSCH — 24

3. A Dialogue between David Novak and Eberhard Busch
   GEORGE HUNSINGER — 37

4. After Barth: A Christian Appreciation of Jews and Judaism
   GEORGE HUNSINGER — 60

5. To Love Tanakh Is Love Enough for the Jews:
   Reflection on *Dabru Emet*
   PETER OCHS — 75

6. Karl Barth and the Early Postwar Interfaith
   Encounters, 1945–1950
   VICTORIA J. BARNETT — 103

7. The Divine Vocation and Destiny of Israel in World History
   THOMAS F. TORRANCE — 118

8. Light from Saint Paul on Christian-Jewish Relations
   C. E. B. CRANFIELD — 128

CONTENTS

9. From Anti-Semitism to Theological Dialogue
   HANS KÜNG                                          138

10. Toward Ending Enmity
    ELLEN T. CHARRY                                   147

    *Appendix*—Dabru Emet: *A Jewish Statement
    on Christians and Christianity*                   173

    *Contributors*                                    177

    *Acknowledgments*                                 179

    *Index*                                           180

*Preface*

This volume arose from a conference held at Princeton Theological Seminary in June of 2014. The highlight of the conference was the papers given by David Novak, the preeminent Jewish theologian, and Eberhard Busch, Karl Barth's distinguished biographer and interpreter. Their papers are included in this volume along with the transcript of an evening dialogue between them. Other papers from the conference are included as well, along with some previously published essays to round things out. Further papers from the conference, more historical than theological in perspective, are slated to appear in a second volume entitled *Karl Barth: Post-Holocaust Theologian?*, edited by George Hunsinger (T. & T. Clark, 2018).

Chapter 1, by David Novak, offers an intriguing account of how Karl Barth might help Jewish theologians to fulfill their distinctively Jewish vocations as Jews.

Chapter 2, by Eberhard Busch, draws on original archival research to enrich our understanding of the risks and challenges that Barth faced in acting on behalf of the endangered Jews in the earliest period of the Third Reich.

Chapter 3 presents the transcript of the conference dialogue between David Novak and Eberhard Busch as moderated by George Hunsinger. The dialogue was not only theologically rich but also moving for both partners as well as for the audience.

Chapter 4, by George Hunsinger, attempts to think with Barth and through Barth, but also beyond and against him, in proposing a new theological basis, based on the love of Christ, for Christians to stand in solidarity with Jews.

In chapter 5, Peter Ochs reflects on *Dabru Emet*, which, along with David Novak, he helped to write. It is a breakthrough document of remarkably generous proportions for renewing Jewish-Christian relations. Ochs discusses it with verve and wisdom.

In chapter 6, Victoria J. Barnett brings her incomparable historical knowledge and research to bear on how Barth made an impact on Jewish-Christian dialogues in the immediate post–World War II period.

Chapter 7, by Thomas F. Torrance, adds depth from the side of Christian theology by implicitly drawing upon but also significantly revising Barth. For reasons of space, this essay appears in an abbreviated form, which required simplifying the syntax and paraphrasing or interpreting elements of the longer original.

Chapter 8, by C. E. B. Cranfield, the distinguished New Testament scholar who often drew upon Calvin and Barth, considers some positive contributions that the Pauline epistles might offer to Jewish-Christian relations today.

Chapter 9, by Hans Küng, the famous Roman Catholic theologian, who, like Busch, Torrance, and Cranfield, was a close student of Barth's works, takes a powerful stand, in a remarkable act of theological repentance, against the grievous history of Christian anti-Semitism.

Chapter 10, by Ellen T. Charry, affords a rare glimpse into what at least one strand of Christian theology might have looked like if some of Paul's earliest opponents had prevailed. The essay, which no Christian can afford to neglect, is provocative, revisionary, and unsettling.

An appendix reprints the text of *Dabru Emet*, which is still required reading, especially by Christians, for any future Jewish-Christian dialogue.

# 1

## How Jewish Was Karl Barth?

DAVID NOVAK

### A Seemingly Impertinent Question

Isn't it rather impertinent of me to question how Jewish Karl Barth was, since everybody knows that Karl Barth was not a Jew? Would it not be more appropriate to ask what Karl Barth thought about the Jews and Judaism (the two were never separate in his theological mind), that is, the Torah that defines the Jews as the people God wants them to be? To ask that question is to look at Barth, the greatest Christian thinker of his time, looking at the Jewish people and Judaism as that which no Christian, certainly no Christian thinker, can ever overcome or be overcome by. For answers to this more evident question, however, we already have the important studies of Friedrich-Wilhelm Marquardt, Eberhard Busch, and Katherine Sonderegger.[1] These studies deal with *what* Barth thought *about* the Jewish people and Judaism.

Nevertheless, my question is not *what* Barth thought *about* the Jews and Judaism. It is *how* Barth thought *like* a Jewish thinker thinks or ought to think *of* the Torah, the object of common concern to both Jews and Christians. This doesn't mean that I am suggesting Barth thought *as* a Jewish thinker, as a kind of "invisible Jew," any more than I am implying that Jewish thinkers who appreciate Barth are to be considered "invisible Christians." That notwithstanding, I not only admire Barth's respectful and insightful treatment of the Jews and Judaism, but even more do I

---

1. F.-W. Marquardt, *Die Entdeckung des Judentums für christliche Theologie: Israel im Denken Karl Barths* (Munich: Chr. Kaiser Verlag, 1967); E. Busch, *Unter dem Bogen des einen Bundes: Karl Barth und die Juden 1933–1945* (Neukirchen-Vluyn: Neukirchener Verlag, 1996); K. Sonderegger, *That Jesus Christ Was Born a Jew: Karl Bath's "Doctrine of Israel"* (University Park: Pennsylvania State University Press, 1992).

*sympathize* with him, that is, I try to think *with* him *of* what gives each of us as a Christian or as a Jew, *mutatis mutandis*, our definition, task, and goal in the world. In that sense, I learn much from Barth for the sake of my Jewish thought, which is like the way some of Barth's living disciples (some of whom are, happily, here with us now) do learn from Jewish thinkers for the sake of their Christian thought. (As is by now well known, Barth himself had very little contact with Jewish thinkers, which might explain some anti-Judaism that emerged from time to time in his work.)[2]

When dealing with what Barth thought about Jews and Judaism, Barth is the thinking subject and we Jews are the object of his thought; but when it comes to sympathy, both Barth and we Jews are the thinking subjects intentionally approaching the Torah, our shared object, similarly. That is why in this enterprise one party is not talking *about* the other. Instead, each of us can truly speak *to* one another *of* a common object of deepest concern, but which neither of us can claim to be their exclusive possession. "Then shall those who are in awe of the LORD speak each to their neighbor, and the LORD will pay attention and listen; and a book of remembrance will be written for him for those who are in awe of the LORD and consider his name" (Mal. 3:16).[3]

To engage in this kind of sympathetic discourse is for each of us to think *like* the other *along with* the other, yet being ever aware that objective commonality does not entail subjective identity. For our discourse is *analogical*, which means that to say that "A is like B" does not mean "A equals B." An analogy is not an equation. For us, this is the true meaning of the much-used word "dialogue." *Dialogue* is our common speaking of the word (*logos*) that is always to be present in our midst (*dia*) even before we speak of it. In fact, the word is there (*dasein*) speaking to us, whether we speak of it or not, even though its truth can only become manifest through our

---

2. See Marquardt, *Die Entdeckung des Judentums*, 335; Michael Wyschogrod, "Why Was and Is the Theology of Karl Barth of Interest to a Jewish Theologian?" in *Footnotes to a Theology: The Karl Barth Colloquium of 1972*, ed. M. Rumscheidt (Waterloo, ON: Corporation for the Publication of Academic Studies in Religion in Canada, 1974), 95–111; and most positively, Kurt Anders Richardson, *Reading Karl Barth* (Grand Rapids: Baker Academic, 2004), 219: "One can only be reminded of the failures of any theologian . . . [but] Barth is neither anti-Semitic nor anti-Jewish. Instead, he is both Pauline and apocalyptic in the vein of Luke." Surely, this is evidenced by Barth's vehement opposition to the Nazis, and by his recognition of the state of Israel (see Busch, *Karl Barth*, 493).

3. All translations, unless otherwise noted, are by the author.

speaking of it together (*dialegein*).⁴ That is quite different from the usual notion of "dialogue" as our talking about our own talking.⁵ Here, conversely, we are speaking to each other about an object we ourselves have not bespoken, but which we have heard spoken to us, sometimes similarly and sometimes differently. Accordingly, being a traditional Jew, I can only engage in a truly sympathetic dialogue with Christians *qua* Christians who affirm that the Hebrew Scriptures express the word of God.

Before getting to Barth, I need to tell you that some in my own tradition would seriously question any traditional, law-abiding Jew having this kind of common theological engagement with any gentile. After all, the Talmud rules that it is forbidden to teach the Torah to gentiles (let alone to learn Torah from gentiles).⁶ And, even though the Talmud permits discussion of the Noachian commandments with gentiles, these commandments are quite practical, mostly what Judaism teaches that gentiles ought not to do.⁷ But what I want to talk with Barth about is quite theoretical. To be sure, it is not without practical implications, yet it is not simply a matter of applied ethics or morality.

Fortunately, Maimonides comes to my rescue. In a responsum, he argues that the Talmudic prohibition of learning Torah with gentiles does not apply to Christians.⁸ Why? Because Christians accept the entire Written Torah, that is, the Hebrew Scriptures or "Old Testament," to be the revealed word of God fully, whereas Muslims (with whom Maimonides seems to have more philosophical commonality) regard it to be at best

---

4. Cf. Plato, *Apology* 29A; *Crito* 48E.

5. See David Novak, "What to Seek and What to Avoid in Jewish-Christian Dialogue," in *Christianity in Jewish Terms*, ed. T. Frymer-Kensky et al. (Boulder, CO: Westview Press, 2000), 1–6; also in David Novak, *Talking with Christians: Musings of a Jewish Theologian* (Grand Rapids: Eerdmans, 2005), 1–7. In this latter volume there are two previous essays on Barth, viz., "Before Revelation: The Rabbis, Paul, and Karl Barth," 108–26 (first published in the *Journal of Religion* 71 [1991]: 50–66), and "Karl Barth on Divine Command: A Jewish Response," 127–45 (first published in the *Scottish Journal of Theology* 54 [2001]: 463–83).

6. Babylonian Talmud (hereafter B.): Sanhedrin 59a re Deut. 33:4.

7. See David Novak, *The Image of the Non-Jew in Judaism*, ed. M. LaGrone, 2nd ed. (Oxford: Littman Library of Jewish Civilization, 2011), esp. 36–143.

8. Maimonides, *Teshuvot ha-Rambam*, no. 149, ed. Y. Blau (Jerusalem: Meqitsei Nirdamim, 1960), 1:284–85); also, David Novak, *Jewish-Christian Dialogue: A Jewish Justification* (New York: Oxford University Press, 1989), 64–67. Nevertheless, despite Maimonides's opinion, generally modern Jewish traditionalists were very uncomfortable with the notion that Jews and Christians could study Torah together in good faith. See, e.g., David Zvi Hoffmann, *Melamed Le-ho'il: Responsa* 2 (Frankfurt am Main: Hermon, 1926), no. 77, pp. 82–83.

a faulty, partial, imperfect revelation. And, as for the pagans whom the Talmud means by the term *goyyim*, they recognize no revelation at all, not acknowledging the unique Creator God, an acknowledgment the acceptance or reception of revelation presupposes. This acknowledgment might well be what Calvin called *sensus divinitatis*.[9] But without this acknowledgment, there can be no true theological dialogue, neither with ancient nor with modern pagans.

Truth be told, though, in this responsum especially, Maimonides sees the purpose of such Scripture-based "dialogue" to be Jews teaching gentiles about what Jews think are your erroneous interpretations of our commonly accepted revelation. In fact, he sees this kind of scripturally based dialogue to have the potential to bring Christians back to their Jewish origins. As such, Jews have everything to teach the gentiles but nothing to learn from them. Nevertheless, if all your interpretations were unacceptable to us, we would have no common text to talk about or even argue about. We would be talking, in fact, about two different texts.[10] Therefore, there must be some significant parts of the common scriptural text that we do or can interpret similarly so we can then designate those other parts of Scripture that we can argue about. But, when we talk together of the Scripture we do hold in common, there need be no proselytizing agenda at all in our dialogue. We can teach and learn together with "no strings attached."

In an age when we had much to fear from one another, we had to defend ourselves from any attempt of the threatening other to take our Torah away from us, to "pull the rug upon which we stand from out under us." That is what made our scripturally centered "dialogues" in reality disputa-

---

9. *Institutes of the Christian Religion* 1.3. Though famous for his rejection of "natural theology," Barth still recognized that for humans to be able to receive the revelation of the one true God, they have to be able to distinguish "that which nothing greater can be thought of" (*id quo maius nequit cogitari potest*) from any other god they might think of (which would be idolatrous if they think of that "other god" as real). Thus humans have to understand the minimal meaning of the name "God," even before they can experience the presence of the real referent of that name. When humans recognize the *possibility* (but not the necessity) of that name having a real referent, it could be said that they are in their prerevelation "state of nature" (*status naturalis*). That recognition might well be a kind of "natural theology" that Barth could accept. See his *Fides Quarens Intellectum*, trans. I. W. Robertson (London: SCM, 1960), passim.

10. The rabbis did recognize that Jews cannot claim exclusive possession of the Written Torah. See Palestinian Talmud (hereafter Y.): Pe'ah 1:6/17a and Hagigah 1:8/76d; *Tanhuma*: Ki Tissa 34 re Exod. 34:27 and Hos. 8:12; also, Saul Lieberman, *Hellenism in Jewish Palestine* (New York: Jewish Theological Seminary of America, 1962), 207-8.

tions. But in our age, due to a variety of historical factors, we have much less to fear from each other. Thus we can concentrate on what the other can teach us of the Torah that is as much yours as it is ours. And, whereas in more disputational times we had to bracket what we had in common while being ever mindful of it, in these more dialogical times we have to bracket what divides us while being ever mindful of it.

In more disputational times, the danger to be wary of, for Christians, was Marcionism: that total break with the God of Israel, the Torah of Israel, and the people Israel. For Jews, the danger was looking at you Christians as if you were no different from the pagans the Talmud warns us to avoid.

In more dialogical times, the danger to be wary of, for both Jews and Christians, is "Religion," which for many in the modern world is a genus of which Judaism, Christianity, Islam, and other "religions" are taken to be species or subsets therein. Yet there is no overarching process that simply envelops each of us, and many others as well. For those who propose such an overarching process, that process takes each of us to be an expendable example or instance of itself, a process that could easily exist without either of us.

I think we needed to carefully delineate the context of our discourse *with* Barth before we can intelligently take up the content of that discourse.

## Revelation and the Imitation of God: Barth and the Rabbinic Tradition

When I first began to read Barth's *Church Dogmatics*, I found myself especially fascinated by the paragraphs in small print. That is where, as you all know, Barth is usually engaged in very close exegesis of biblical texts. And what fascinated me most was how he interpreted passages from the Old Testament, where he seemed to be talking like a rabbi (and, oh, what a rabbi he would have made!). Yet I soon learned that Barth had no real contact with the rabbinic writings. So, was I reading into Barth what I wanted to see in him, perhaps justifying my reading him when all my time should have been devoted to the Talmud? But then it dawned on me that this similarity between Barth and the rabbis, though not intended by Barth nor even something of which he was likely aware, was because Barth was reading Scripture *like* the rabbis read Scripture. *How* the rabbis read Scripture, that is, as a revealed seamless garment, is *how* Barth read Scripture. Hence their concurrence on many key points of doctrine was not accidental. Not only did the rabbis and Barth revere the same text, but they also struggled with the same theological problems their careful reverential reading of the text raised in their minds.

Let us now look at a rather well-known scriptural text and do three things in connection with it: (1) See how some rabbinic interpreters of this text and Barth were thinking quite similarly. (2) See how Barth interprets this text in a way that enables him to better differentiate between Hebraic theology and Hellenic philosophy (even when that philosophy is appropriated by Jewish or Christian theologians) on the question of *what is good*. (3) See how the one Jewish thinker with whom Barth did have profound contact—his Marburg teacher, Hermann Cohen (but with whom Barth studied philosophy, not Jewish theology)—was actually less Jewish in his interpretation of this text than was his Christian student.[11]

The scriptural text is from Micah 6:8. "It has been told to you, O man [*adam*], what is good [*mah tov*] and what the LORD requires of you [*doresh mimmekha*]: but to do justice [*asot mishpat*], loving kindness [*ahavat hesed*], and walking humbly [*hatsne'a lekhet*] with your God." Note carefully what Barth says about this scriptural verse. "The man who, according to Micah 6:8, has been told what is good, is not man as such and in general [*im Allgemeinem*], but Israelite man, the people of Israel. That which is required of him ... is not, therefore, the compendium of a natural duty incumbent on men [*Menschenpflicht*] generally, but ... the demand which is proclaimed and established and enforced by the fact that God has chosen this people, and Himself to be the God of this people."[12]

Let us now analyze and explicate the points Barth is making here in this comment, in which no word seems to be wasted.

First, "the man" (*adam*) being told what is good is not the humankind per se personified in the first "Adam," but it is the Jewish people personified in each and every individual Jew.[13] That is implied by the words "it has been told to you [*higgid lekha*]," that is, this truth has been given to you,

---

11. See Busch, *Karl Barth*, 44–56, about Barth's student days at the University of Marburg, where his theology professor, Wilhelm Herrmann (1846–1922), was a close colleague of and interlocutor with Hermann Cohen (1842–1918).

12. *Church Dogmatics* (hereafter *CD*) II/2, trans. G. W. Bromiley et al. (Edinburgh: T. & T. Clark, 1957), 572 = *Kirchliche Dogmatik* (hereafter *KD*) II/2 (Zürich: Evangelischer Verlag, 1948), 635.

13. Actually, there are places in the rabbinic writings where *adam* is interpreted as "man" or "human being." See, e.g., B. Sanhedrin 59a re Lev. 18:5 and *Tosafot*, s.v. "ela he'adam"; B. Yevamot 61a and *Tosafot*, s.v. "v'ein."

then received by you, not taken by you at your own initiative, and it is certainly not your own invention. It is not, as Barth puts it, "a matter for our own discovery [*Entdeckung*] but for His revelation [*seiner eigenem Offenbarung*]."[14] However, if this verse were speaking of man in general, there would be no need to speak of what the Jews have "been told," for since the Tower of Babel there has been no united human community that could be the recipient of any such general revelation. Revelation is a special event, occurring at a unique time and place, and experienced by a unique people. As Barth emphasizes (in the large print): "We do not know God otherwise than as acting God—we have to understand divine action, and therefore an event [*ein Ereignis*]—not a reality which is, but a reality which occurs [*eine geschehende Wirklichkeit*]."[15] Humans in general, though, are the subjects of only ordinary experience, what regularly occurs anywhere at any time and place. It is from this ordinary experience that some philosophers try to infer some timeless truth that, in principle, could be found by anyone. But that is not what—better, Who—finds or locates some but not others. In other words, the people of Israel and revelation are correlates: the people's identity, task, and goal in the world are the result of being elected by God to be given his Torah; and the Torah would remain in heaven were there no people on earth to whom it could be given and who were capable of receiving it and living by its teachings, however imperfectly.

Second, not only is the subject of this telling somebody rather than anybody, not only is their being told different from their discovery (and certainly from their invention), but "what" (*mah*) they have been told is different from what they could have told themselves or could have been told by anyone else but God. Just as those directly addressed by God are unique and not "men as such and in general," and just as the method of this address is unique and not a process of general experience and inference therefrom, so the content of the message being addressed to this people is not "a natural duty incumbent on men generally." But what differentiates a commandment from this choosing God from a "natural duty"? And, what is a natural duty?

It would seem that a natural duty is something ordinary people, who are not sociopaths, can accept as the minimal requirements of a decent human life lived with others, because it is others whom such a decent person needs and therefore wants to live with in peace (what some have

---

14. *CD* II/2, 666 = *KD* II/2, 742.
15. *CD* II/2, 548 = *KD* II/2, 609.

called *mitsein*). A "duty" is something I owe others (best expressed by the Hebrew word *hovah*, meaning both a "debt" and a "duty").[16] Minimally, I owe these others not to do "what is hateful to me," for if they were to do that to me, I could not live with them in peace.[17] Without the acceptance of this natural duty, which is the duty humans, as naturally social beings, owe one another, our lives together would become a Hobbesian state of war (*bellum omnium contra omnes*), where persons live in a state of paralyzing terror of each other.[18] But that in and of itself does not require an acknowledgment of the commanding/requiring God. As Maimonides put it, this is a matter to which "human reason inclines" (*ha-da'at noteh*).[19] This is what Thomas Aquinas called *inclinatio naturalis*, which for humans is primarily *inclinatio rationalis*.[20] Nevertheless, that does not necessarily involve an acknowledgment that this is what God commands, that this is what God requires of us.

Now, in the rabbinic tradition, there are two different ways of acknowledging what God has commanded one to do.

The first way is the way of halakah, that is, the commandments of God represented as law (which is what *torah* means *qua nomos*), that is, as precepts (*mitsvot*).[21] In performing a commandment or precept this way, one acknowledges God to be the source of the commandment by reciting the prescribed blessing (*berakhah*) immediately beforehand. One is to say: "Blessed art Thou, O Lord our God, king of the cosmos [*melekh ha'olam*], who has sanctified us through His commandments, commanding us to do X." Nevertheless, Maimonides rules that the recitation of this blessing is required only when performing a time-bound commandment involving the direct relationship of a Jew with God, like the sanctification of the Sabbath day (*qiddush*) over wine at the outset of the Sabbath on Friday evening.[22] But in commandments involving interhuman relationships—like "doing justice" and "loving kindness" (i.e., doing acts of kindness to one's neighbor

---

16. See, e.g., Y. Pe'ah 1:1/15d re Exod. 20:12.
17. B. Shabbat 31a, i.e., "What you would hate to have done to you, do not do to somebody else." For the difference between this universal, natural duty and the specifically commanded "You shall love your neighbor as yourself" (Lev. 19:18), see David Novak, *Covenantal Rights* (Princeton: Princeton University Press, 2000), 119–21.
18. See Hobbes, *Leviathan*, chap. 13.
19. Mishneh Torah (hereafter MT): Kings, 9.1.
20. *Summa Theologiae* 2/1, q. 94, a. 2.
21. See Lieberman, *Hellenism in Jewish Palestine*, 83–84.
22. MT: Blessings, 11.2.

lovingly)—then the blessing is not to be said.²³ Now there could be two reasons for this differentiation. (1) Since the direct object of the commandments involving interhuman relationships is another human person, that other person deserves our full and undivided attention. God, as it were, is willing to step back in this kind of human interpersonal situation and let the human persons there confront one another directly.²⁴ (2) Since doing justice and loving kindness could be done and are done by persons who do not acknowledge their acts to be divine commandments, one cannot say that at the prima facie level the act itself requires an acknowledgment of its divine source. Thus, in another discussion, Maimonides states that only when one wants to affirm the metaphysical foundation of the law is the acknowledgment of the divine source necessary.

The second way of acknowledging the divine character of the commandment is the way of haggadah (which is what *torah* means *qua Lehre*, or "teaching").²⁵ Now haggadah refers to the narrations—the stories or "tellings"—in Scripture and the rabbinic writings: Talmud and midrashim. The best-known expression of haggadah is the Passover haggadah, or "Passover story," which is to be retold by every Jewish family on the first nights of the Passover festival. These narrations are especially significant theologically when they speak of God's interactions with humans in the world. "Haggadah" comes from the verb "to tell" (*nagad*), as in "It has been told to you" (*higgid lekha*), which is the beginning of Micah 6:8. Along these lines, Barth is quite insightful when he speaks of "the demand which is proclaimed and established and enforced *by the fact* that God has chosen this people of Israel to be His people."²⁶ Indeed, that is what the Passover haggadah is all about.

But how is a command that has been "told" different from a commandment that has been prescribed through law? Well, the telling that is

---

23. See Joseph Karo, *Kesef Mishneh* thereon.
24. See, e.g., B. Berakhot 19b–20a; B. Shabbat 127a re Gen. 18:3.
25. That *torah qua* "teaching" is more than "law" (*nomos* or *lex* or *Gesetz*) is obvious when looking at the rabbinic writings: teaching (*Lehre*) is not reducible to law in the strict sense. The question for modern Jewish theology, though, is whether teaching is more than but not less than law, or whether teaching can overcome law when the two seem to be in conflict. For the former, more conservative option, see Abraham Joshua Heschel, *God in Search of Man* (New York: Farrar, Straus and Cudahy, 1955), 321–42. For the latter, more liberal option, see Hermann Cohen, *Religion of Reason out of the Sources of Judaism*, trans. S. Kaplan (New York: Frederick Ungar, 1972), 338–39, 353–59.
26. *CD* II/2, 572 = *KD* II/2, 635.

haggadah tells us what God has done, what God does, and what God will do with us and for us. And the purpose of this telling is to seek us out, to invite us (the meaning of *doresh*, as in "what the Lord *requires* of you") to imitate God's goodness.[27] Here God is the original exemplar, not as an example or instantiation of something greater than himself, but as the God who sets the paradigm *qua* divine praxis, which lends itself to imitation by the people to whom this praxis has been revealed in their history.[28] Thus when Scripture speaks of the command "to love the LORD your God: to walk in his ways" (Deut. 11:22), an early rabbinic midrash explains: "God is called just [*tsaddiq*], so you are to be just. God is called kind [*hasid*], so you are to be kind."[29] And how does one know what God does, and that what God does is imitable? The text continues: "Those who interpret the narrations [*haggadot*] say that if you want to acknowledge [*le-hakir*] the One-who-spoke-and-the-cosmos-came-to-be, learn *haggadah*, from out of which you shall recognize the One-who-spoke-and-the-cosmos-came-to-be, and cleave to His ways." Even only hearing of what God does through Scripture is certainly better than God's goodness not being made known to us at all.

Unlike the way of the law or halakhah we saw above, where God is in the background as the foundation or source of our action, the way of haggadah is one in which God is in the foreground, leading our action, action by which we follow in God's paths. And how rabbinic of Barth to see this divine beneficence in God's election of his people Israel! What greater beneficence, what greater love, could there be in the world than God's election of his people?! It is not so much that God elects his people *and* then loves them; instead, God's love and God's election are one and the same act. Indeed, elective love is always elective selective love. One loves somebody, not everybody. Someone who loved everybody would in effect love nobody. To everybody one owes elementary justice, that is, doing to them what we want them to do to us, minimally. That often means just to be left unmolested. That might be justice, but it is certainly not love.

---

27. See Isa. 16:5 and comment of David Kimhi (Radaq) thereon re 2 Chron. 14:1.

28. "It is . . . with the theory of this divine praxis . . . that theology and therefore theological ethics must deal" (*CD* II/2, 531) This seems to reflect the post-Kantian notion that *theory*, which is concerned with what *is*, is of less philosophic import than *praxis*, which is concerned with what *ought to be*. See Kant, *Critique of Pure Reason*, B828–32. Cf. Aristotle, *Nicomachean Ethics* 6.7/1141a20–1141b1; 10.8/1178a10.

29. *Sifre*: Devarim, no. 49, ed. Finkelstein, pp. 114–15.

How do the people Israel respond to God's loving election? They are to walk in the ways they originally saw and subsequently heard as God's concern for their situation in the world, especially for their vulnerability in the world. This comes out in the command in Micah 6:8 to "do justice." But what makes divine justice different from human justice? Well, human justice is usually reactive, that is, it is a righting or correction or restoration of the social order that has been wronged.[30] Divine justice, on the other hand, is proactive: it is meant to transform the world into something infinitely better than it had been before. This is how God first revealed his justice to Abraham, the first of God's elect: "Do I hide from Abraham what I am doing? . . . For I know him, that he shall command his children and his household after him, that they shall keep the way of the LORD to do righteousness and justice [*tsedaqah u-mishpat*]" (Gen. 18:17, 19). But how does Abraham know what this "righteousness and justice" is, that is, how does he know *how* it is to be done? Well, he knows it by hearing from God what God is doing here and now. So, when Abraham questions God: "How can the judge of the whole earth not do justice?" (Gen. 18:25), what he is saying to God is that if God's justice appears to be irrational and contradictory, then how can God expect Abraham to imitate what seems to be inimitable?[31] Furthermore, Abraham's *imitatio Dei* is not a return to any *status quo ante*. His imitation of God's justice will be something by which "all the nations of the earth will be blessed" (Gen. 18:18). That is something that has never happened before, and that is what makes God's justice awesome. Most of us, however, "fear the justice of God less than the injustice of men," as the Christian poet T. S. Eliot so insightfully put it.[32]

The same is the case for the command in Micah 6:8 "to love kindness" (*ahavat hesed*). When writing about the commandment "You shall love your neighbor as yourself" (Lev. 19:18), Maimonides saw this general commandment being specified as what the rabbis called *gemilut hasadim*,

---

30. Hence the first universal, Noachian commandment is *dinim* (B. Sanhedrin 56b re Gen. 18:19), i.e., the communal obligation to set up courts of law to adjudicate cases of injustice. In other words, the first business of those coming together politically is to rectify injustice and protect themselves from violence. In fact, that is why they come together there in the first place, and that is why those who are close to the Torah should not live in a place where there is no law court (B. Sanhedrin 17b).

31. See David Novak, "Divine Justice/Divine Command," *Studies in Christian Ethics* 23 (2010): 6-20.

32. *Murder in the Cathedral*, pt. 2, *Complete Poems and Plays: 1909-1950* (New York: Harcourt, Brace and World, 1971), 221.

usually translated as "acts of loving-kindness."[33] One of the most important such acts is what the rabbis designated as "caring for or attending to the sick" (*biqqur holim*). On this point, a Talmud text states: "How is it possible to walk after the divine Presence [*shekhinah*]? . . . But one should follow after God's qualities [*middotav*]. . . . God attends to the sick as it written: 'The Lord appeared to him at the oaks of Mamre' (Genesis 18:1), so you too attend to the sick."[34] Abraham's sickness was the result of his circumcision at the age of ninety-nine, and circumcision is the sign of the covenant that God elected Abraham and his clan.[35] Here again, this is not a return to a *status quo ante*, since God had not elected any other people before—and will not replace the people of Israel with any other people thereafter (a point Barth strongly affirmed by his nonsupersessionism).

## Divine Humility

The prophet Micah said that the good to be done is threefold, and that doing this good is in imitation of God's goodness, revealed to Israel during their history (what some call *Heilsgeschichte*) and recorded in Scripture. We have just seen how this imitation of God works in the case of *doing justice* and *loving kindness*. But what about "walking humbly with your God," the third imperative? Is that, too, acting in imitation of God? Does God walk "humbly" with us?

Now the rabbis see in Scripture statements of divine humility. But, as we shall soon see, whereas humans need to practice humility before God to continually remind us that we are not God's equals, God chooses to practice humility to show humans he is with us when we are most alone in the world. Thus the Talmud presents the dictum of Rabbi Yohanan bar Nappaha: "Everywhere you find a statement of God's might [*gevurato*], you also find thereafter a statement of His lowliness [*anavtanuto*]. . . . In the Torah it is written: 'For the Lord your God is God-supreme and Lord-supreme' (Deuteronomy 10:17), but thereafter is written: 'who executes justice for orphans and widows' (10:18)."[36] In other words, God comes down from his pedestal and involves himself

---

33. MT: Mourning, 14.1.
34. B. Sotah 14a.
35. B. Baba Metzi'a 86b.
36. B. Megillah 31a.

intimately with the most vulnerable, the most lowly, of his people. As the great twentieth-century Jewish theologian Franz Rosenzweig taught: by his very involvement with this lowly world, God comes out of and down from his primordial self-sufficiency.[37] And that is what is to be imitated by those who, like God, have the power to effect justice and kindness in the world. The humility in both cases is that the justice and kindness being effected in the world are for the sake of those who need this justice and this kindness most. It is not to be an occasion of using those in need for the sake of one's own self-aggrandizement. So, according to this interpretation, we could translate "to walk humbly with your God [*im elohekha*]" as "to walk humbly with your God as your God walks humbly with you." Indeed, the word translated as "humbly" (*hatsne'a*) in the rabbinic tradition is called *tsni'ut*, or "modesty," like the modesty of a husband and wife who resist any kind of exhibitionism for the sake of their intimate (what some would call private) communion.[38] This is what the medieval theologian Nahmanides called the "secret miracles" (*nissim nistarim*).[39] In fact, one midrash sees "walking humbly with God" to refer to God's preference for the intimacy (*ha-tseni'ut*) of the tent of meeting (*ohel mo'ed*) for his revelations to and conversations with Moses.[40] And, as one commentator notes, God's presence (*ha-shekhinah*) is more awesome in this intimate setting than even the more splendid public revelation at Mount Sinai, which is a revelation some rabbis believe was witnessed by the gentiles too.[41]

## What Is Good?

The statement "It is told to you, O man, what is good [*mah tov*]" seems to mean that there is some entity called "the good" about which one can ask *what* it is. In other words, the adjective "good" can easily be hypostatized into a metaphysical reality, designated by an abstract noun. If this is the case, then the three acts of (1) doing justice, (2) loving kindness, and

---

37. *The Star of Redemption*, trans. B. Galli (Madison: University of Wisconsin Press, 2005), 31–48.

38. See B. Shabbat 140b; B. Nedarim 20a–b.

39. See his *Commentary on the Torah*: Exod. 6:2; also, David Novak, *The Theology of Nahmanides—Systematically Presented* (Atlanta: Scholars Press, 1992), 61–75.

40. *Bemidbar Rabbah* 1.3 re Num. 1:1.

41. Joseph Zundel, *Ets Yosef* thereon.

(3) walking humbly with God are all instantiations of this metaphysical entity. That is, those who do these acts participate in this higher reality called "the Good" or "Goodness." Nevertheless, in the larger-print section of *Church Dogmatics* II/2, to which the exegesis of Micah 6:8 is attached, Barth explicitly rejects any such notion of what is good, representing this notion as follows: "It might be said that God is the essence of the good, the eternal good itself. He therefore claims [*Anspruch*] man for himself to the extent that man as man participates [*Anteil hat*] in God from the very first... from the very outset [this] is the desire, the longing [*die Sehnsucht*] to be equal to God.... Finally, it might be said that God is simply the all-sufficient being whom I have selected [*erlesen*] as my supreme good... the God whom he [man] has chosen [*den erwählten Gott*]."[42]

Actually, for Plato and Aristotle *the* Good as the end of all ends, the *summum bonum*, is not chosen nor does it choose. What it does is simply show itself to be irresistible to those who can see it with what Plato called "the eye of the soul."[43] I think Barth understood that when he spoke of actual choosing (*erlesen* or *erwählen*) of God by humans, whereas God's "claim" (*Anspruch*) on humans (in this view anyway) can simply mean the irresistible attractiveness of the Good and whatever or whomever a human identifies with it.[44] But even if this "good god" is the Absolute, as it is for Aristotle, this is still a god who does not engage in any transitive action *toward* the created world, and all the more does not engage in any transactions *with* humans, who are the only beings we know a god could transact with.[45] But God's most important transaction with humans, from a scriptural perspective, is his election of Israel, which is a covenantal transaction. It is a transaction conducted in a mutual though unequal relationship. For its validity it requires God's initiating choice, and for its effectiveness it requires Israel's acceptance of being chosen. In the rabbinic tradition, this is epitomized by God's giving the Torah (*mattan torah*) and Israel's reception of the Torah (*qabbalat ha-torah*) at Sinai and thereafter.[46] However, that transaction is totally distorted when it is presumed that Israel did the choosing and that God is the one

---

42. *CD* II/2, 554 = *KD* II/2, 615.
43. *Republic* 519B.
44. See Aristotle, *Nicomachean Ethics* 10.7/1177b26–29 and 10.8/1179a25.
45. See Aristotle, *Metaphysics* 12.7/1072a25–35.
46. See B. Berakhot 58a; also, Solomon Schechter, *Some Aspects of Rabbinic Theology* (New York: Behrman House, 1936), 116–69.

they chose. That inversion was first proposed in modernity by the Jewish renegade Baruch Spinoza.[47]

We shall return to the question "what is good?" in the final section of this paper. But now we need to look at God's goodness as an act of love.

## Divine Eros

For Barth, to assume that the God-human relationship is founded in the human desire to participate in the life of God is to claim God for ourselves; but that is "not the God who really claims [*Anspruch nimmt*] us."[48] So, indeed, "what begins with the human self cannot end with the knowledge of God and His command."[49] Here I think of two correlated terms of the kabbalists: the "awakening from above" (*it'aruta de-l'ela*), which denotes God's attraction to us, and the "awakening from below" (*it'aruta de-le-tatta*), which denotes our attraction to God.[50] Barth does speak of "the awakening of faith" (*das Erwachen des Glaubens*), which is akin to the kabbalistic "awakening from below."[51] Barth also speaks of what could be called an *awakening from above* when he speaks of "the divine truth that seeks us [*der uns aufsuchenden Wahrheit Gottes*], the truth of the divine command that desires us [*uns verlangenden*]."[52] And here I think of the great work of my late revered teacher, Abraham Joshua Heschel, *God in Search of Man*—my teacher who was so imbued with the theology of the kabbalists and their Hasidic heirs.[53]

---

47. See his *Tractatus Theologico-Politicus*, chap. 17; also, David Novak, *The Election of Israel* (Cambridge: Cambridge University Press, 1995), 22–49.

48. *CD* II/2, 557 = *KD* II/2, 618.

49. *CD* II/2, 554.

50. This is a *leitmotif* in the *Zohar*, the fundamental kabbalistic text. See *Zohar* 1:78a re Gen. 12:1; 1:164a re Num. 28:2; 1:239b re Lev. 1:2; 3:271a; also Gershom Scholem, *Major Trends in Jewish Mysticism*, 3rd rev. ed. (New York: Schocken Books, 1954), 233. For the kabbalah, though, the relation of "above" and "below" is an inner divine relation, since there is no real world outside God. Everything is *ad intra*. But, for the rabbis, the relation *between* "above" and "below" is *ad extra* for both *separate* parties. So, my use of kabbalistic terminology here is selective, more beholden to rabbinic theology than to the metaphysical presuppositions of kabbalistic theology.

51. *CD* II/2, 557 = *KD* II/2, 618.

52. *CD* II/2, 649 = *KD* II/2, 722.

53. See supra, n. 25, for full reference. Nevertheless, Heschel speaks of divine *pathos* rather than divine *eros*. His preference for *pathos* seems to be because he sees human ap-

The idea of "awakening" as thought by the kabbalists and by Barth has definite erotic meaning. It means that our desire for God has been *awakened* by God's desire for us. This *eros* is a divine initiative that continually tries to elicit an appropriate human response; and when there is such an appropriate human response, God responds to that response. "Return [*shuvu*] to me, says the LORD of Hosts, and I shall return to you, so says the LORD of Hosts" (Zech. 1:3). On the one hand, this is unlike what for some is divine love as *agape*, that is, selfless giving, without any desire for or attraction to its object.[54] But could anybody respond to love that is not the lover's attraction to what is unique about the beloved (even if the beloved is not yet aware of his or her attractiveness)? Surely, the God who reveals himself in Scripture is a desiring God. Thus divine *eros* calls for—it requires—a response, even though that required response is not and could not be an equal *quid pro quo*. It is thus the archetype of all true *eros*, in which the lovers both affect and are affected by each other interchangeably. Nevertheless, this true *eros* is not at all like lust or libido (*epithymia*), which is the active desire to subsume the other or the passive desire to be subsumed by the other.[55] In either case, whether love is *agape*

---

prehension of God to be *sympathetic* with God, who is "emotionally affected by the conduct of man" (*The Prophets* [Philadelphia: Jewish Publication Society of America, 1962], 320). This is best expressed in his earlier work, *Die Prophetie* (Krakow: Polnische Akademie der Wissenschaften, 1936), 70: "Das prophetische Grunderlebnis ist als Miterleben von Gefühlen Gottes, als Mitfühlen mit dem göttlischen Pathos, dem Grundmotiv der Prophetie, als Miterleben, das durch seelische Nachahmung oder Einfühlung zustande kommt, zu bestimmen."

54. In his famous work *Agape and Eros*, trans. P. S. Watson (Chicago: University of Chicago Press, 1982), the Lutheran theologian Anders Nygren characterizes human *eros*/desire for God as "acquisitive" and "egocentric" (175), even when it is quite different from sensual desire (49–52). God's *agape*, by contrast, is "unmotivated" (75–76). But, in Scripture, God's love is clearly revealed as *eros*. "Not because you are the most numerous of all the peoples does the LORD desire you [*hashaq bakhem*], does he choose you [*va-yivkhar etkhem*]" (Deut. 7:7). Martin Buber and Franz Rosenzweig in their translation of the Pentateuch translate this verse as "Er sich an euch gehangen, hat euch erwählt" (*Fünf Bücher der Weisung* [Cologne: Jakob Hegner, 1954], 497). The German verb *hangen* means "be attracted to" or "depend on." (See, also, B. Yevamot 63a: the statement of Ben Azzai.) Moreover, when human *eros* is a response to divine *eros*—a response and not an apotheosis—it is not a one-way ascent to an unresponsive, disinterested God, but part of a mutual interaction. It is certainly not "acquisitive" or "egocentric." Indeed, humans' desire for God (*bi hashaq*) is because they have recognized God's name/manifestation already made known/revealed to them (Ps. 91:14). Because humans have responded to God, God responds to them in turn in covenantal mutuality.

55. The difference between erotic desire and lustful desire lies in *who* is desired, *how*

or whether it is *epithymia,* both I and the other lose our ability to confront each other, to be present to each other, as distinct persons. In both cases, then, there is no true covenantal relationship.⁵⁶

Along these lines, I think of the way a great modern midrash—Thomas Mann's *Joseph and His Brothers*—deals with the phenomenon of *eros* in its discussion of the relationship of Joseph and Potiphar's wife in Genesis 39.

The usual interpretation of Mrs. Potiphar is that she is the bored, jaded young wife of a much older man, a man whose career kept him away from home and from her much too often.⁵⁷ One usually sees her desire as some sort of libidinal potential, of which she was fully aware, and this potential was there just waiting for its object, who could be just about any young, good-looking man who happened to cross her path at an opportune, discreet time, even if this young man was unaware of his attractiveness to her.

Mann, however, sees her desire to be altogether different. For him, she is the very young, sexually naive wife of an older, neglectful husband. (In fact, one rabbinic interpretation assumes that Potiphar was more in-

---

the one *who* desires actually desires this other person, and *what* is so desirable about him or her. See Deut. 21:11, where the verb *hashaq* (the verb used in Deut. 7:7; see supra, n. 54) is used to denote acquisitive, egocentric, human lust. LXX translates *hashaq* in Deut. 21:11 as *enthymēthēs* (desiring), but translates *hashaq* in Deut. 7:7 as *proeileto* (chose), possibly because it did not want to ascribe desire to God. Buber and Rosenzweig (*Fünf Bücher der Weisung*, 530), conversely, do want to ascribe desire to God, hence they translate *hashaq* in Deut. 7:7 using the same verb they use when translating *hashaq* in Deut. 21:11, viz., *du hängst dich an sie.* The problem with desire, whether human or divine, is whether it seeks a respectful relationship with its object or whether it seeks to subsume the other or be subsumed by the other. Is desire extending oneself to the other, or is it using the other or being used by the other to fill an emptiness (*kenōsis*) in oneself (see Plato, *Philebus* 35B)?

56. Barth explicitly criticizes Augustine on the question of the God-human relationship originating in human desire for God (*CD* II/2, 555 contra *Confessions* 1.1 and passim). Furthermore, one can see Barth's frequent theological adversary, Paul Tillich (1886–1965), as siding with Augustine on this point. See his *Systematic Theology* (Chicago: University of Chicago Press, 1951), 1:281–82. In an earlier work, *The Election of Israel*, 119–20 and n. 32 thereon, I sided with Augustine and Tillich against Barth (and Nygren too on the question of human desire for God). However, because I now see authentic human desire for God to be subsequent, not prior, to God's desire for us, I am now much more in sympathy with Barth (though, I think, he is quite different from Nygren on the question of God's desire for us; see *supra*, n. 54).

57. Mann speaks of "this false portrait of unbridled lasciviousness and seduction devoid of all shame." *Joseph and His Brothers*, trans. J. E. Woods (New York: Knopf, 2005), 816. Cf. Louis Ginzberg, *Legends of the Jews*, trans. H. Szold (Philadelphia: Jewish Publication Society of America, 1910), 2:44–58.

terested in Joseph than he was in his own wife.)⁵⁸ As Mann sees it, Mrs. Potiphar does not know what desire is until it has been awakened in her by Joseph's very presence, which especially attracts her when they finally find themselves alone together. Mann writes: "She now gave herself over to this novelty ... to realize the thrill of its awakening [*Erweckung erfahren*] ... awakened now from its slumber."⁵⁹ In other words, she knows her own desire only *after* she herself has been desired. And that, moreover, is consistent with a rabbinic treatment of what happened that day between Joseph and Mrs. Potiphar. Joseph is there portrayed as quite consciously desiring her, and being willing and able to consummate his desire for her.⁶⁰ He is only prevented from doing so by an epiphany in which his father and his mother warn him that if he follows his desire for her, he and his progeny will be forever removed from God's covenant with the people Israel.⁶¹ In other words, true *eros*—as distinct from untrue lust—is only valid when it is in harmony with, when it truly reflects, God's love for Israel.

So, too, Song of Songs is not an allegory comparing God's love for his people to the love between a man and a woman. Instead, God's initiatory love for Israel and Israel's responsive love for God are the archetype that is then symbolized in the mutually erotic relationship of a man and a woman.⁶² It is the symbol, though, that reflects the reality it symbolizes, not vice versa.⁶³ The ostensive meaning of the text (*peshat*) is only what appears to be its meaning; but it only lies on the surface.⁶⁴ The deeper meaning of the text that must be plumbed (*derash*) is the real meaning, the text's truth that has been uncovered. That is why Song of Songs deserves to be Scripture, to be in the biblical canon.⁶⁵

---

58. B. Sotah 13b re Gen. 39:1 and Rashi, s.v. "l'atsmo" thereon.

59. *Joseph and His Brothers*, 904 = *Joseph und seine Brüder* (Oldenburg: S. Fischer Verlag, 1959), 2:1113.

60. B. Sotah 36b re Gen. 39:11.

61. Y. Horayot 2:5/46d and B. Sotah 36b re Gen. 49:24.

62. See *Shir ha-Shirim Rabbah* 1.11 re Song of Songs 1:15–16.

63. That is why Song of Songs is not to be sung like an ordinary song (*zemer*). See B. Sanhedrin 101a.

64. See David Weiss Halivni, *Peshat and Derash* (New York: Oxford University Press, 1991), 3–22.

65. Mishnah (hereafter M.): Yadayim 3:5.

## Divine Partnership

In this relationship, according to Barth, "Man is determined [*bestimmt*] only to be the partner of the gracious God."[66] The concept of partnership here is significant.

Partnerships are constituted by the coming together of two parties, when one party makes an offer that a second party accepts. Partnerships can be of two kinds: either a relationship of two equals, or a relationship of a senior partner with a junior partner. Clearly, in the God-human relationship, God is the senior partner and humans are the junior partners. As such, God's superiority comes about not only because God initiates the relationship, but also because God continually directs the relationship and judges it.

The fundamental difference between a humanly initiated and maintained partnership and a divinely initiated and maintained partnership is emphasized by the rabbis. A humanly initiated partnership with God is condemned. Thus "whoever partners [*na-meshattef*] the name of God with anything else is uprooted from the [God's] world."[67] Another rabbinic text states: "Why were humans created last [in the order of creation]? So that the heretics [*ha-minin*] couldn't say that humans were the partners [*shuttaf*] in God's creativity."[68] Nevertheless, the rabbis also speak of God's "partnering [*meshattef*] His great name with Israel so they might live" in a world that would otherwise swallow them up.[69] And, concerning the pursuit of justice, which is to be done in imitation of God's justice, it is taught: "Any judge who judges truthfully [*din emet*], from a scriptural perspective [i.e., who judges according to the word of God], it is as if [*k'ilu*] he has become the partner [*shuttaf*] of God Himself in the work of creation."[70] Therefore, humans who make themselves God's partners are condemned like idolaters are condemned; yet humans whom God has chosen to be his partners are included in the greatest activity of God that we could conceive: the creation of the cosmos from nothing into everything. Whether partnering with God is good or bad depends on who is doing the initial partnering: God or man.

But what is "the good" that this divine-human partnership is to accomplish? Does this good itself determine what God or humans are to

---

66. *CD* II/2, 575 = *KD* II/2, 639.
67. B. Sanhedrin 63a re Exod. 22:19.
68. Tosefta: Sanhedrin 8:7.
69. Y. Ta'anit 2:7/65d.
70. B. Shabbat 10a re Exod. 18:13 and Gen. 1:5.

accomplish by it? For Barth, "this duty signifies the good which man is to perform."[71] That is, it is a *mitsvah*, not initiated by man, but in "conformity [*Gleichförmigkeit*] with the grace of God," and which "must be determined by the fact that he [man] accepts the gracious action of God as right."[72]

For scripturally based theology, God is not the chief participant in the Good (Plato's view), nor is God identical with the Good (Aristotle's view).[73] We cannot define what God is. That is beyond the ability of any human: "No human shall see me and live" (Exod. 33:20). So we must see God's relation to the adjective "good" (*tov*) in an entirely different way. Since the God of Abraham, Isaac, and Jacob is an active subject and not a passive object, God is better designated by a verb than by a noun. If that is the case, then "good," when predicated of God *qua* agent, is best taken to be an adverb that modifies a verb rather than an adjective that modifies a noun. Thus immediately before God tells Moses what humans cannot know, he shows Moses how God benefits humans: "I will make all my beneficence [*tuvi*] pass before you, and I will proclaim the name of the LORD before you. I will be gracious to whom I will be gracious, and I will be merciful to whom I will be merciful" (Exod. 33:19).

Along these lines, Maimonides insists that we can only say what God does, not what God is.[74] That means we cannot speak of divine attributes in the sense that attributes of *what is* are qualities that modify a substance, which are designated by adjectives that modify a noun. But, if we can only describe what God *does*, we are really describing *how God acts*, adverbially. Unlike adjectives, adverbs are much more indigenous components of the verbs they modify by stating *how* the subject of the verb acts rather than *what* it is. Thus the word *tuvi*, which I have translated as "my beneficence,"

---

71. *CD* II/2, 678.

72. *CD* II/2, 579 = *KD* II/2, 639. See M. Avot 2:4.

73. For Plato, God as *dēmiourgos* is "good" (*agathos*), but that is because God "looks to the Eternal" (*to aidion*), which is what is "the best" (*ho aristos*), as "the model" (*paradeigma*) to be copied in God's good work of making the cosmos (*Timaeus* 28B–29B). This is like the Bible saying, "God *does good* for all; his mercy is over all his works" (Ps. 145:10), i.e., "good" (*tov*) functions as an adverb, describing *how* God acts. Furthermore, Plato's God, like the God of the Bible, does good *for* somebody else (*Timaeus* 29E–30A). Nevertheless, unlike Plato, the Bible does not subordinate God to some higher better/best reality above him. Also unlike Plato, for Aristotle, God is the highest good (*to ariston*), but God does not do anything, either good or bad, to anything outside himself (*Metaphysics* 12.7/1072b25–30). Thus from both Plato and Aristotle we see that what is good per se does not act transitively, and what acts transitively and beneficently is not what is good per se.

74. *Guide of the Perplexed*, 1.52.

includes both the act and the quality of the act together in one word. Moreover, God's beneficence is not inferred from or discovered in our ordinary experience of the world. Instead, God reveals to us just as much of his beneficence as he wants us to know and be able to imitate. Unlike adjectives that answer to the question *what*, adverbs that answer to the question *how* are much less likely to be made into some higher metaphysical entity in *which* the subjects they originally modify now participate. That is because, unlike adjectives in relation to the nouns they modify, adverbs are much harder to separate from the active verbs of which they are more integral.

Since biblical Hebrew seems to be quite deficient in adverbs, what often looks like an adjective is actually functioning as an adverb. This is especially true of the so-called adjective "good" (*tov*). So, for example, note how the words *mah tov* ("how good") are used in this verse: "Behold how goodly [*mah tov*] and how delightful [*mah na'im*] it is when brothers dwell together!" (Ps. 133:1). Here the word *mah* does not mean "what" but rather "how," that is, it designates the good and pleasant *way* brothers can dwell together. As such, we could (somewhat awkwardly) translate the verse as: "How well and pleasantly do brothers dwell together." Thus *tov* and *na'im* function as adverbs not just describing but declaring or exclaiming *how* brothers (like Moses and Aaron) can act with one another. The word "how" (*mah*) here and elsewhere functions vocatively. Yet one could not turn "well" and "pleasantly" into supernouns like "Goodness" or "Pleasantness" (as in Plato's *t'agathon*).[75] Therefore, that brotherly solidarity cannot be viewed as a participation in some higher metaphysical state, since these adverbs don't modify any *thing* (whether physical or metaphysical).

To ask *what* X is doing is to ask *how* X is doing. So, too, when Scripture states that "God saw all that he made and found it to be very good [*tov me'od*]" (Gen. 1:31), that might mean that God is pleased with how well he has created and how well his creation pleases him.[76] Yet God is not answerable to or identifiable with any standard that could be thought of as being outside of himself. Instead, God's action itself generates the standard that can be imitated by those to whom God's action is revealed. Thus we read: "For how great is his goodness [*mah tuvo*], and how great is his beauty [*mah yofyo*]!" (Zech. 9:17).

---

75. *Republic* 505A–509B.

76. Scripture is replete with statements of God's pleasure or displeasure, which means that God chooses to both affect the world and be affected by the world, especially with his beloved people. For rabbinic emphasis of this doctrine, see M. Menahot 13:10 re Lev. 1:9, 17; 2:2; B. Zevahim 46b; also, Heschel, *The Prophets*, 221–67.

Nevertheless, this divine goodness and beauty are not inferred from our gazing at nature (the original meaning of *theōria*). From nature one can only infer God's multifaceted power. For example, "How manifold [*mah rabbu*] are your works, O LORD. . . . The earth is full of your creatures" (Ps. 104:24). God's goodness and beauty are revealed, not inferred.

## More Jewish Than Hermann Cohen?

I don't know whether Hermann Cohen, Barth's Jewish philosophy professor in Marburg, ever discussed with Barth his interpretation of Micah 6:8. Nevertheless, as Barth rejected many of Cohen's views (quite respectfully, though), I see his interpretation of Micah 6:8 in sharp contrast to Cohen's interpretation of it in his book *Religion of Reason*, which was published posthumously in 1919, a number of years after Barth had studied with him. Cohen writes there: "Thus, with regard to the problem of the good [*des Guten*], God and man come into a necessary community [*notwendige Gemeinschaft*]. God has to proclaim the good. . . . Reason with its principle of the good unites [*verbindet*] God and man, religion and morality [*Sittlichkeit*]."[77] A little earlier, Cohen reiterated a point he made throughout his thought: "Religion itself is moral teaching [*Sittenlehre*] or it is not religion, and moral teaching is autonomous [*selbständig*] only as philosophical ethics."[78] Here in critical agreement with Kant at his most Platonic, Cohen speaks of *the Good*. That is the *tertium quid*, the key third factor, that brings God and man together. But the Good can only do that if it transcends both God and man. It could only do that by being metaphysically prior to them both. Thus Cohen's view of God (*Gotteslehre*) as the supreme subject of any metaphysics is admittedly based on Parmenides's identification of God and Being.[79] Barth, on the other hand, develops his metaphysics out of Scripture.

In fact, I would consider one of Barth's greatest contributions to both Christian and Jewish thought to be his retrieval of metaphysics from its abandonment by almost all modern philosophers, not by an anachronistic return to the kind of metaphysics that is beholden to a worldview that

---

77. *Religion of Reason*, 33 = *Religion der Vernunft aus den Quellen des Judentums*, 2nd ed. (Darmstadt: Joseph Melzer Verlag, 1966), 39.

78. *Religion of Reason*, 33 = *Religion der Vernunft*, 38.

79. *Religion der Vernunft*, 48: "Nur Gott hat Sein. Nur Gott ist Sein." See LXX on Exod. 3:14.

nobody in the world today can speak of but by radically reconstituting it theologically.

Unfortunately, too many modern theologians, whether Jewish or Christian, have followed the lead of the modern philosophers and have given up on dealing with metaphysical questions altogether. Indeed, metaphysics is only important (let alone even interesting) when it deals with *the* metaphysical question: whether God exists (*quod sit Deus*). So, why should theologians deal with what seems to be a truly "philosophical" question when the philosophers no longer challenge them with their own counterarguments on this very question? Nevertheless, Barth is not willing to let theology become as metaphysically anemic as philosophy has now become. Instead, he restores metaphysics to its ancient role as "queen of the sciences" (*regina scientiarum*). I might add, though, that there are two types of modern philosophy that are nonmetaphysical but not necessarily antimetaphysical, that is, analytic-linguistic philosophy and phenomenology. The methods of these two types of modern philosophy are very much evident in Barth's own work by his critical use of them.

For all this, Jewish and Christian thinkers must be grateful to Karl Barth for the rigor, clarity, and depth of his theological project.

# 2

# Karl Barth and the Jews: The History of a Relationship

EBERHARD BUSCH

## Finding a Connection

The question of Jewish-Christian relations first arose for Barth through the so-called Patmos Circle of baptized Jews. He met them during the turbulent times that preceded the second edition of his Romans commentary. They acquainted him with their Jewish friend Franz Rosenzweig, who, like Barth, had been a pupil of the Jewish philosopher Hermann Cohen. They appear to have directed him to Rosenzweig's essay from 1914 with the startling title "Atheistic Theology."[1] One cannot read this brilliant piece without sensing in it the same spirit as would be evident in Barth's soon-to-be-famous Romans commentary. Rosenzweig urged that modern theology, whether Jewish or Christian, was grounded in the notion of "religion," and so was atheistic, whether in its rationalistic or its mystical forms. "The difference between God and humankind—an offense to all unbelief, whether ancient or modern—has been blotted out. The encounter between divine revelation and human unreadiness" was redefined into a "tension immanent within humanity." But, in fact, revelation really meant "the great eruption of the Spirit into the non-spiritual world." Because its content was God himself, only *one* revelation was given, only *one* way of salvation: the way that ran from God to his people, from heaven to earth. But this revelation appeared in two forms. Through their mission of universal love,

---

1. Franz Rosenzweig, "Atheistische Theologie," in *Die Schrift: Aufsätze, Übertragungen und Briefe*, ed. K. Thieme (Frankfurt am Main: Europäische Verlagsanstalt, n.d.), p. 215.

---

Several years ago I gave a lecture at Princeton Seminary about Karl Barth's theological understanding of how Christians are related to the Jews. Now I want to speak about the history of his relationship with them.

Christians were called to work in society for the world's redemption. The Jews for their part had a vital though different role to play. Although they lived largely closed off from the rest of the world, their insular communal life symbolized the coming redemption of all things.

The Patmos group saw a bridge at this point to Barth's theology as they had encountered it in his 1919 Tambach lecture. In those days there were intense contacts between them and him. Barth saw in this circle "a hopeful bond . . . with the Synagogue's point of view."[2] In 1920 he reflected: "Surely, the people of Israel-Judah are a people like any other," yet a people "in whom a tremendous awareness of the *Wholly Other* was never quite lost." Like Rosenzweig, Barth lumped Jews and baptized Jews together over against Christians, who stemmed from the gentiles. Barth remarked: "If we attend to the Jews and baptized Jews still living among us, massively tossed to and fro, we may learn at all events that new and strange things once took place. . . . As those who believed like Abraham, as foreigners in the promised land like Isaac and Jacob, they devoted themselves like Moses to the God they could not see, as if they did see him. We are reminded of John the Baptist in Gruenewald's painting, with his almost impossibly outstretched finger, endlessly pointing to the Crucified."[3] In the thirties Rabbi Leo Baeck picked up on Barth's insight when he retorted: yes, this finger *is* "the peculiarity of the Jewish existence," but "it is in danger of being broken off from this pointing."[4] While Barth was writing his *Church Dogmatics*, a copy of the Grünewald painting hung over his desk. In it he saw his judgment confirmed. It was, he declared, "the peculiar honour of Israel to bind the Christian Church to the Word of the Cross."[5]

In 1920 Rosenzweig presented Barth with the gift of a prayer book containing texts from the Psalms. In the dedication he wrote: "To the Jewish Christian of Safenwil."[6] This inscription had a double edge. For, according to Rosenzweig's close friend Eugen Rosenstock, the "facts of salvation in the New Testament sink down in Barth's theology to the level

---

2. Karl Barth and Eduard Thurneysen, *Briefwechsel*, vol. 1 (Zürich: Theologischer Verlag, 1973), p. 366.

3. Karl Barth, *Das Wort Gottes und die Theologie* (Munich: Chr. Kaiser, 1924), pp. 78-79.

4. Leo Baeck, *Die Existenz des Juden* (March 3, 1935), in Leo Baeck-Institut, Bulletin 81 (1988), pp. 10-12.

5. Karl Barth, *Church Dogmatics* II/2 (Edinburgh: T. & T. Clark, 1957), p. 262 (translation revised).

6. The booklet *Der Tischdank* in the Barth-Archive Basel.

of the Old Testament."[7] Nevertheless, Barth's theology was soon of no account for the Patmos group, as if swept away by a deluge. They wanted to set up a curious cult around sensuality, around Cybele, and around an ideology of Germanic thinking, none of which Barth found congenial. Rosenstock would declare that his friend Rosenzweig had "grown out of the 'Barthanism' which he had learned ten years ago."[8] That could not be quite right, however, because he had known little about him at that point. In any case, while Barth found this turn of affairs disappointing, he did not abandon what he had learned from the Patmos Circle about a Christian connection with the Jews.

In the twenties Barth was drawn to make the idea of "covenant" into a central feature of his theology. When Adolf von Harnack, the renowned modern liberal theologian, visited Barth in Münster, he was irritated to find his former pupil reading Johannes Coccejus with sympathy. Coccejus was the seventeenth-century theologian who (like Calvin) had taught that there was only one covenant in two different dispensations. He held that already in the Old Testament God had entered into an alliance with his people, the Jews. For Barth it became important that this covenant was instituted by God before the Fall. Such a thesis deviated from the views of Friedrich Schleiermacher. According to him, the more the Christian faith was distanced from the Old Testament, with its primitive superstitions, the better off it was. Schleiermacher contended that including the Jewish law code in the Christian canon could only lead to construing Christianity as continuous with the Jewish religion, a grave mistake.[9] Christianity and Judaism were seen as radically different. Judaism was a matter of servile subjection to the letter—it was even an "imperishable mummy"[10]—while the Christian religion was a free expression of the spirit. Barth would depart from Schleiermacher at many points, including here.

---

7. Rosenstock to Nelly Barth (Nov. 20, 1920), in the Barth-Archive Basel.

8. Rosenstock to Martin Buber (Feb. 14, 1923), in Franz Rosenzweig, *Gesammelte Schriften* I/2, p. 893.

9. Friedrich Schleiermacher, *Kurze Darstellung des theologischen Studiums*, 4th ed. (Darmstadt, 1961), p. 47.

10. Friedrich Schleiermacher, *Über die Religion: Reden an die Gebildeten unter ihren Verächtern* (1799) (Göttingen, 1967), p. 191.

## Affirming an Inseparable Bond

In 1933 it became necessary to affirm all the more that Christians were connected with the Jews by an inseparable bond. Yet this idea was difficult, not only because of the anti-Semitic Hitler regime, but even more because German Protestants were deeply infected by a rigid, traditional anti-Judaism. Three beliefs, widespread and obstinate, needed to be opposed: first, that Christ was the founder of a new religion that split Christians off from the Jews; second, that because of their no to Christ the Jews were rejected by God and replaced by the church (Barth called this supersessionism the specifically Christian form of anti-Semitism);[11] and finally, that God's law was mediated to Christians in a normative way through the secular orders of *Volk* and race. As can be seen from his statements in 1933, Barth opposed these beliefs openly.

In March 1933 he delivered a lecture in Copenhagen entitled "The First Commandment as a Theological Axiom."[12] This theme established the ground on which Barth would speak and act in the years ahead. In the Barmen Declaration of 1934, he would develop his theme with reference to "Jesus Christ as he is attested for us in Holy Scripture," while adding that he is "*the one* Word of God," thus placing him in line with the first commandment. In Copenhagen Barth had explained that this commandment—"You shall have no other gods before me"—was no less normative for Christians than for Jews. He urged Christians to take seriously that "the God of the First Commandment is the God of Israel." The first commandment could never be overridden by any human law. But how should Christians understand it? Barth posited that "Jesus Christ is the meaning of the law of Sinai." The law of God was essentially gracious, thus differing from other laws. It was gracious because it was determined by the gospel. Barth's famous move of giving priority to the gospel over the law arose in this context—as did his stress on their inseparable unity.

Shortly before his trip to Copenhagen Barth had come into contact with the Jewish theologian Hans-Joachim Schoeps. Schoeps would write perceptively of Barth that his theology was "marked by a sense that his *own* speaking about God is always in danger. It follows that one must always tremble when seeking proper words for the truth."[13] Perhaps it is no

---

11. Barth, *Church Dogmatics* II/2, p. 290 (translation revised).
12. Karl Barth, *Theologische Fragen und Antworten, Ges. Vortr.*, vol. 3 (Zürich, 1953), p. 143.
13. Hans Blueher, *Hans-Joachim Schoeps: Streit um Israel* (Berlin, 1932), pp. 110–11.

accident that it was a Jew who discerned this virtue in Barth. In the fateful year 1933, Barth would declare his solidarity with Schoeps against an anti-Semitic scholar who had attacked him. The reason for this comradeship, Barth explained, was that Christianity sees the revelation at Sinai as validated in Christ. Therefore the church would always be more closely connected with Judaism than with any other religion. "The substance of your convictions occurs in the framework of faith," stated Barth, "which, though not the Christian framework, is seen positively from its perspective."[14] He went on to list some questions he hoped to take up with Schoeps. Why did he not focus more on the covenant in which the commandments were given; why did he say so little about the importance of sacrifice in the First Testament; and why did he seem to sidestep the significance of God's name as it resided in Jerusalem? Finally, were not his ideas of revelation, election, grace, and law in line with what Paul had termed "the righteousness of the law" (*dikaiosyne ek nomou*)? Barth adopted the idea that God's name resided in Jerusalem from Rabbi Emil Cohn of Berlin, whom he had invited to Bonn to speak in his seminar.

During the year 1933 Barth often criticized an idea held by many German Protestant theologians and churchgoers, namely, that the law was divorced from the gospel. On this ground they claimed that in the church one had to listen to the gospel, but in political life one should follow the law of Hitler. In April 1933 an ordinance was passed against all groups that did not agree with the Hitler regime. But this law, it was said, should not be opposed by the Protestant churches, because they were not affected, and in any case they supported the Nazi regime. In the same month Barth wrote to Georg Merz, an influential theologian in Munich: "The assumption that you can first agree with the 'Deutsche Christen' [German Christians] (in their Yes to Hitler), but then expect to have a pure church — this assumption will one day prove to be one of the most evil illusions in a time that is so rich in illusions. Put this idea away, honestly and radically, and then we can speak about what follows."[15]

In that same month Dietrich Bonhoeffer published his article "The Church and the Jewish Question." It appeared in the National Socialist journal *Der Vormarsch* (*The Forward Advance*), of which he was then co-editor. In it we read "that the (so-called) 'elected people,' which nailed our

---

14. Karl Barth, *Briefe des Jahres 1933*, ed. Eberhard Busch (Zürich, 2004), pp. 64-70; on p. 66.

15. Ibid., pp. 176-77.

Savior to the cross, has to bear the curse of its deed through a long history of suffering, until it returns to God by converting to Christ."[16] Barth could not agree with this article. Moreover, he encountered such ideas again when he was asked to write in support of a text that was dubbed "The Bethel Confession" by Eberhard Bethge after the war.

## Reflecting on the Law

Barth was convinced that the biggest obstacle preventing Christians from grasping their God-given bond with the Jews was their false conception of the law. As long as they persisted in this error, they would be hindered from understanding the Jews truly in the light of Scripture. At the same time, they would be prevented from seeing another important point: that their bond with the Jews involved them in political consequences. Therefore Barth criticized the so-called Bethel Confession (August 1933) mainly for its idea of the law. In a passage written by Bonhoeffer, it stated: "To preserve human beings from their unbridled selfishness and keep them from destroying themselves, God imposes firm orders upon human life." No one was permitted to transgress these God-given "orders": "The orders of preservation have the unconditional value of being divine institutions, and their transgression makes us enemies of God." "Human beings cannot escape from any of [them].... Marriage remains marriage, Volk remains Volk, government remains government." "Volk remains Volk" was the fateful line. "The Christian Church," the text concluded, "never hovers above the Volk." Instead, all church members were connected with their *Volk* "inextricably"—with their *Volk* but apparently not with the Jews (or so it seemed). These statements, though not without ambiguities, were unfortunate in the context of the times.

Barth rejected this theory of created "orders" by which divine obligations were supposedly imposed. On the contrary, he argued, we have to allow "free space for the operation of God's commandment." For "the demand of the *one* Word of God has a direct bearing on the secular sphere, even on supposedly pre-arranged 'orders.' Why don't you speak first and foremost ... about the 'concrete claims of God's power' as they pertain to what are humanly called 'orders'? According to the First Command-

---

16. Dietrich Bonhoeffer, "Die Kirche vor der Judenfrage" (April 1933), in *Gesammelte Schriften*, ed. E. Bethge, vol. 2 (Munich: Chr. Kaiser, 1965), pp. 44-53; on p. 49.

ment," he insisted, "even the orders cannot claim to have a fixed divine validity that can be known in advance!" Here Barth was opposing the two-kingdoms doctrine, in its Bethel version, on the basis of the first commandment. The force of his critique was political, because he believed that such a statement had direct *political* consequences. Therefore Barth asked the drafters of the confession: "Is the systematic treatment of the Jews by the German government today something about which 'we' have nothing to say? Do 'we' have to accept it and to take part in it as divinely ordained, just because it is decreed from on high by the '*Obrigkeit*' [state authority]?"

The root failure of German Protestant theology toward the Jews, as Barth saw it, rested on its faulty two-kingdoms doctrine. German church historians say today that because of his fight against this doctrine he was not interested in the question of the Jews. Let us hope they will understand some day that Barth's no to the two-kingdoms doctrine was the source of his yes to solidarity with the Jews. For he was convinced, as he wrote in September 1933: "Theologically speaking, the question of how to relate to the Jews is surely *the* pivotal question of the whole history of our time. . . . And just here I cannot countenance even the smallest compromise with National Socialism. At no other place do you see more clearly the immovable boundary whose transgression can only mean 'betraying' the Gospel."[17]

In those days German Protestant theologians and bishops tended to identify *the* law with the decrees of the political government. Therefore they could not speak out when inhumane laws were promulgated. Indeed, they often consented to them on the grounds that they were necessary for the German *Volk*. Against this mind-set Barth insisted that no human law should ever be confused with God's will. The decrees of any government had to be tested against God's gracious commandments. On Reformation Day 1933, in his address to a packed lecture hall in Berlin, Barth put his convictions into practice. It was because of what he said on that occasion that a German court in Cologne would dismiss him a year later from his post as a university professor in Nazi Germany. "What has been going on in the concentration camps?" Barth intoned. "What has been done to the Jews? Isn't the Christian church guilty because of its silence?" He invoked the decisive norm: "Whoever is called to proclaim the Word of God in such circumstances has to make clear just what the Word of God requires."

In the winter semester that followed, I assume, in December 1933,

---

17. Barth to Fr. Dalmann (Sept. 1, 1933), in Karl Barth–Archiv, Basel.

Barth spoke in his lectures at the university about the First Testament; the material later appeared under the heading "Time of Expectation" in *Church Dogmatics*, volume I, part 2. The next section, about the New Testament, did not have the heading "Time of *Fulfillment*" but "Time of *Recollection*," so that it was again in effect still a matter of renewed expectancy on the basis of memorial. This emphasis meant that Christians did not replace the Jews in God's covenant, for what was at stake was "only their incorporation into the one covenant."[18] In the section about the First Testament, Barth referred to Jewish writers and texts such as Martin Buber, *Kingship of God* (1932), Hans-Joachim Schoeps, *Jewish Faith in Our Time* (1932), and Emil Bernhard Cohn. He wrote: "Just because they are 'pure' students of the Old Testament, they are instructive to listen to for our question, both in what they say as earnest Jews, and in what they cannot say as unconverted Jews."[19] This remark did not mean converted to *Christ* in any patronizing sense. If you were to open those Jewish books, you would see that Barth was standing alongside them, listening to them, and speaking with them.

In this same section he returned positively to the points he had missed in Schoeps's book. Barth seemed to ask him quietly whether it was true that

> the Torah . . . is not an instrument put into man's hands by whose means he can manipulate God and gain control of God's goodness and succour. The Torah is God's instrument of his own compassion. . . . As law, the covenant itself is grace; even as grace, it is also law. The covenant is grace, that is, it doesn't compel God. . . . It is God's free faithfulness if he doesn't abolish the covenant, just as it is God's mercy if he punishes and forgives sins, if after having punished he always likewise blesses again. If the nation for its part is faithful, if it keeps God's commandments, if it honours his name, if it brings him sacrifices, it does nothing out of the way. It merely acknowledges that the decision has been made, that God has adopted his own, that from him it may from time to time receive forgiveness and help. Sacrifice is possible only on the basis of the covenant, not vice versa. . . : As always, all human obedience can only be a copy, a repetition, a confirmation of what God does for human beings with incomparable majesty.[20]

---

18. Karl Barth, *Church Dogmatics* I/2 (Edinburgh: T. & T. Clark, 1956), p. 115 (translation revised).
19. Ibid., p. 80 (translation revised).
20. Ibid., p. 81 (translation revised).

We turn now to Martin Buber's *Kingship of God*. It is still exciting to read, just as it was when Barth encountered it. According to Buber, the Sinai covenant did not bring God and Israel into relation for the first time, but rather into a new *kind* of relation. After Sinai Israel was freshly distinguished as the people of God. It was enabled to be God's partner in a new, reciprocal relationship that was at once both sacral and legal.[21] Barth seemed to take up this idea and sharpen it. "This covenant," he wrote, "does not find Israel already existing as such. It *creates* Israel as a national unit. And only with respect to this covenant does the Old Testament take an interest in this nation, and this nation in particular."[22] The reciprocity between God and Israel, Barth thought, was not quite as Buber had depicted it. For God's people would henceforth depend completely on their Creator in a way that would not be true in reverse of their Creator on them. God was free to enter into full reciprocity with his people without being conditioned by them.

While he agreed that God revealed himself in and through the covenant, Barth explained this revelation in a surprising way. "The Old Testament like the New Testament," he wrote, "is a witness to the *revelation* in which God remains a *hidden* God, who indeed declares himself to be the hidden God precisely by revealing himself."[23] Barth was describing the mysterious name of God as given to Moses: "I am who I am" (Exod. 3:14). Buber also discussed this passage, proposing that it meant "I will be-there howsoever I will be-there."[24] I doubt whether Barth and Buber understood this passage in the same sense. Both were together, however, in the conviction that God in his revelation did not become a mere possession in the hands of his people. Barth would stress this point more strongly than Buber. He argued that God's self-revelation was "the radical de-divinization of nature, history and culture — a remorseless denial of any other divine presence than the one that occurred in the event of establishing the covenant. If there were any pious Canaanites — and why should there not have been? — the God of Israel must have appeared to them as death incarnate, and the faith of Israel as irreligion itself."[25]

Barth noted, furthermore, that according to the Old and the New Testaments, the God whose presence was attested by revelation was always the

21. Martin Buber, *Königtum Gottes* (Berlin: Schocken, 1932), p. 118.
22. Barth, *Church Dogmatics* I/2, p. 81 (translation revised).
23. Ibid., p. 85 (translation revised).
24. Buber, *Königtum Gottes*, pp. 83-84.
25. Barth, *Church Dogmatics* I/2, p. 85 (translation revised).

## Karl Barth and the Jews

very God who was also yet to come. Barth explained this idea in relation to the kings in the First Testament. In and through them Israel was waiting, implicitly, for the *one* true king. The advent of this king would bring peace, victory over sin, and even the renewal of a ruined cosmos. According to Barth, this hope was accomplished in the redemption and reconciliation of Jesus Christ, the Messiah. Remarkably, when he wrote these lines about the kings and the coming king, it seems that he had Buber's book in mind. Indeed, it is astonishing to see how close Buber came to this very idea in the final sentence of his book *Kingship of God*. There he spoke about a future crisis "out of which there emerges the human king of Israel, the follower of JHWH, as his 'anointed,' the *meschiach* JHWH, *christos kyriou*."[26] With those final words, the eschaton almost seemed just around the corner.

### Assessing Church and Synagogue

Barth closed his section about the First Testament on two remarkable notes. First, he entered into conversation with the contemporary synagogue. Adopting the form of a dialogue and dispute, he raised a number of questions.

> To this day the Synagogue waits for the fulfilment of prophecy. Is it really waiting? Is it waiting as the fathers waited? The fathers' waiting was no mere abstract, infinite waiting, but a waiting which already participated in fulfilled time. Ought it not to have been in this knowledge that the Synagogue closed the Canon as the document of this waiting? Did it not thereby confess that there is a time for waiting but that waiting has only its own time? Could the Canon be closed and Christ yet be rejected? Can the closed Canon of witness to an expected revelation be read with meaning apart from the counter-canon of revelation that happened? Is an infinite waiting, such as is the result of an abstracted Old Testament faith, a real waiting and not rather an eternal unrest? Is revelation that is only awaited real revelation?[27]

Second, Barth took up a thesis of Franz Rosenzweig, who wrote: "Israel, who is the people elected by his Father, looks resolutely across the world and

---

26. Buber, *Königtum Gottes*, p. 181.
27. Barth, *Church Dogmatics* I/2, pp. 100–101 (translation revised).

its history to the uttermost goal, whereupon his Father will be 'all in all.'" Until then the synagogue had to exist in isolation, "immortal, but with a broken staff and blindfold over her eyes." This was how she was depicted above the portal of the Strasbourg cathedral, whereas the church was portrayed with open, worldly eyes. Nevertheless, Rosenzweig argued, the church would always be in danger of adopting norms from the nations, and so be compromised by them. Therefore the church needed the synagogue as a silent admoniser, a unique counterpart acquainted with grief. The synagogue was a warning to the church not to forget about speaking the word of the cross.[28]

In concluding his discussion of the First Testament, Barth would pick up on Rozenzweig's statements and vary them. "The Church," he wrote, "may *also* be a figure with bandaged eyes and a broken lance, even though she holds in her hands the New Testament." Likewise, in a 1935 lecture entitled "The Gospel in the Present Time," Barth urged that Christianity existed only by an undeserved grace—a grace that, as Paul said, not only derived from Israel but also promised to include them in the end (Rom. 11:20-23, 26).[29] As he had done in 1933, Barth insisted that free grace was what bound the church of the New Testament inseparably to the people of the Old Testament. The church shared in Israel's blessing solely by grace. Precisely this mystery, the mystery of grace, was what not only distinguished the church from, but also joined the church to, the synagogue, and the synagogue to the church.

As previously noted, in thinking about these questions Barth, like Rosenzweig, once alluded to the portal of the Strasbourg cathedral. He suggested that "the Synagogue of the time after Christ is more than the ... uncannily pitiful figure" depicted there. Barth was closer to Rosenzweig, who portrayed the Jews as a silent admonition, than to Schleiermacher, who dismissed them as an "imperishable mummy." According to Barth, the Jews *remain* elected by God. As witnesses to God's election, they play an important role for the church. They remind her that there is no grace without judgment even as there is no judgment without grace. The church needs this witness, Barth contended, just as she needs the First Testament. "Without the Word of God in the Old Testament," he stated, "the Church would be believing in a different Christ from the New Testament witnesses."[30]

---

28. Barth, *Church Dogmatics* II/2, p. 262 (translation revised).

29. Karl Barth, "Das Evangelium in der Gegenwart," *Theologische Existenz Heute* 25 (1935), p. 31.

30. Barth, *Church Dogmatics* I/2, pp. 93-94.

During Advent of 1933, and thus during the winter semester when he lectured about the First Testament at the university, Barth preached in a Bonn church. His sermon set forth what he was developing in his dogmatics. It considered Romans 15:5–13, which read in part: "For I tell you that Christ became a servant to the circumcised to show God's truthfulness, in order to confirm the promises given to the patriarchs, and in order that the Gentiles might glorify God for his mercy" (Rom. 15:8–9). When the sermon was printed, Barth sent a copy directly to Hitler. In the accompanying letter he told him he could learn from it what the Christian church was really about. There are reasons to assume that the chancellor read the sermon, unfortunately without success. In it Barth interpreted the Jews in light of Christ. He explained that Jesus Christ did not start a new religion that replaced them. On the contrary, Jesus was the indestructible bridge connecting Christians with the Jews, even if they did not recognize him as the Christ. The central sentence avowed that "Jesus Christ was a Jew." Barth did not mean this avowal merely as a matter of historical provenance, as it is said in Germany today and as it was said by Schleiermacher. He meant that the Jewishness of Jesus must be seen as something essential and necessary. He saw Jesus himself as the bridge between Jews and Christians.

After the sermon a woman asked Barth to explain what he meant. He answered in writing: "If you believe in Christ, who was himself a Jew and who died for Gentiles and Jews alike, you *cannot* take part in the disdain and the ill-treatment that the Jews are suffering today."[31] In the sermon Barth had quoted the Gospel of John: "Salvation is from the Jews" (John 4:22). During the Second World War, through his initiative, this verse became the motto for the relief efforts conducted by the Swiss Reformed Church on behalf of the persecuted Jews. In his sermon Barth boldly proclaimed: Jesus Christ "looks on us as Jews, struggling with the one true God [which is what the name Israel means]. He even looks on us heathens as those who have made peace with the wrong gods. But he sees Christians and Jews together as 'children of the living God.'" Therefore we can only "shake hands with one another, and we can only praise God for his faithfulness to us despite all our unfaithfulness to him. When we grasp this, we will accept one another."[32]

Barth's convictions had many practical consequences during the Second World War. I mention only one. When in 1944 the German army trans-

---

31. Eberhard Busch, *Karl Barths Lebenslauf* (Munich: Chr. Kaiser Verlag, 1975), p. 247.
32. Karl Barth, "Die Kirche Jesu Christi," *Theologische Existenz Heute* 5 (1933), pp. 16–17.

ported nearly a million Jews from Hungary to the concentration camps in order to exterminate them, Rabbi Zwi Taubes of Zurich hurried to Karl Barth to show him the documents about it. Barth immediately contacted the Swiss authorities, because he felt that only they were in a position to help. Indeed, for the first time they became active in such an affair. So some thousands were saved.

## Baptized into a Holy People

During the seven-day war of Israel with its neighbors in June of 1967, Barth was extremely restless. One night he dreamt he was called to take up his rifle and help the Israeli army. When he awoke in the morning, he was disappointed that he was too old for this kind of task. Therefore he went to the post office and sent a considerable sum of money to the army of the Jewish state. Throughout the day he kept turning on the radio for news. He was happy to hear the names of the old places known from the Bible. Upon learning that the Israeli army had defeated its enemies, he handed my wife a piece of chocolate with a little card that said "Victory!" But he gave it, he said, in the hope that one day those enemies would cease to be enemies and become friends.

At the end of this dramatic day he announced: "Now I am ready! I must finish the final corrections of my baptism ms. before it goes into print." The final sentence, which he dictated to me on the evening of that very day, is astonishing. Note that these are literally the last words that he ever wrote for the whole of his *Church Dogmatics*: "In sum, in baptism a person becomes an active member of the holy people of Israel, which is appointed to serve as 'a covenant to the people, a light to the nations' (Isa. 42:6)."[33]

---

33. Karl Barth, *Church Dogmatics* IV/4 (fragment) (Edinburgh: T. & T. Clark, 1969), p. 201 (translation revised). The subsequent text, as it now stands in the printed volume (pp. 201-13), had been written earlier.

# 3

## A Dialogue between David Novak and Eberhard Busch

GEORGE HUNSINGER

At Barth Center conferences we have sometimes shown a BBC video interview with Karl Barth. When the BBC first asked him for an interview, he declined. When they persisted, he agreed but insisted that it would be "60 minutes, no more!" (In the event, it was two hours and not a minute more before he excused himself, explaining, "I am busy with *Church Dogmatics*; the angels and the demons watching.") And then he wanted them to send their questions in advance. On those terms, he did the interview.

With Barth's example in mind, I prepared questions in advance for Eberhard Busch and David Novak. What follows is a transcript of our conversation.

**Hunsinger:** In what sense do you believe that the Jews are the chosen people of God?

**Novak:** Well, if belief means affirmation, then I affirm it because this is what Torah and the Jewish tradition have taught. But I think that when one talks about "the chosen people," one has to understand that the true *leitmotif* of the Old Testament, the Hebrew Bible, is election. God elects to create a universe. God has freedom of choice; God doesn't have to create a universe. God elects to create the human person in his own image and likeness. He doesn't have to. God elects the people of Israel. Now what does God elect Israel for? And there I think that the election is either retrospective or prospective. In other words, if God elected the people of Israel, then what makes the people of Israel different from other people? Is there some kind of genetic component? Is there some kind of cultural component? Well, if that's the case, then for the Jewish people, it could be a source of great pride. "Look at us, we're better than anyone else, and that's why God chose us." The fact is that God does not reveal his reasons for choosing the people.

Therefore, the choice of the Jewish people—and I will use two German expressions—is not a *Gabe* (gift), but an *Aufgabe*—it's a task. The people are to live up to God's election. God has a plan, not only for all of humankind, but for the whole universe, in which somehow the people of Israel play a central role. But clearly, it says in Deuteronomy, "I haven't chosen you because of your great numbers. You're the smallest of the peoples, the most insignificant of the peoples."[1] So in that way, it is not a question of a kind of racism. It's not a racism because anyone who wants to become a part or a member of the people of Israel can. And it's the covenantal logic that one can check in, but one cannot ever really check out. And that is simply a factor. I think that to live a Jewish life in the world that's coherent on the part of the Jew, one must understand that God has elected his people for a purpose: to be faithful to his covenant, to be in the vanguard of the time when all humankind and the entire universe will be reconciled with God.

And I think that all efforts of modern Jewish thinkers to argue out of election, to indicate that this is some kind of chauvinism or racist vestige, are actually wrong, and I think that it actually began with the quintessential modern Jewish renegade, Baruch Spinoza, who inverted it. It was not God who chose the Jews; it was the Jews who chose God. And therefore, if the Jews chose God, they could un-choose God. But if God chose the people of Israel and said that his covenant is everlasting, then those of us who have been born into the covenant and chosen to remain in the covenant have to take that not as something that we can use to say, "Hey, look at me, I'm a part of that, I'm chosen," but rather, to remember that this is always a task. This is always—to use a German phrase—an *Aufgabe*, a task placed upon us, rather than something we can claim was given to us.

**H:** Thank you. Professor Busch?

**Busch:** It is interesting to hear your answer. But if I understand the election of the Jews, then it is in my view, first of all, a gift of God. They have not elected themselves. God has elected them. And that was not because of anything special. You can read it in what I call the First Testament, the Old Testament. Often it is said, "You are the fewest of all peoples; *therefore*

---

1. Deut. 7:7.

## A Dialogue between David Novak and Eberhard Busch

has God chosen you." And I see this election, first, as a gift of God. And I would say that if you see it only as a task, then you have the problem which prophets raised, "How is it that this elected people fails to correspond to its election?" I like very much the words of the prophet Hosea which I spend a long time in reading: "My people are determined to turn from me. . . . My heart is changed within me; all my compassion is aroused. I will not carry out my fierce anger," and now the wonderful bit, "for I am God, and not man—the Holy One among you. I will not come in wrath" (Hos. 11:7-9). I think that is, in my understanding of the First Testament, an accent that what comes first is not the task, but the task then follows. The task is to correspond to the gift of God. This is my answer.

**H:** [To Professor Novak] Would you like to respond at all?

**N:** What I mean by task is as follows: It's very interesting that this *Shabbat*, this upcoming Sabbath, the reading from the Torah is from the sixteenth chapter of the book of Numbers where Korah rebels against the authority of Moses. He makes the statement, *"Ki kal haedah kulam qedosim ubetowkam Yahweh umaddua titnasseu al qehal Yahweh."* All of the congregation are holy! So who are you and Moses and Aaron to have this kind of hierarchy? We're all holy! God is in our midst! *Gott mit uns!* And Martin Buber has a wonderful critique of that; he said that holiness in the Bible is always used with "shall be holy"—it's a task. Yes, it's a gift, but it's not something I can claim as a possession. Because if it's a gift, then I say, "I must have done something to deserve this gift." The fact is, God says, "You didn't deserve it." Therefore the task means that it's always something I need, not to earn in the sense of getting a reward, but it's something that I always have to demonstrate.

In other words, if God chose me, then God chose me for some kind of purpose. Probably one of the greatest rabbinic scholars is a survivor of Auschwitz. And when he was taken to the camp, they immediately divided you in two lines. There were people who immediately went to the gas chamber, and there were those who immediately went on work detail. And he said that he made a vow to God. He said, "If God will let me survive, I will devote the rest of my life to the Torah." If God will let me survive. And he is convinced, that if he was saved by God, then God saved him for a purpose. So if God elected him to live, it was for the purpose of studying the Torah, applying the Torah, and living according to it. So I agree with you—it's not a kind of works piety. It's not, "Guess what, I'll prove to you

I'm chosen by how righteous I am." But it means that it's a gift, but I can't claim it as a possession.

**B:** I think that we are not so far apart. We are close together. But it is a fundamental point, I think, in the First Testament that Israel has not elected itself. In this sense, I say it is a gift of God.

**N:** Yes.

**B:** Then it follows that this is a task. And what you related about the man who devoted his life to the Torah is wonderful. It's very moving. But I think in the books of the prophets the problem is: What happens when they do not follow the gift? Indeed, it is right, I agree, that the problem is there.

**N:** Yes, yes.

**H:** Good, let's move on. My next question will be a little different for each of our guests. It has to do with the idea of the one true religion. So to Professor Busch I will ask, "Is Christianity the one true religion? Or is it one of several true religions?" And to Professor Novak, "Is Judaism the one true religion? Or is it one of several true religions?" Let's begin this time with Professor Busch.

**B:** That is a point that is surely interesting. But I would say regarding the phrase "Christianity is the one true religion," that this is old thinking which is not right in this form. In the nineteenth century the liberal theology in Christianity said that everything is relative, but at the end, Christianity is the absolute religion. In the thinking of the nineteenth century, there is a claim for absoluteness. In a radical way I want to answer this question: it depends not on service to God, but on service from God to all humans. A religion may survive; it may survive in a sense that it is "true." I would say "more." The Christian religion is more true, the more it gives witness to this truth: only that we depend on that which God does with us.

**N:** The question is whether I think Judaism is the one true religion. Professor Busch alluded to nineteenth-century liberals, which was not only nineteenth-century liberal Christian theology, but nineteenth-century Jewish theology as well, both of which have survived. And that was basically, "Let's avoid all truth claims altogether. And you have yours, and I have mine. And we'll all live in harmony and peace." But of course we all know that traditions that are based on revelation like Judaism, Christianity, Islam do make truth claims. So that becomes the question.

There's an ancient debate in the Talmud. There's a verse from the eighth psalm, which can be translated, "All of the gentiles have forgotten God," which would imply that only Judaism is true and that is all. Or "All the gentiles *who* have forgotten God." Some have, some haven't. Some of the Jews have, and [some] haven't. The opinion that was accepted by someone like Maimonides, although there were those who disagreed with it, was that basically, all of those gentiles who live according to the law of God as they understand it have, as he put it, a portion in the world to come. Obviously, he thought that the Jewish revelation had the best claim to truth, but that doesn't mean that everyone else's was false.

Now how does that translate into practice? One type of practice is that I can go out and proselytize and tell people that what I have is true and what you have is false. Therefore you should accept what I have as true. Even though it's not prohibited in Judaism, generally Jews, for a variety of reasons, both internal and external, have avoided proselytizing. But we do accept converts. Therefore the only time it really becomes a practical issue is that if a gentile decides that they want to convert to Judaism, we have to say to a certain extent that we think you made a correct decision. You're rising at the level of truth. And if a Jew decides to convert out of Judaism, as it were, we have to say that we think you've made a very bad decision. If they ask us. Most Jews who leave Judaism don't ask us. You know, they are absent without leave. So in that sense, it really only becomes an issue when you're either trying to, in effect, persuade people to come to what you have, or you're trying to persuade people not to leave the covenantal community.

But if you're not engaged in that, then the gauge is, yes, obviously if I thought that something like Christianity, or Islam, or whatever, had a closer relation to the one true God, I would become that. I don't think that. In other words, I was born a Jew. But I came from a relatively nonobservant Jewish family. I mean they were not atheists, but Judaism was not terribly important to them, and I decided to become much more of a Jew than most of my family. That was my choice. And even though you cannot—there's a Talmudic expression, "Even those who have sinned, become apostates, are still part of Israel"—yet de facto people have left the Jewish community either for some other religion or no religion. And we haven't sent a posse after them. That becomes their de facto choice. So I think the task is, number one, if you really want to become a committed member of your faith community, yes, you have to believe that it has the ... it's been given, as it were ... the best take on truth possible in this world. Even though the final truth won't be revealed until the world to come.

On the other hand, that is something you have to do. Because if you're not going to make truth claims, then religion becomes a matter of taste and subjective preference. However, it should not lead to the type of triumphalism which basically goes, "I have the truth, and whatever you have is inferior or totally false." But it always seems to me that that approach—especially when done by Christians—is an example of works piety of the worst kind. Basically, "Here I am, I'm saved!" You know? And that sort of thing. But to bear witness, there's a different story. I mean every time I have to say at a Jewish conference, "I'm sorry, it's getting dark on a Friday afternoon, I have to keep the Sabbath," I'm bearing witness. I'm bearing witness to God who has created the world and has rested on the Sabbath and commanded the people of Israel to keep the Sabbath. I'm not proselytizing, but I'm bearing witness. I'm bearing witness by saying that this takes precedence over whatever we're doing. I'm not saying whatever we're doing is wrong; I'm saying this takes precedence. And I think that becomes the question.

However, if truth is understood as logical demonstration, I don't think that our respective faith commitments are conclusions from premises. I don't think that anyone was ever argued into faith. I think that one has to have the experience of grace, and faith is a response to grace. I think that's the way it has to be handled.

**B:** The most problematic word here is "Christianity." What does it mean? It is very dark for me. Is it everything that falls under the heading of Christianity? Does it mean real in the sense of Jesus Christ? It is a very heavy question. And if you look at Christianity, I often think it might be better if I were not a Christian, because I don't belong to this or that circle. Therefore we have to define very clearly what the subject is in this question. And I would say that if we think in terms of the congregation, in the name of Christ, then we have to think about the question of true religion.

If you look at the different forms of Christianity that appear in the world, you could say there are only relative differences between Christian forms, and Buddhist forms, and so on. There are different ways of living it out. Today, maybe in this country too, the tendency is to connect them eclectically. People especially experience something like this in Japan. At a birth, you follow this religion, for the burial ceremonies, it is better to be a Shintoist or something, and for the marriage ceremony, you go to a Christian church. But I think that is a problematic way of thinking also for Germany. They are mixing it up today. It's a very important question for Christianity in my region; it becomes . . . but I don't mean to set myself up as a teacher for you because I don't know exactly what's going on in this country. But Christianity assumes a face, a clear public profile.

What is meant by the Christian life is first the congregation. And then you will not be able to say, "Here is the only true religion," because as a pastor in a congregation I can think of people who don't belong to the church, or who may have left the church, and perhaps they understood better what Jesus was about than all the people who paid their tithes and offerings to become a member. The question is very complicated which you pose here.

**H:** Again, a two-part question. Or one different for each of our speakers. For David Novak: In what sense do you believe the Torah to be divine revelation? And for Professor Busch: In what sense do you believe the gospel to be divine revelation?

**N:** Yes. When it comes to the question of divine revelation, there is always the question that was raised by what is called biblical criticism, beginning actually with Spinoza and then going up through Wellhausen, "How can you believe a strong revelation?" These are different documents. In that sense I take a more phenomenological approach. The philosophy that I find most helpful for my theology is phenomenology. And that is, I really don't know how the text was put together. There are all kinds of theories. Even if there were separate authors of the parts of the Torah, they all clearly believed that what they were transmitting was divine revelation. I don't think they themselves thought this was something they themselves were making up. And the Jewish people have experienced the revelation of the Torah as a seamless garment. As a datum. As what Husserl called a *cogitatum*, something that we know as a whole, a *gestalt*; I mean there are all these kinds of terms. And therefore the question becomes: How does one interpret this revelation?

This revelation has to be interpreted by those who are members of the community who've accepted this revelation. And they use all kinds of tools. They use hermeneutical tools, they use philosophical tools. This is very much a *credo ut intelligam*. I accept it in faith, as a whole, as a datum, and then I attempt to understand it, what it means, how it's to be applied, and whatever. But Judaism stands and falls on the most important Jewish dogma, which is the dogma of Torah Min-Hashamayim: "the Torah comes from God." And you can understand the process of revelation in a variety of different ways; indeed, it was in the rabbinic tradition. How much did the people, all of them, hear, how much of it was mediated through Moses, and so on.

But without revelation there is simply no Judaism. It becomes a human-made phenomenon which humans can make and humans can take away, to paraphrase Job. And this is what I found most exciting in Barth: Barth's unapologetic approach, that the Logos appeared, that the Logos in this case became flesh—certainly the word became flesh for Christians—that this is the word of God, this is the word of God which claims us, and claims us not only to do it, but to understand it and to interpret it and to struggle with it. That is the most important in Jewish dogma. Franz Rosenzweig said, "Das Judentum hat keine Dogmatik aber Dogmen."[2] "Judaism had no dogmatic structure"—actually the dogmatic structure of Judaism is the halakah, it's really the law, which is very structured—"but it does have dogmas." And the dogma of Torah Min-Hashamayim, it can be interpreted in a number of ways, but once that is given up, I think that Judaism has become incoherent.

**B:** The first question is: What is the gospel? The gospel is the message of God, by which you become a free human being. It makes you free from fear of death, and it makes you free from your sin, and free from the powers which want to rule over us. That is the gospel. It is not something you can do by yourself; once more, it is a gift from God to you. But the gift is not only swimming in the pure air of the gospel; you meet it if you read the Bible. In Old and New Testament. The gospel is given to us in the first and decisive line of the Holy Scripture. And it is very moving to see this perception emerge during the Reformation.

At first the reformers had no article about Scripture, but they were speaking about what happens when the Bible meets us. Calvin writes, "You have to read it. But if you read it, it happens as an event which grasps you, and you cannot avoid hearing it. And you become happy to hear it. It is an event which encounters us." What does it mean in a theological sense?

---

2. "Das Judentum hat namlich Dogmen aber keine Dogmatik." Franz Rosenzweig, *Kleinere Schriften* (Berlin: Schocken Books, 1937), p. 31.

*A Dialogue between David Novak and Eberhard Busch*

Calvin says that we need the Holy Spirit; the Bible speaks in this way to us. And what does it mean? When you have to make a sermon, you read the Bible—indeed, you have to read it—but at the same time you have to pray that God should open this word for us, for without this opening of the word of God by the Holy Spirit you understand nothing. You can read it in Calvin. He said it in this way.

And if you read the Bible—we will speak later on, I think, about the problem, too—you don't need only the Bible, but you also need to have open eyes to what is happening and what is surrounding you in nature and in history and so on. But the first step is always and remains decisive: reading Holy Scripture.

And what I wish for German worship services would be for them to become open for this: simply reading the Bible. When I go to the Reformed services, for I am Reformed, the preacher tells us what we have read in the day before in the newspaper. And so I hear it again. It can of course be very interesting to hear it again from the pulpit. At the end, however, we do have a biblical text for the day, but it's in the last part of the reading. I learned, from Karl Barth, that you have to *begin* with it! And not bring up a story which is nothing. If you open the Bible, I think the most important thing is that sometimes we find a verse which is very important for us. In the Lutheran Bible, these verses are printed in boldface letters. And then you think only this is important for you. But my experience is, if you continue to read, you learn much more than before. At the end you think, "My initial understanding was too small." The Bible opens up a wide horizon.

**H:** Next question: Do Christians and Jews believe in the same God?

**N:** Is the question belief or worship? There's a difference.

**H:** What's the difference?

**N:** This was a tremendous debate in medieval Judaism. The debate was never the question of the same God. Christians say they worship the Lord God of Israel. That was never held in dispute. How can you say that they're not if they say that they are? What was held in dispute in the early Middle Ages—in the middle and later Middle Ages it became different—what was held in dispute is as follows: in the Bible itself, there is really no explicit prohibition of gentile idolatry. The understanding is that the people of Israel have the covenant with the one creator God; the gentiles have their own gods. So any criticism of idolatry is that Jews are attracted to gentile idolatry or the moral faults. Look at the beginning of the book of Amos. I'm criticizing the gentiles for the same reason I'm criticizing the Jews: their moral faults. In the rabbinic tradition, even sources in the Hellenistic Jewish tradition, now the prohibition of idolatry is considered to be universal. Now this is something that God prohibits for both the gentiles and the Jews. Now idolatry in the rabbinic tradition is called *avodah zarah*. Strange worship. It's not the worship of a strange god, but it's the worship even of the right God in an inappropriate fashion.

Now the debate in medieval Judaism wasn't, "Are the Christians worshiping the God of Israel?" We don't dispute that. But are they worshiping the God of Israel in a way that's inappropriate for any human being? Or are they worshiping the God of Israel in a way that's appropriate for them but not appropriate for us? Why? Because they have a different relationship. Their relationship with the God of Israel is mediated by Jesus the Christ. Our relationship with God is mediated by the Torah. In that sense, that became the question. You can line up with these theological options. I am on the side that *avodah zarah*, strange worship, means that it is the prohibition of strange worship for a Jew to worship the God of Israel in any other way than is developed by the Jewish tradition. It is not strange worship for a Christian whose connection to the God of Israel is different than mine, even though I do believe it is one covenant, but it's one covenant that is lived by two very distinct communities and traditions. So that is really the debate.

But what happened in modern times was that the whole question—this is going back to the truth question—that maybe we shouldn't talk about this at all. Maybe we're not going to get anywhere with this, let's talk about something else, and Franz Rosenzweig, who, like Karl Barth, had a remarkable capacity to utter a *bon mot*, said that the reason many modern liberals like the idea of monotheism is that one is the closest number to zero. You know the old joke about the Ten Commandments: we got 'em down to ten! So in that way, this becomes a very important point, because it means, are gentiles ... are Christians, let's say, in this case, worshiping God in a way that we consider to be inappropriate for anybody? Or are they worshiping God in a way that is perfectly appropriate for them but is not appropriate for us? And I am on the side of the latter option.

The document *Dabru Emet*, which was given to you in your packet, [was written by] Peter Ochs and I—there were four authors, unfortunately only two of us are still alive—Tikva Frymer-Kensky and Michael

Signer died rather young of illness. But clearly we could not have written that article, that statement, which has been translated into eight different languages, if we thought that Christianity was a form of strange worship for everybody. But understanding that difference means we worship the same God. We worship the same God out of the same book, the Bible. But we worship that God differently. Now when God comes at the end of days, or returns at the end of days, depending on which version you wish, then the whole earth will worship God in one way. But until that time, any attempt to pressure others into worshiping God your way is, I think, pseudomessianism.

**H:** Some Jews believe that Christians are guilty of idolatry.

**N:** Yes, I guess you open up idolatry, but there are two words for idolatry. One is *avodat elilim*, that's generally the biblical term, worship of other gods. Now clearly, other than certain, perhaps, forms that are marginal to Christianity that have tritheism, clearly the idea of the Trinity is not three different gods. And the interesting thing about worshiping the same God, in the early Middle Ages, Jewish and Muslim polemics against Christian Trinitarianism were as follows: What do you mean by one in three and three in one? This makes no sense; we are strict monotheists, you have compromised monotheism.

When the kabbalah emerged in the thirteenth century, with its talk of the multiplicity of God, and kabbalah became the *leitmotif* of Jewish theology from the thirteenth century all the way into the nineteenth century, it's amazing how all Jewish anti-Trinitarian polemics vanish, virtually. Because now Jews are talking about divine multiplicity. It's very interesting; you have to trace the history of this. But clearly, even those who would say that Christians are a form of wrong worship, it is still wrong worship of the right God. And those who would say that Christians are worshiping another God altogether from the perspective of what I'm going to call these "right-wingers"—and I'm hardly left wing on anything, but there are people to the right of me, believe it or not—it becomes: How is this sorted out?

This is very much a factor and has to be sorted out. Maimonides, for example, talks about three revelations: Jews, Christianity, and Islam. So which is the best? His argument is a very philosophical argument. It's the revelation that coordinates the relationship between God and humans best, and he's convinced that Judaism did that best. But he does not deny that Christians or Muslims are not illegitimate worshipers of the one God.

**B:** I agree with many things which you wrote, but I want to answer the question in another direction. I am a little critical over against my own Christian tradition and the Christian life in my region. Because often, very often, Christians worshiped the wrong god. And therefore it is difficult to answer the question: Is it the same God? And you can sometimes see a disparity of views in a room full of Christians about what is named God. When a prophet would come—I am not a prophet—but would come to us, I think that this prophet [would have] many things to do like Amos or others. And say, "What you do is wrong! You do service to the wrong god." And I think that is a source of the answer to your question of the same God. But I want not to lament about the Christianity in Europe. I think to *myself*, which service do *I* live or follow? Is it the wrong god? That is a deep question. And I have to put it to myself. Then I have to pray such things as the Lord's Prayer, and I cannot quote it in your language, "Und führe uns nicht in Versuchung, sondern erlöse uns von dem Bösen."

**H:** Lead us not into temptation, but deliver us from evil.

**B:** Yes, I think there is a concrete necessity for me—I will not speak for anyone else—but for me to pray it. That God will lead me out of this danger. And when—I make it slow now—and when this prayer is heard, by God, then God's name, God's word, will speak to me. And then I think the question of whether we have the same God in the Old Testament and New Testament—that means also the question of whether Jews and Christians have another God—is not so deep a question. Because we see then it is a gift to see it. Indeed, thanks be to God, it is indeed the same God. [In] different forms he is understood by Jews and Christians, but thanks be to God, it is the same.

**H:** Let's begin with Professor Busch this time. What is your view of natural theology?

**B:** It can mean different things. What does natural theology mean? If you think that it's knowledge, cognition of the nature as creation of God, then indeed I think we have to discover it again and again, and today especially that nature is something made, and made by God. We need continually to ask about and discover what makes men and women persons with a God-given nature. But maybe you think in another way. And then it becomes more difficult. In the eighteenth century especially we had the development of a theology or a way of thinking in which it was posited that we don't need God to speak to us by revelation, because we can discover everything from the given nature of the world. Immanuel Kant, to give only one example, said that the principle of his thinking was the starry heaven above him and the moral law in his heart.[3] In other words, you don't need a Bible, revelation. Is there then a problem? We can see it in the development of the eighteenth and nineteenth century in theology, that they became great problems. And more and more the thinking of theology departed from Christian theology. Therefore we have to decide, in our thinking, where do we see what nature is? In what way can we see what God has given in the creation? At that point we have to start with revelation, and think from there: this is the framework in which God sets his people, working with his grace and his law.

**N:** On the question of natural theology, I agree with Karl Barth on one point and disagree with him on another. On the notion of natural theology, that somehow or other we can get a knowledge of God and even a relationship with God, which does, as we say in English, an end run around revelation, it is best illustrated—Professor Busch referred to the eighteenth century—by the great German poet Friedrich Schiller in his poem "An die Freude," "Ode to Joy," which was set to music by Beethoven in the Ninth Symphony. The line is "über'm Sternenzelt/Muss ein lieber Vater wohnen" (over the starry skies/the loving Father lives), and by the way—Kant may have liked the starry skies, but whether the loving Father was on top, that is a question—and then the line, "Deine Zauber binden wieder/Was der Mode Schwert geteilt."[4] In other words, your magic, this natural theology, does away with custom, which is based on revelation, tradition. We don't need all of that. We have a direct relationship. I think, by the way, the one who defeated that whole notion was Kant, quite clearly. So in terms of natural theology, yes, I think that the only possible positive relationship with God is through revelation.

And even natural theology, when Karl Barth gave his Gifford Lectures in 1936—and I'm preparing for my own, so I reread them—and it was marvelous! He said, "Lord Gifford talks about natural theology. Has anyone read anything that I've written? I don't know why you invited me. But I'm here." So what did he do? He didn't do natural theology. He did a theology

---

3. Found in the conclusion in Kant's *Critique of Practical Reason*, 1788.
4. Thy magic powers reunite/what custom's sword has divided.

of nature. Which means basically that from revelation, which is a miracle, the only God who could possibly perform these miracles is the God who has created nature. And therefore an opening for it to happen. Therefore we appreciate God as creator of nature in retrospection from revelation. Not that we go from creation to revelation, but it's revelation that therefore informs us about creation. So in that sense of natural theology, I pretty much agree with Barth.

Where I disagree with Barth is that Barth assumed in all of his arguments against natural law that natural law presupposes natural theology, which it does certainly in Thomistic natural law theory, and therefore if you can't have natural theology, natural law goes with it. There I think that Barth was wrong. And in fact in my own writing I've indicated that Barth really does have a natural law theory even though he protests to the contrary. It might be very minimal, but it's there. Therefore when Barth talks about *Allgemein und Menschenrechte*, general human obligation, this is something that human beings, as political beings, can have some understanding of how they are to live in the world. What revelation gives to them is "you're in the image of God." It's not just works and society. But this is how God wants this world, and you have some inkling of it. But it's revelation that really gives you the foundation. Therefore I agree with Barth that there's a theology of nature and not a natural theology, but I don't think that natural law, contrary to the Thomistic tradition, even though I was educated by Thomists, is connected thereto. And that would be very much a difference.

But the greatest natural theology, the most impressive natural theology, was the natural theology of Alfred North Whitehead. And Alfred North Whitehead, who was a theist but clearly neither a Christian or a Jew, basically goes back to the god of Plato. And the god of Plato, the god of philosophers, is not the God of Abraham, Isaac, and Jacob. Therefore in terms of natural theology, yes, there's a theology of nature, no, natural law does not presuppose natural theology. I think they have to be sorted out.

**H:** What can Christians and Jews learn from each other?

**B:** Indeed, we can learn as Christians from Jews and Judaism. It is right, in this conference, that we can learn. And you show at the same time, that you have learned from the Christians, and that is a wonderful experience for me in these days. I knew a man in Switzerland. He's not known in this time. His name is Paul Vogt. He worked together with Karl Barth to save

*A Dialogue between David Novak and Eberhard Busch*

Jews in Switzerland in the dark time. And I headed the service when he was buried. And the rabbi of Zurich came after I had spoken in the pulpit, and he said to the whole congregation there, "I don't like the Christians. But . . . Paul Vogt was a Christian." He wanted to underline this; this was his negation. Because he had a clear view of this: what it means to follow the bond of connection with the Jews.

I often read Psalm 1, where it is written, "Blessed is the man who does not walk in the counsel of the wicked. . . . His delight is in the Law of the Lord. And on this law he meditates day and night. He is like a tree planted by streams of water . . ." and so on. Read it. It is such a wonderful speaking of the gift which is given to the Jews. There I think oftentimes of a picture which is made from—I forgot the name—from a Jewish painter and you see there a Jew meditating by day and by night. And in the Jewish life, we discover such persons, and we have to learn from them. You spoke in the beginning of a Jew who after he was saved from the concentration camp, he spent his life for the Torah. And I think that connects—I want to learn it, to concentrate on it, to the Word of God, to the Torah.

**N:** What can Jews learn from Christians? I'd like to give two personal anecdotes that I think can illustrate it better than something abstract. The first anecdote is that my initial connection to Karl Barth—and I actually met Karl Barth very briefly at his one appearance at Princeton University in 1962—but my first connection to Karl Barth was actually when I was an undergraduate at University of Chicago, and I took a course on the New Testament taught by his eldest son, Markus. What I learned from Markus Barth was very interesting. I wrote a paper on Romans chapters 9–11 for Markus Barth's course. And don't forget I was at the University of Chicago, which was still in the heyday of the neo-Aristotelian philosophy of Robert Hutchins and Richard McKeon. And I was a major in classics, Greek. So I decided that what Paul was doing was that the Jews are the potential, using Aristotelian terms, and the Christians are the actualization. Markus Barth returned my paper and wrote the following, "You are a Jew. Why are you using terms of Greek pagans? Why don't you use Jewish terms of creation, promise, and redemption?" So there a Christian told me, Stop using this type of language and be more authentic.

And that reminded me of my childhood. As I mentioned before, I did not grow up in an observant Jewish family. My parents belonged to a synagogue. And I got religion, as they say, at an early age. And my father and mother were kind of concerned about it, you know? "He's getting too religious, what is this?" My mother had a friend who comforted her and told her, "Oh they all go through that stage, he'll outgrow it! Don't worry, my son did that too, and now he's an atheist." It's like acne, or something like that. So anyway, we had a very close family friend, the Jones family. And they were—some people find this bizarre today—but they were actually very devout low church Episcopalians. They were very serious about their Anglican faith. And they were my—as it were—rescuers. They said to my parents, "You should be proud that your son is a better Jew than you are! You should be proud that he's becoming part of the tradition! This is not something that you should be concerned about. This is something you should be proud of." So at a very early age, these very devout Christians were basically arguing for my becoming more of a Jew than my family background. And therefore I have always, throughout my life, resonated most to those Christians who want me to be most Jewish.

The second thing, more abstractly, is that I deal a lot with questions of public morality—questions of war and peace, marriage, and this sort of thing. And in fact, when I came to the University of Toronto, about a year after I came there, somebody said to me, "You're so theological. How did they ever hire you here? Why did they give you a professorship?" And I said, "Theological? I don't know what you're talking about. That's what Christians do. I just do universal ethics." Got a big laugh, but anyway. But the point there is that when you read Jewish treatments, classical Jewish treatments of these subjects, they're all academic. Jews did not have political power. They were really not in the world at all. We were in a ghetto somewhere. And therefore, like on just war theory, when I read Augustine and other Christians on just war theory, these were people who had real live experience with political power. And therefore I can learn a lot from them on how the law of God can be in the world but not of the world. The discussions in my own tradition, which are interesting, are basically by rabbis sitting in a synagogue off in a corner somewhere who had no notion of political power. So in that sense, this is something that I've learned from Christians: how to be in the world, which Jews since modern times are, without the world "doing you in," becoming of the world.

H: What do you most appreciate about Karl Barth? And what do you most regret about him?

N: What do I appreciate? I basically mentioned in the talk I gave last night, I appreciate, first of all, what Michael Wyschogrod appreciated: Karl Barth's audacity.[5] Karl Barth's simply saying, I am not going to tailor my theology to your point of view. I am going to speak its inner logic, and if you see the point you see the point. If you don't see the point, then I can't dispute that. There's a wonderful rabbinic phrase: if the Torah is empty, the emptiness is from you, not from the Torah. That kind of audacity. And I think part of that came from his personal experience of being German-speaking but Swiss, rather than German itself, in the time of the First World War. He was very much a minority; he was very much a foreigner like the Jews were foreigners. So in that sense, but I mean the tremendous power of Barth's theology, and the tremendous power is especially that Barth insisted that God had not broken his covenant with the Jews, which means we have a lot in common with Christians, and we have differences, and they can't be underestimated. There's a dialectic there. There is a *ja* and a *nein*, a *sic et non*. And that is something I think will take place until the end of time.

My only regret about Barth, and this has been pointed out a number of times, is that at times Barth seems to fall into a kind of classical Christian anti-Judaism; you find it in a number of the church fathers. And it is kind of chilling to read some of the statements that are written in 1942 and 1943 [with] what was going on in the world. And that's something I do regret in Barth, but as my friend Kurt Richardson, who's a Barth scholar, pointed out, Barth was a human being, and very fortunately, Protestant Christians have not done to Karl Barth what the Catholics did to Thomas Aquinas. You didn't canonize him. Which means you did not turn him into revelation. You can't disagree with revelation; you can only interpret it. But you can agree and disagree.

So I would say that I agree with most of Karl Barth. There are points that I disagree because I'm a Jew and he's a Christian, namely, who was the Messiah. I mean that's a big point of disagreement; that is the *différence même* (essential difference), as they say in French. But I think basically, I thank God that God sent Karl Barth to the Christians, and enabled us Jews to overhear a lot of what he had to say to you.

**B:** Thank you. I will stress other points. What is impressive for me is especially his formula: you have to begin with the beginning, always. And I think it was a principle of his thinking, and also in his personal life. He said, "I close every evening with a sigh because I am a sinner. And I'm happy every morning anew that I can start with a new day, and new opportunity

---

5. See Michael Wyschogrod, *The Body of Faith* (New York: Seabury Press, 1983).

to live." It was very strong in his thinking, this element: you have to begin, always, with a new beginning. Begin always with the beginning.[6] And it was a principle of his theology, too, but I want not to demonstrate it in newer form, but say what is a negative, what is a problem.

I think that he had, from the beginning of his life, a very hard head — like a stone, sometimes. There's a nice story. When he walked with a friend in Basel, through the street — Gottlob Wieser was his name — said, "You always want to be right." And he said, "I always *am* right!"[7] And this had the consequence that, I think, every man or woman who would want to be a follower of his thinking had various difficulties with him, because he was always criticizing. He would start with a critique of the nearest persons around him.

**N:** I just wanted to add one point. One of the things that impressed me about Barth — a sort of personal parallel — for the first twenty-three years of my career, I was a congregational rabbi and a part-time academic. And then in midlife I made the move to academia. And one of the things that impressed me in learning about Barth, from his son Markus, is that he began life as a pastor and regularly preached. In fact, in his last days, he was regularly preaching in the jail in Basel. Michael Wyschogrod told me a wonderful story. When he came to see Barth, he phoned and Frau Barth answered the phone, and he said, "I'm Michael Wyschogrod," and she said, "Aus dem Gefängnis?" From the prison? She automatically thought, "Where is he from? He's late."

But in terms of that, there are two factors. And that is, that as somebody who had been a pastor and was regularly, his theology was coming from within the community. And one of the things I would always think about — if I was working on some idea, some theological concept — I would think to myself, this something, this idea — granted, in a simpler form — could I present this in a sermon, and would it make any sense to the people sitting in the congregation? And if it didn't, then it's really not authentic. It's really not authentically Jewish; it's something that is an intellectual con-

---

6. Cf. K. Barth, *Church Dogmatics* I/2, *The Doctrine of the Word of God* (Edinburgh: T. & T. Clark, 1956), p. 868: "In dogmatics strictly speaking there are no comprehensive views, no final conclusions and results. There is only the investigation and teaching which take place in the act of dogmatic work and which, strictly speaking, must continually begin again at the beginning in every point."

7. Busch, *Karl Barth: His Life from Letters and Autobiographical Texts* (Philadelphia: Fortress Press, 1976), p. 395.

struct. And I think the theological circle was not just in Barth's thinking, but that he was from within the community. And that, I think, influenced very much the way he wrote. It is always good to think that Barth was basically speaking to a Christian congregation, and I was very happy that he was allowing non-Christians like me to overhear the sermon.

**H:** Was the Holocaust unique, or simply the latest example of tragedy in Jewish history?

**N:** Of course there are those who have attempted to explain the Holocaust as unique. One of those has been—actually, I knew him—the famous Jewish philosopher Emil Fackenheim, who for many years taught at Toronto University, my university. I will say the following: there is no serious person, whether he's a Jew or a Christian, or anything else, who does not have to confront the Holocaust. This was evil to the nth degree. I think that those thinkers, Jewish thinkers and even some Christian thinkers, who've made the Holocaust the center of their thinking—it's a black hole. It eats you up. It has to be looked at—but like an eclipse of the sun, it has to be looked at sidewise or it will blind you.

I certainly don't think there's an explanation for the Holocaust. I think the explanation is that basically when all is said and done, we Jews especially—but really everybody is the victim—have to thank God that we're alive and try as much as possible to prevent things that seem to look similar. It became very clear to me a number of years ago, when I was invited to give a lecture at the University of Munich. It was a celebration in memory of the Weiße Rose, which was the student anti-Nazi movement. And I gave a talk in the Große Halle, the Great Hall, of Munich, and there was a podium there, not like this podium that you can move around; it was clearly stone, in the floor. And a chill went up my spine, because I remembered a picture of Hitler speaking from the same podium. And then, at one point, I had to say, "Thank God. Because he's dead, and I'm alive. It was supposed to be the other way around."

I don't think the question of the uniqueness—the problem with saying the Holocaust is so unique is that then there's nothing we can learn from it. It's a *sui generis*. On the other hand, the problem is, is the Holocaust just one tragedy among many? But at the end of the day, because there are many Jews who have formed an opinion that the whole survival of Judaism is, as Fackenheim put it, not to give Hitler a posthumous victory, my approach is that I thank God every morning for having elected me as a Jew. God elected me as a Jew. That's my identity; my identity is not that Hitler selected me for annihilation.

**B:** It is very difficult for me to speak to this question. I belong to the generation in which it happened. And it is a very, very deep question. It is moving, every time I have to speak of it. There are tears now. It is so awful! And it is academic, the question whether it is unique or not. But you spoke about it. You cannot bring it in your head why there were millions of men and women and children and so on. It's awful. The real hell in our century, in our time. But I will stress two points. I can't speak about it directly. The first, this is very important to me, because you say, Hitler and some animals did it. No. Thousands and thousands of people worked with them to do it. And they have forgotten it! At the end of the war, they were free and helped to restore the state. This is awful.

And the second point. The church was not very good after the war. The Christian church abdicated its responsibility. Let me mention, because it was typical, the lecture of a famous theologian, which was published in 1948, some time after the war: "The Guilt of the Others."[8] And I think it is awful. A Christian who cannot repent but speaks of the guilt of the others. I think it is so awful that Christianity destroyed itself in order to live; the possibility is so dark, this—not only for the Jews, but also in this other form, the guilt of the Christians was again imponderable. Let me stop here.

**N:** Just one point—one of the things that I find very, very moving was Karl Barth's coming back to Germany right after the war, speaking in bombed-out churches. Telling the German people—I'm sure he took his life in his hands, he could have been killed; this is the Barth who in 1935 was expelled from Germany—speaking of the fact, recalling God's punishment, and yet that repentance was possible. That God had not abandoned the German people. But there had to be a genuine repentance. It couldn't just be business as usual. So he brought a very prophetic message, and the prophet's message is always, yes, there must be genuine repentance, which means the acknowledgment of sin, but that God does not reject anybody's true repentance. And I found that to be quite brave on his part. Somebody could have taken a gun to him. And I found that quite moving, in terms of his sense of prophetic responsibility for the German Christians, who had rejected him!

---

8. Helmut Thielicke and Hermann Diem, *Die Schuld der Anderen: Ein Briefwechsel* (Göttingen: Vandenhoeck & Ruprecht, 1948).

*A Dialogue between David Novak and Eberhard Busch*

**H:** My next question may be something we can pass on. It was, "What is the impact of the Holocaust on Judaism and Christianity, and what impact *should* it have?" Do you have anything to add to what you've already said?

**N:** Not really, other than the fact that, again, with all due respect, I think Fackenheim was a great thinker. And I knew him personally. The Holocaust cannot be the center of Jewish existence. It cannot be. Because it's a black hole. It's a black hole. It just swallows up everything that happens to it. Therefore the survival of the Jewish people is because the covenant did not die in Auschwitz. The covenant has showed those of us who have survived that they therefore have the obligation to live on. But to take this seriously, I give a course—in fact, I'm giving it again this fall—called "Philosophical Responses to the Holocaust," which deals with the writings of Jews, Christians, and secular thinkers. And I tell the students at the beginning of the course, there are two groups of people that I think really . . . I mean, I can't tell you to leave the course, but it's not for you. First of all, if you think it didn't happen or that it's grossly distorted, we have courses on the history of it, take them. This course is not for you. And if you think you, or I, or anybody else has a grand explanation that will explain all of it, you're in the wrong course. All we can do is help people respond.

**H:** [To Professor Busch] Would you like to say something about the impact?

**B:** I think that there are many things we must do, and the first is to be well informed about what was done. And it is astonishing that now in Germany, in the last years, many books came out from the time of suppressions of the Jews, and I told my children, please give me no books for my birthday, I have enough. But everyone came with a new book of news about the Hitler time and the persecution. I have a big library about this matter. And then the second is, we have to change many ways of thinking, not only in the public realm, but especially in the church. It is a good sign that many have discovered anew the First Testament, the Old Testament, and they write sermons about it. And I think you would agree, if you heard this. This is a change, indeed.

Then, I think on the whole, there are many different tasks to do; I think in Göttingen it was very awful at the time. We had very ugly professors of theology who agreed with what happened. There were many. I will name three: Otto Weber, Emanuel Hirsch, and Friedrich Gogarten, among others. These are theologians.

But now, it is wonderful to see, every year, there is a place where in former times a synagogue existed. And now the youth come together; the students have the memory of the Jews in our town. And we have a new synagogue, and there are many problems because . . . funding mostly comes from Russia, and many don't know what it is to be a Jew. They don't know. But there is good help for this, and I think there is a science of renewal which happens. The most important thing is, I think, that Christians have to learn in theology and in the realm of the congregations, not only to speak about Jews, but to speak with Jews.

**N:** I hope this is not considered to be in any way patronizing. But we're here at Princeton Seminary, which is a Presbyterian seminary. Busch has indicated that he's of Reformed background. So we have this Calvinist background. I think that the fact that Calvin was a nonsupersessionist and Barth was a nonsupersessionist has some very practical ramifications. And I think of one in particular.

Some of you may have heard of the group of villages called Le Chambon-sur-Lignon in southern France. These were Calvinists, organized by a pastor, André Trocmé. These were French Calvinists who were in the mountains in southern France, southwestern France primarily because—after the Saint Bartholomew's Day massacre, in the slaughter of French Protestants—it's easy to hide out in the mountains. It's harder to find you. And of about five thousand people, they sheltered almost as many: five thousand Jews. And they are very old, and they are very poor people. And I saw an amazing documentary about it—some of you may have seen it—they were interviewed.

**H:** We're showing it tomorrow night in this room. It's called *Weapons of the Spirit*.

**N:** Yes. And I remember this. And to the credit of the Jewish community, there's a principle [at 01:32:55 in the film], remembering when good has been done for you, and actually these people to a large extent are being supported in their old age by Jews who are grateful for what they did. But they asked them, "Why did you do this?" And they gave two answers. One answer, which was just basically, and is a good enough answer: These were human beings! And we can't just sit around when human beings are being murdered. And then they said, and this is what comes out of their Calvinism, "They were the people of God. To the extent, that if they're murdering the people of God, then this is the anti-Christ doing it." Now that comes out of their Calvinist theology.

And it's interesting that in the Netherlands especially, the overwhelming number of those who risked their lives to save Jews were Dutch Calvinists. I'm not saying there weren't Roman Catholics and others who risked lives. I'm not saying that. But I think that here's an example of where the rejection of replacement theology—I mean the church is Israel—is something that had very practical implications in terms of this. But I remember when I saw this documentary, I wept. I mean, it was really utterly incredible. Because during the Holocaust, we Jews didn't have a choice. Our only choice was how to survive. But these people really did. It really was a choice. They had options. They could have done nothing. Or cooperated. But the fact that they didn't, they had this choice; to a certain extent, their choice was a greater choice than ours was—ours was just how to survive. Theirs was really a choice between good and evil. And for that, there is no doubt about it, there is a definite connection to the type of theology that is part of the Reformed Calvinist tradition. I wish to thank Calvin, Barth, and all those in the tradition.

**H:** Well, thank you very much. I did have a few more questions, but we've been here an hour and a half, and this would be a wonderful note on which to end. That documentary is called *Weapons of the Spirit*. It was produced by a filmmaker named Pierre Sauvage, whose life was saved as a child in the village of Le Chambon. And you can see the documentary tomorrow night, here at 7:30. So thank you for coming, and let's thank our speakers again.

# 4

## After Barth:
## A Christian Appreciation of Jews and Judaism

GEORGE HUNSINGER

Is a non-anti-Judaic Christianity possible? That is the question I hope to address in this paper. A lot will depend, in the end, on what counts as "anti-Judaic." I am going to argue that Christianity enters into profound self-contradiction whenever it is anti-Judaic, as it regrettably has been throughout most of its history. I am going to go further, however. I am going to argue that Christianity cannot love Jesus Christ without also loving the Jews, who are his people, and that when Christianity does not love the Jews, it corrupts its love of Jesus Christ at the very core. Loving Christ, I will argue, is inseparable from loving the Jews, and where the Jews are not loved, Christ himself is dishonored. I am therefore going to argue for a form of philo-Semitism or Judaeophilia as governed by a center in Christ.[1]

### The Case for a Soft Supersessionism

Because of that same Christocentrism, however, I am also going to argue for a form of supersessionism. Despite the almost universal conviction in contemporary theology that supersessionism is the inevitable cause of anti-Judaism, to say nothing of its more repellant cousin anti-Semitism, and that therefore any form of supersessionism is unacceptable, I am going to argue that the inner logic of the Christian faith cannot dispense with supersessionism in some form. The form that I will advocate is the one

---

1. For the history and potential dangers of philo-Semitism, especially in its abstract forms, see Jonathan Karp and Adam Sutcliffe, eds., *Philosemitism in History* (Cambridge: Cambridge University Press, 2011).

David Novak has called "soft supersessionism."² According to this view, the new covenant does not replace the old covenant, but it does fulfill, extend, and supplement it, while also fundamentally confirming it.

Along these lines, I will suggest that there is only one covenant, and thus only one people of God, and yet there are also two faiths. The presence of two faiths—which in some ways, though not in all, are diametrically opposed—represents a festering wound in the one people of God. No one knows how this wound can be healed. Neither Christians nor Jews know how to heal it. Only God can heal it.

The day is long since past when Christians might hope to alleviate this wound by adopting Saint Paul's strategy of "making Israel jealous." Today this strategy, which was scarcely ever adopted, smolders in ruins. After the long and unbearable history of Christian anti-Semitism, and especially after the Shoah—for which Christian history was the dreadful background, if not the direct cause—Christianity would be delusional if it thought it could any longer do anything to make Israel "jealous."

It would be a major step, and one that cannot be taken for granted, if Christianity were to *systematically* commit itself to contrition, confession, and (insofar as possible) reparations. It would be a major step if Christianity were to commit itself not to making the Jews jealous, *per impossible*, but somehow simply to making them less terrified, less isolated, less vulnerable to existential threats in the world. It would be a major step, in other words, if Christianity were to enter fully into solidarity with the Jews. But as I will argue, solidarity is not enough.

Perhaps I should mention, as an aside, that I do not believe the necessary solidarity should be uncritical. How to enter into solidarity with the Jews today in a way that accords with a larger commitment to justice and peace is not an easy question. I cannot go into it here, and in any case I have no special wisdom. As the founder of the National Religious Campaign against Torture, I tend to align myself with Israeli groups like Rabbis for Human Rights that work against torture and other injustices in their own country, and with spin-offs in the United States like T'ruah that do similar work against solitary confinement and torture by our own government here at home.

I now return to my main theme. What the gospel asks of Christians

---

2. David Novak, "The Covenant in Rabbinic Thought," in *Two Faiths, One Covenant? Jewish and Christian Identity in the Presence of the Other*, ed. Eugene B. Korn (Lanham, MD: Rowman and Littlefield, 2004), pp. 65–80.

is solidarity, yes, but more than solidarity, it requires love. Christ must be loved and honored in the Jews, because the Jews must be loved and honored in Christ. They must be loved and honored in Christ, precisely because he has made them his own. While there are precious few examples of what this solidarity and love might look like, for the sake of clarity I will mention at least one.

During the Nazi occupation of France, the lives of as many as two thousand Jewish children were saved in the southern mountain village of Le Chambon, under the leadership of a Reformed pastor named André Trocmé. Le Chambon stands as an emblem of what Christianity is called now more than ever to become. It stands as an emblem of Christian solidarity and love toward the Jews as grounded in love for Christ. The people of Le Chambon did not try to convert the children. They simply tried to help them by taking the necessary risks of love.

Love for Christ is also the ground for the soft supersessionism that I am advocating. Love for Christ, according to Nicene Christianity, is tantamount to love for God, because Christ is God with us in human flesh. He is the eternal Word of God who became incarnate for our sakes without ceasing to be God. He is thus the beyond in our midst. He encounters us as God's self-revelation, as the reconciliation of the world with God, and as the proper object of our worship. He himself is the Savior of the world. According to Christian faith, however, he is what he is as the world's Savior only because he is also Israel's long-awaited Messiah. The universality of his saving significance is grounded in the particularity of Israel.

It was one of Karl Barth's signal achievements to insist that God's covenant with Israel is irrevocable. Although he arguably kept too much anti-Judaic baggage in his theology, he can at least be credited with this much. He invalidated every form of "strong supersessionism," according to which Israel is replaced by the church in God's covenant. Insofar as his softer supersessionism retained anti-Judaic elements, however, he cannot be followed by Christian theology today. What needs to be worked out is a soft supersessionism purged of every anti-Judaic element.

Soft supersessionism is unavoidable, because there is only one covenant and only one people of God. It is impossible to read Holy Scripture in any other way. There is no other covenant than the one established by God with Israel, and thus no other people is, or could possibly be, the elect people of God. By virtue of the divine election, Israel's unique status is irrevocable and indeed eternal. Nothing Israel can do, whether in obedience or disobedience, can revoke its status as God's elect.

*After Barth*

Christianity—and not least Karl Barth—has said far too much about Israel's disobedience and far too little about its ongoing obedience, even after its rejection of Jesus Christ. Even worse, Christianity—and not least Karl Barth—has said far too much about the church's obedience and far too little about its disobedience, most especially its historic disobedience in the form of anti-Semitism, mass persecution of Jews, and the teaching of contempt. All other forms of churchly disobedience, I would argue, are contained in this one toxic form.

If there is indeed a disobedience of Israel to the Lord their God, then that is between Israel and the Lord their God. Christians have long since discredited themselves in this arena. If it is somehow a form of disobedience for Jews not to accept Jesus Christ, Christians at this point have only themselves to blame. They need to attend all the more to the log in their own eye. Every possibility of Christian triumphalism was consumed in the fires of Auschwitz.

Nevertheless, according to apostolic authority, God's covenant with Israel is fulfilled in Jesus Christ for the sake of the world. All the promises of God are Yes and Amen in him. Not even Christian disobedience can overturn the covenant's fulfillment in Christ. Like Israel's election, it is grounded solely in the free grace of God. Nor can it be overturned by well-meaning Christians today in their quest for a meaningful repentance. Repentance, yes, but not at the expense of the Word of God. There is only one covenant, and according to apostolic authority, it has been fulfilled in Jesus Christ—for Jews, for Christians, and for the world—by grace alone.

Just as there is only one covenant, so also is there only one people of God. Karl Barth's doctrine of the one twofold people of God is another signal contribution. As I have already suggested, however, it cannot be carried out in the way he suggested. Israel cannot be the type of disobedience that is destined to pass away while the church is the type of obedience that is destined to prevail at the close of the age. The disobedient type should have been represented by Adam with the obedient type being represented by Christ. Christ would then have his own twofold relationship to the one elect people of God as constituted internally by both Israel and the church.

There is only one indivisible people of God, I would contend, and yet everywhere it is riven into factions. The unity of this one people is displayed neither among Jews nor among Christians—nor, to say the least, in the wounded relations between Christians and Jews. Among the Jews, we have divisions of varying degrees and stripes in at least the following groupings: secular Jews, synagogue Jews of various denominations, and baptized Jews in Christian congregations, including the recent phenomenon of messianic Judaism. Among Christians, the fragmentation is if possible even worse. In Nicene Christianity, as I would like to think of it, we have Roman Catholics, Eastern Catholics, and Reformational Catholics, including innumerable subdivisions and factions within each of them. In this situation, Nicene Catholics are seeking to recover a lost unity today, at least among those who are ecumenical. We would then also have non-Nicene forms of Christianity, including a number of modern liberal Christians as well as, at the other extreme, those evangelicals, charismatics, and Pentecostals not in accord with Nicaea.[3]

Notwithstanding all these sorry divisions, subdivisions, and factions, I want to suggest that Jews and Christians, whether separately or together, cannot undo their divine election as the one indivisible people of God. In a way that passes all understanding, Jews and Christians together are one in Christ, from a soft supersessionist standpoint. For the time being, and apparently until the end of history, they are more perfectly in Christ than he is in them. This would be as true (though in many and different ways) for the Christians who acknowledge Jesus Christ as for the Jews who do not (or do not yet) acknowledge him. In one way or another they are all one in Christ, by Christ, despite their being riven into factions. *Sub specie aeternitatis*, what is true *de iure* in Christ overrides all that exists to the contrary in history, and what is not yet true in history will be severely judged and forgiven, transcended and overcome, at the end of all things.

No doubt Jews will immediately fear at least two things about this latest turn in my argument. They will tend to fear their coercion by Christians and their disappearance as Jews. If these fears, which are understandable, cannot be convincingly addressed, then my argument for a soft supersessionism will turn out to be anti-Judaic after all, despite my best intentions. I must therefore explain why I think my argument supports neither the dreaded coercion nor the feared disappearance.

As is well known, Karl Barth discouraged all Christian missions to the Jews. Evangelical missions are appropriate, he believed, only where per-

---

3. No Jews were present at Nicaea, presumably because there were no longer any Jewish-Christian bishops. Moreover, as my colleague Ellen Charry points out, the Nicene-Constantinopolitan Creed would have been improved if it had added a phrase about the exodus: "We believe in one God, the Father Almighty, Maker of heaven and earth, and of all things visible and invisible, *who delivered Israel from slavery in Egypt*." The absence of Israel from the creed reflected the general disappearance of Jews and Jewish consciousness from the churches.

sons need to be delivered from idolatry. He argued that the Christian community can never presume to proclaim the one true God to Jews in place of an idol. As the people of the covenant, they already know, worship, and serve the one true God even after they have rejected Jesus Christ. He argued that the Jews need to be shielded against well-meaning but finally insulting efforts to convert them. The Jews in their own way are witnesses in the world to God's love. They are witnesses in their very Jewishness, for their preservation as a people despite all that has assailed them throughout history attests, Barth argued, the covenant faithfulness of the God who will not let them go. On these grounds, my own argument would rule out any Christian coercion of Jews to convert and any proselytizing efforts that would specifically target them. As exemplified by the people of Le Chambon, what the Jews need from Christians is not evangelism but solidarity in times of need and above all the practice of love.[4]

Let me ask a difficult question. Would it be possible for Jews to become Christians without ceasing to be Jews? Insofar as Jews became Christians, would their Jewishness not simply disappear into the predominantly gentile Christian community? Is not Torah observance essential to maintaining the Jewishness of the Jews? I have no easy answers to these questions. Consider that today Christians in the aggregate represent about one-third of the world's population; they number roughly 2.3 billion people out of a total of 7.0 billion people. Place alongside that the far smaller number of Jews, who total about 14 million people, or less than 0.2 percent of the world's population. On these grounds alone it is easy to see how Jews might simply disappear on the absurd hypothesis that they all became Christians.

Theologically, furthermore, it seems that there are good reasons for believing that God wills the continued existence of Israel. It is hard to see how the Jewish people could retain their Jewish identity apart from their ongoing Torah observance. As Bruce Marshall has argued, "In permanently electing Israel, it seems that God has also permanently willed the practice of Judaism."[5] If Marshall is correct, as I believe he is, how would that comport with the form of soft supersessionism that I am advocating?

---

4. For a sensitive approach to this question that is neither anti-Judaic nor anti-evangelical, and thus one with which I am in substantial agreement, see Gavin G. D'Costa, "What Does the Catholic Church Teach about Mission to the Jewish People?" *Theological Studies* 73 (2012): 590–613.

5. Bruce Marshall, "Elder Brothers: John Paul II's Teaching on the Jewish People as a Question to the Church," in *John Paul II and the Jewish People*, ed. David G. Dalin and Matthew Levering (Lanham, MD: Sheed and Ward, 2008), p. 122.

Again, the matter is delicate and complex. A narrow path needs to be charted, as I see it, between anti-Judaism, on the one hand, and what I will call anti-evangelicalism, on the other, by which I mean a position contrary to the gospel. A position would be anti-Judaic if it led to the disappearance of the Jews, while it would be anti-evangelical if it compromised on the imperative that Jesus Christ be recognized for who he is as confessed by faith. In principle, as I see it, this imperative is incumbent upon all peoples, the Jew first, as Paul put it, and then also the Greek. At this point I would invoke the Pauline theme of the hardening of Israel, though this needs to be done, if possible, in a careful and charitable way.

The mystery of the Jewish rejection of Jesus as the Messiah remains, from a Christian standpoint, a painful mystery. It was a mystery especially at the time of Christian origins, though, as I have suggested, it can hardly be looked on merely as a mystery today. When Paul pondered this mystery in his own historical moment, he could not do so without anguish. This was in part surely the anguish of love. The monumental failure of Christianity toward the Jews in the subsequent history of the church can largely be traced, I believe, to a loss of the empathic bond that Paul felt toward his fellow Jews, as expressed in his cry of anguish. The Christian loss of empathy was accompanied by a progressive loss of love. At the very point where love ought to have prevailed, it was notoriously twisted over time into animosity, hatred, and contempt.

With regard to the rejection of Jesus Christ by the Jews, and then the rejection of the Jews by Christians, which I have contended is tantamount to their own rejection of Jesus Christ, I would take solace in the words of Augustine. "For in a strange and ineffable way," he wrote, "nothing is done without the will of God, even that which is done contrary to it."[6] From the standpoint of my soft supersessionism, both Jews and Christians have done something that is contrary to the will of God, each in their own way. If Augustine is right, however, neither the one rejection nor the other can finally escape the overruling providence of God. The Pauline theme of the hardening of Israel in order that gentiles might be grafted in, and so join the people of God, was arguably a beginning in this direction. Paul was trying to make sense of God's strange and dreadful providence.

It seems that in early Christianity it was possible to become a Christian without ceasing to be a Jew. The earliest Christians were predominantly

---

6. Augustine, *Enchiridion on Faith, Hope, and Charity*, book 26 (New York: Fathers of the Church, 1947), p. 454.

Jews who remained law-observant. Even Paul did not reject this form of Christianity in principle. His mission was to establish another form of Christianity alongside the first, a form in which gentiles could become Christians without needing also to become law-observant. Paul could not have known that by the vicissitudes of history, or the inscrutable providence of God, the law-observant Christian community in Palestine would soon be decimated by the Romans when they laid siege to Jerusalem and destroyed the temple in 70 CE, and that such communities would cease to survive in dispersion past the first few centuries, not merely because they died out but because they were actively resisted by both gentile Christianity and the newly emergent rabbinic Judaism.[7] Paul could not have known (and in my opinion would certainly have opposed) the intolerable development that the gentile Christian communities he was establishing would soon lose their Jewish-Christian counterpart forever.

Where does all this leave us? It is the will of God that the Jews should not cease to exist. Since Torah observance is a necessary condition for the preservation of Jewish identity, it is the will of God that Torah observance should not cease to exist. At one point in history it was possible for Jews to become Christians without ceasing to be law-observant Jews. Most Jews refused this option, which in any case soon disappeared. Nevertheless, the imperative did not disappear that all persons and peoples should acknowledge Jesus Christ for who he is as confessed by faith. Paul believed that in some sense all Israel would be saved, and that God desires all others to be saved along with them by coming to a knowledge of the truth. In the Latin West, and in our own day, Karl Barth then, almost single-handedly, revived the long-lost prospect of a universal hope, though he was actually in accord with much Greek patristic teaching. According to this hope, the day will come when Jesus Christ is thanked and praised without exception for who he is. "At the name of Jesus," we read, "every knee will bow, in heaven and on earth and under the earth, and every tongue confess that Jesus Christ is Lord, to the glory of God the Father" (Phil. 2:10–11).

It is to the abiding shame of Christians that because of their lovelessness, hatred, and contempt throughout history, almost no Jew today can hear these words without something like horror, revulsion, and dismay. As Barth once said in a slightly different connection, perhaps in the end

---

7. See David G. Horrell, "Early Jewish Christianity," in *The Early Christian World*, vol. 1, ed. Philip F. Esler (London: Routledge, 2004), pp. 134–67, on pp. 159–60.

the Lord God will have a little less trouble with them than he had with us. The emergence of messianic Judaism in our own day is an important and unexpected sign that it might still be possible for some Jews to become Christians without ceasing to be Torah-observant Jews. It would be quixotic, however, to expect this movement to catch on very widely. Messianic Judaism is a sign, not a model. It attests in practice the kind of thing I am affirming theoretically, but, humanly speaking, it has little or no prospect of becoming more than a tiny minority.[8] Until this movement learns to locate itself within the churches of catholic Christianity, moreover, instead of standing as a mere sect outside it, it will not be ecumenically viable.[9] For all practical purposes, therefore, it is the institutions and practices of rabbinic Judaism that are necessary for Jews and Judaism to survive. According to my version of soft supersessionism, every actually existing form of Jewish existence—whether secular, rabbinic, or baptized—has its own relative validity and invalidity this side of the eschaton, and the same would need to be said all the more about every actually existing division of Christian existence in and among the churches.[10]

I believe I have said enough, however, to establish my two main points in this section. It is possible, at the theoretical level, to construct a version of soft supersessionism that is neither anti-Judaic nor anti-evangelical. It is not anti-Judaic because it eschews every form of religious coercion, and because it respects the indispensability of a Torah-observant Judaism. It therefore respects the ongoing necessity, by the providence of God, of rab-

---

8. If messianic Judaism were ever to locate itself within and not outside the churches of catholic Christianity (whether Roman, Eastern, or Reformational), perhaps it would need to be in the form of something like a "religious order." It seems that some messianic Jews are sympathetic to this idea. Theoretically, I could see something similar happening for Protestants relative to the churches of Roman and Eastern Catholicism, that is, they would not disappear but would become something like a religious order. For the ecumenical divisions among the Christian churches, and some suggestions about how they might be overcome, see George Hunsinger, *The Eucharist and Ecumenism: Let Us Keep the Feast* (Cambridge: Cambridge University Press, 2008).

9. "From a Christian theological point of view it is fully possible to have a Jewish Christian community established on equal terms with Christians from other cultural backgrounds. Since a Jewish Christian community was a reality in the first century, there seems to be no reason why it cannot be reintroduced." George C. Papademetriou, "Jewish Rite in the Christian Church: Ecumenical Possibility," *Scottish Journal of Theology* 26 (1973): 466-87, on p. 466.

10. To a certain extent, therefore, my soft supersessionism is like Wittgenstein's philosophy. It leaves everything as it is. It describes but does not resolve the existing tensions while finding something of value in each of the major tendencies or traditions.

binic Judaism, which has been the mainstream form of Judaism since the sixth century CE. Again, it is hard to see how Jews could survive as Jews without it. My proposal is not anti-evangelical, on the other hand, because it upholds the imperative that Jesus Christ should be acknowledged by all for who he is, by the Jew first and then also by the Greek, and the hope that this imperative will one day be accomplished universally by the inscrutable grace of God—through and in spite of the church.

Let me review my larger argument. I have suggested that there is only one covenant and thus only one people of God. I have also contended that within this one covenant two faiths coexist. The two faiths converge in some ways while diverging in others. According to my soft supersessionism, the covenant established by God with Israel was fulfilled in Jesus Christ. Israel did not cease to be God's people when it rejected him, but it was supplemented and fulfilled by the inclusion of Jews and gentiles who did believe in him. In the course of history, the one indivisible people of God suffered, among other things, the infliction of a mortal wound it could not heal, not only because some accepted Jesus Christ while others did not, but even more because they mostly turned against one another in enmity, with the burden of guilt resting most heavily on the Christians as history progressed. Christian enmity toward the Jews then came, directly and indirectly, to an unspeakable culmination in the Shoah.

I have not yet developed the essential christocentric grounds that I see for philo-Semitism or Judaeophilia. Before doing so, however, I want to examine a little further the indivisible oneness of God's people. I have argued that there is only one covenant, not two—in other words, not, as some have urged, one for Christians and another for Jews. There are not two parallel covenants, but rather one covenant in two forms, namely, the old form and the new. Over against the Lutheran tradition, which tended to pit the new covenant sharply against the old, the Calvinistic or Reformed tradition, to which Barth belonged, always insisted on one covenant in two forms. From the standpoint of a soft supersessionism, the deep wound within the one people of God means that some of its members continue to adhere, in various ways, to the old form, while others, also in various ways, embrace the new.

Strictly speaking, therefore, I need to modify what I said earlier about there being two faiths within a single covenant. There are not really two faiths but, again, only one faith in two forms, namely, the old form and the new. Today the old form is represented in various ways by Judaism, while the new form is represented by various versions of Christianity. Those who adhere to the old form of faith will see the others at worst as idolaters, or as interlopers, or, perhaps in the best of cases, as fellow travelers. Those who adhere to the new form will—if they subscribe to my version of a soft supersessionism—look on their opposite numbers with empathy, respect, patience, contrition, and love, for the sake of Christ.

Gentile Christians in particular will be stricken by their need to find that godly grief that leads to repentance, as Paul described it, to reach at least a modicum of reconciliation, however partially, with the long-suffering Jews. They will all—Jews and Gentiles alike—call upon God for the grace that might heal their unhealable wound, but they will resist every form of premature closure. They will resolve instead to live out their days in the unbearable pain of their wounded body, the pain of the open questions that each one must pose to the other. Together they will bear the pain of the wounded body of faith, and, in the midst of this pain, persevere. Only God, as I said before, can remove this pain.

## The Template of God's Covenantal Love

From the standpoint of a soft supersessionism, how are the universality of Christ and the particularity of Israel related? Karl Barth offers the following suggestion, one that I believe is seminal for the scope of his entire theology: "God is he who [loves his Son Jesus Christ], in his Son Jesus Christ all his children, in his children all human beings, and in human beings the whole creation."[11]

This proposition specifies the objects of God's love by means of a graded scheme. Starting with radical particularity, it ends in complete universality. We might picture it as a series of concentric circles that are centered on Christ, as if on a bull's-eye. With Christ at the center, the first circle around him is comprised of "all God's children," by which Barth means Israel and the church. The second concentric circle then widens out to include "all human beings," while the outermost circle embraces the whole creation. The result is three concentric circles centered on Christ.

Note that the syntax hinges on the words "in" and "all," which provide the grammar governing the whole proposition. The word "in" suggests relations of both participation and mediation. Let's begin with participa-

---

11. Karl Barth, *Church Dogmatics* II/1 (Edinburgh: T. & T. Clark, 1957), p. 315 (translation revised).

tion. When joined with the adjective "all," the word "in" serves to incorporate universality into particularity. The whole creation participates in God's relationship to humanity, all humanity participates in God's relationship to his children (Israel and the church), while all God's children—the one twofold people of God—participate in his unique relationship to Jesus Christ. This would comprise the movement from the universal to the particular.

The reverse movement would run from the particular to the universal. It describes the event by which God's love is mediated from the one to the many, or from the particular to the universal. Christ the center represents the point of radical particularity. As God's Son, he is seen as the direct and supreme object of God's love. In him God's love is then mediated to all God's children (Israel and the church); in them it is mediated to all humanity; and finally, in humanity it is mediated to the whole creation. Just how this mediation is thought to occur is left open, but that it occurs in these terms is the salient point.

With this scheme in mind, I want to focus on the pattern of unity that governs how Jesus Christ is related to God's children. The elect children of God, as conceived by Barth, constitute one twofold people. Although they are one, they are also internally differentiated. Their internal differentiation can be worked out in a way that goes somewhat beyond Barth. Within the one people of God, Israel would arguably have priority as the ground, while the church would have priority as the goal. The church would belong to the one people of God only as it was grafted into Israel. Israel would thus stand out as the original and proper object of God's love, through whom, along with the church, that love would be mediated to the world.

In Barth's scheme, God's love for Israel is grounded in his love for Jesus Christ. Therefore, God's love for Jesus Christ would be inseparable from his love for Israel, just as God's love for Israel would be inseparable from his love for Jesus Christ. Together they would constitute an unbreakable bond. Their unity cannot be destroyed because it is grounded in divine election. The direct object of election, as Barth conceives of it, is of course Jesus Christ, but in him the original object of election would be Israel. The election of Israel is exemplified by the fact that Jesus Christ was born a Jew. The love of Jesus Christ has made the people of Israel his own by virtue of divine election. Election represents a kind of covenantal ontology of love that binds Jesus Christ to the Jews.

This bond of Jesus Christ with the Jews in covenantal love is, I would suggest, the ground of Christian philo-Semitism or Judaeophilia. Jesus

Christ cannot be loved without also loving the Jews. The one cannot be loved without the other, nor can the one be held in contempt without dishonoring the other, because election has forged them into an inseparable union of love. Jesus Christ's undying love for the Jews, regardless of whether it is acknowledged and reciprocated or not, means that loving Jesus Christ while holding the Jews in contempt is a contradiction in terms. The blindfold that Christian iconography would place around the eyes of the Jews belongs more properly to the eyes of the church in its anti-Semitic and anti-Judaic moods.

Barth did not make this logic of Christian philo-Semitism explicit, although I believe it is implicit in his theology. He did, however, assert, if not a robust union in love, as least a corresponding union in suffering. Jesus Christ suffers in the sufferings of the Jews, he claimed, and those who inflict suffering and abuse on them secretly inflict it on Christ himself. Before I quote Barth to this effect, let me try my hand at a variation on his seminal proposition. It might run like this: "God is the One whose love suffers in his Son Jesus Christ. In and through Jesus Christ his love suffers in the sufferings of all his children. In and through his children it suffers in the sufferings of all human beings, and in and through human beings it suffers in the sufferings of the whole creation."

I believe this variation represents the spirit if not the letter of Barth's theology. Jesus Christ participates in the sufferings of all these others, even as the sufferings of these others is mediated to him, in the same graduated and differentiated pattern of unity-in-distinction that we saw before. And just as before, we might give the sufferings of the Jews pride of place.

Barth was uncompromising in connecting the sufferings of the Jews to Jesus Christ. During the church struggle against Nazism, he wrote: "Whoever rejects and persecutes the Jews rejects and persecutes him who died for the sins of the Jews—and then, and only thereby for our sins as well. Anyone who is a radical enemy of the Jews, were he in every other regard an angel of light, shows himself, as such, to be a radical enemy of Jesus Christ. Anti-semitism is sin against the Holy Ghost. For anti-semitism means rejection of the grace of God."[12]

As powerful as this statement is, it nevertheless focuses on rejection and persecution. Those who reject and persecute the Jews are rejecting and persecuting Jesus Christ. An inseparable union between them is clearly

---

12. Karl Barth, *The Church and the Political Problem of Our Day* (New York: Charles Scribner's Sons, 1939), p. 51.

*After Barth*

implied. As far as I know, however, Barth never explored the larger implications of this insight. He never pressed Christ's union in suffering with the Jews forward to include their inseparable union in covenantal love. He did not quite see that the very logic of his Christ-centered rejection of anti-Semitism implied an equally Christ-centered affirmation of the Jews, that is to say, a philo-Semitism grounded in covenantal love.

Here is a similar statement from the same period: "In Israel the really suffering One who bears the wrath and judgment of God is not Israel itself but He to whose advent Israel looks forward and who furnishes the clue to the inner meaning of its existence: Israel's Messiah in the one day of His passion. He and not Israel is also the One who really suffers in all that the Jews of today have to endure. He is the One who is intended, aimed at and smitten, hated and pushed aside."[13]

What I wish to focus on from this statement is the preposition "in." Jesus Christ is said to be the one who really suffers "*in* all that the Jews of today have to endure." This can only mean that Jesus Christ suffers in the unspeakable sufferings of the Jews. It can only mean that he has truly made the sufferings of the Shoah his own. From the standpoint of my soft supersessionism, it could even be taken to imply that he is the hidden Messiah of Israel. He himself, states Barth, "is the One who is intended, aimed at and smitten, hated and pushed aside."

In this line of interpretation an obvious danger exists. It is the danger that the unspeakable sufferings of the Jews might be eclipsed. Unfortunately, this danger is not entirely absent from the tenor of Barth's remarks. Nevertheless, the preposition "in" could be taken in a different direction. It could be taken to imply a strong unity-in-distinction. It could allow that full weight be accorded to that which is unspeakable while still believing with fear and trembling that the unspeakable has been taken up by the hidden Messiah of Israel into the very heart of God. It could therefore be taken as a sign of hope against hope.

The preposition "in" points beyond solidarity to *participatio Christi*. According to this view, Jesus Christ participates fully in the sufferings of the Jews. When they are despised and rejected, he himself is despised and rejected, not merely in solidarity, but by an ineffable union of covenantal love. He takes them into his wounded body that they might be given a share in his risen body. They are not without hope because through his sufferings he has overcome the world. God is the One whose suffering love

---

13. Barth, *Church Dogmatics* II/1, pp. 395–96.

triumphs in his Son Jesus Christ. In him this suffering love triumphs in the sufferings of all his children. In his children it triumphs in the sufferings of all human beings, and in human beings it triumphs in the sufferings of the whole creation.

This is the scope of resurrection hope. It ends in complete universality. But it begins, I am bold to say, in the ineffability of God's covenantal love for the Jews.

# 5
## To Love Tanakh Is Love Enough for the Jews: Reflection on *Dabru Emet*

PETER OCHS

My assignment is to address the themes of this volume by reflecting on *Dabru Emet* fourteen years later. My address will be a reflection in light of Barthian directions in both Christian and Jewish theology. I will ask, "How Barthian was and is this Jewish-Christian theological exchange?" And I will answer, "Very." Those of you born after 2000 may not have heard of *Dabru Emet* (or the '60s or the Beatles!). So I shall begin with a brief review of what happened way back then.

The title, *Dabru Emet*, comes from Zechariah 8:16: "These are the things you are to do: Speak the truth (*dabru emet*) to one another, render true and perfect justice in your gates." The statement appeared as a full-page ad in the *New York Times*, coauthored by David Novak (the main force in its wording), Peter Ochs, and of very dear and blessed memory, Tikva Frymer-Kensky and Michael Signer. The statement represented the fruits of four years of work under the sponsorship of the Institute of Christian and Jewish Studies (ICJS), headed by Chris Leighton and guided as well by Rosann Catalano, David Sandmel, Charlie Obrecht, and Joel Zaiman.

The full text of the statement is given in the appendix to this book.

### A JEWISH STATEMENT ON CHRISTIANS AND CHRISTIANITY

In recent years, there has been a dramatic and unprecedented shift in Jewish and Christian relations. Throughout the nearly two millennia of Jewish exile, Christians have tended to characterize Judaism as a failed religion or, at best, a religion that prepared the way for, and is completed in, Christianity. In the decades since the Holocaust, however, Christianity has changed dramatically. An increasing number of official

> Church bodies, both Roman Catholic and Protestant, have made public statements of their remorse about Christian mistreatment of Jews and Judaism. These statements have declared, furthermore, that Christian teaching and preaching can and must be reformed so that they acknowledge God's enduring covenant with the Jewish people and celebrate the contribution of Judaism to world civilization and to Christian faith itself.
>
> We believe these changes merit a thoughtful Jewish response. Speaking only for ourselves—an interdenominational group of Jewish scholars—we believe it is time for Jews to learn about the efforts of Christians to honor Judaism. We believe it is time for Jews to reflect on what Judaism may now say about Christianity. As a first step, we offer eight brief statements about how Jews and Christians may relate to one another.

The eight statements were accompanied by more detailed explanations. I shall note only the statements themselves:[1]

(1) Jews and Christians worship the same God.
(2) Jews and Christians seek authority from the same book—the Bible (what Jews call "Tanakh" and Christians call the "Old Testament").
(3) Christians can respect the claim of the Jewish people upon the land of Israel.
(4) Jews and Christians accept the moral principles of Torah.
(5) Nazism was not a Christian phenomenon.
(6) The humanly irreconcilable difference between Jews and Christians will not be settled until God redeems the entire world as promised in Scripture.
(7) A new relationship between Jews and Christians will not weaken Jewish practice.
(8) Jews and Christians must work together for justice and peace.

## A Touch of History, or at Least Memory

According to Alice Eckardt and Franklin Sherman, "In Fall 1969 the Faith and Order Commission of the National Council of Churches called into

---

1. The full text is available on the World Council of Churches website: http://wcc-coe.org/wcc/what/interreligious/cd36-04.html.

being a 'Study Group on Christian-Jewish Relations' to undertake an in-depth study and consideration of topics relevant to Christian-Jewish relations both historically and currently. This was the origin of the Christian Scholars Group."[2] The Scholars Group included many of the most well-known Christian theologians who responded to the events of the Holocaust and to American anti-Semitism. For a while the group was sponsored by the National Conference of Christians and Jews. "From the spring of 1988 until the spring of 2002, the Institute for Christian and Jewish Studies in Baltimore hosted the group's scholarly activities." Reexamining the history and theology of the church, the group sought in those years to remove marks of anti-Judaism and supersessionism from church literature and liturgies. These scholars sacrificed much, even work that was more central to their scholarly disciplines, to undertake the practical work of care for Jews in an individual, civilizational, and spiritual sense, and often sacrificed their standings in church bodies that were not quite ready for their interreligious outreach. This was ecumenism in the broadest sense, displaying the courage to press on in the name of care for the Jews.

In 1996, the ICJS gathered a group of Jewish scholars to respond to the efforts of the Christian scholars over so many years. The gathering failed to generate a common spirit of action, except for a small group of us who remained afterward to propose a multiyear effort in honor of the Christian scholars; this effort generated the *Dabru Emet* project.

**Memory**: What moved us to this work?

- We were moved by gratitude to the Christian scholars who had done so much for us as a people against such sacrifice and without recognition from the Jewish people.
- We were moved by our own deep relationship with Christian theologians who were representative of this turn to Christian concern for the Jews. Many were already our close colleagues.
- We were moved to address the negative stereotypes that fellow Jews had of Christianity: to alert them to what these Christian scholars have done and to explain that these actions are representative of significant turns away from Christian anti-Judaism and supersessionism. We understood that Jews tend to identify Christians the way they identify Jews: through their identities as members of some people rather than as those who professed some finite set of beliefs. We recognized, fur-

---

2. See the group's website at http://www.ccjr.us/members/christian-scholars-group.

thermore, that a majority of Jews tended to identify "Christians" with members of a civilization that is defined by its actions through history and that these actions have included many things, some praiseworthy, but some evoking utter horror, including the Crusades, pogroms, and the Holocaust.[3] This meant that Jews would long associate Christianity and the Crusaders' cross as emblems of murderous hatred against Jews. We sought to counter that image: not to change Jewish understanding of religion as inseparable from action and from familial inheritance, but to change Jewish understanding of the habits of action that could appropriately be associated with Christianity.

- We were embarrassed that our people, associated with a tradition of learning, were so ignorant of their neighbors' Christianity. We were moved to help resocialize our people to take responsibility to learn about the religions of their neighbors, in particular about Christianity.
- We sought to awaken our Jewish neighbors to the enemies that faced us today rather than in the past and to the fact that in confronting these enemies Jews very much needed the help of the Christian neighbors and of Christian theologians.
- Who were these enemies? Here I switch to my own voice, lest I misattribute certain claims to others. I considered our major enemy to be one major civilizational tendency within the modern West: that which theologians close to Augustine may label human self-absorption or even self-deification; that which Barthians see epitomized in natural theology and which I call the either/or logic of modernity, both religious and nonreligious. I like to call this our civilization's "binary logic," a behind-the-scenes tendency that some of us can diagram in the form of strictly two-valued logics, but that otherwise makes itself known by two effects. It is a positive force when conventional thinking is called for (such as asking folks around the table to pass the salt—rather than the pepper—when someone asks for salt). And it is a disastrous force in times that call for repair. In times of crisis or deep need, when human life and language is already divided against itself, binary logic strides onto the scene to make things worse: replacing the one redeemer who can heal division with humanly constructed ideals that promote ways of solving what turns out to be only one-half of the

---

3. We recognized that Jewish populations tended to identify the cross with the sign of marauding crusaders, an image associated with the place of Christians in the pogroms of nineteenth-century eastern Europe and in the Holocaust.

problem, stimulating angry proponents of the other half to arise from slumber and produce a wonderfully inflamed higher division, generating new false redeemers and so on. A case in point is the tendency of Euro-Western civilization to spawn such embodied contrast-pairs as reactionary fundamentalism versus radical secularism, and so on.

Before I ask what all this has to do with Barth, I shall ask a preliminary question: What has all this to do with Jews and Christians? I shall answer in both a polite and a not-so-polite way.

The polite answer—also true—is that *Dabru Emet* and its accompanying books received considerable attention over the years. The scholarly book version of *Dabru Emet* sold thousands; many essays and some books and dissertations were written in response to it. Many churches and synagogues have held talks and dialogues in the name of *Dabru Emet*; the ICJS has made a good business of extending such dialogues. In all, *Dabru Emet* made its lasting mark on Jewish-Christian theological dialogue. It is significant that, early on, *Dabru Emet* stimulated greater interest among European churches, especially in Germany and Poland, than among American churches or synagogues. It is most significant that the dialogue was and *is* theological, as distinguished from the focus on social ethics and getting-to-know-one-another that marked dialogue before *Dabru Emet*. The great champions of Jewish-Christian dialogue from the 1960s on were primarily liberal Christians, by which I mean Christians, at first Catholics especially, who were wary of theological instruments of dialogue, were predominately concerned to make amends for the long history of Christian anti-Judaism culminating in the Shoah, and argued that some aspects of the biblical and liturgical literature of Christianity contributed to anti-Judaism and some anti-Semitism and needed, urgently, to be amended. These pioneers sacrificed much in their standing with the church to promote this work. They also provided a context for the subsequent turn that made theological dialogue possible, even though the turn to theology tended to make them uncomfortable: especially the type of theology that emerged as the strongest complement to *Dabru Emet*: postliberal Christian theology, whose strongest single source was the work of Barth complemented by Nouvelle Théologie. But more on this later.

My less polite answer is that, although responses from American churches have been okay (not remarkable, but okay), the most disappointing responses have, from the very start, come from the American Jewish public. The only truly bad memory of our work at ICJS was that the major

Jewish federations at the time not only declined to offer financial support for the project but in several significant cases worked—shockingly, I feel—against our getting support.

So what, in sum, did *Dabru Emet* have to do with Christians and with Jews? The lesson I learned is that neither Jews nor Christians tended to find reasons for *Dabru Emet* self-evident in their readings of the plain sense of Scripture. Nor did they find self-evident reasons in the primary ways the plain sense has been interpreted in the two-thousand-year history of Christianity and of rabbinic Judaism.

But there is a helpful hermeneutical lesson in this. The lack of self-evident reasons for theological dialogue has deepened my sense that the intimate behavioral instructions of Torah are not displayed in the plain sense but only in its performative force, as displayed in context-specific interpretations. This has deepened my sense of the profound hermeneutical difference between conventional rules for reading Scripture and rules displayed only *b'et laasot lashem*, or in cases of urgent need for the sake of repairing inadequacies in the conventional rules of a given generation. I am convinced, moreover, that this difference is occluded by the dominant, binary logic of modernity and by the practices of religious and secular groups who obey that logic consciously or unconsciously (and usually it is unconsciously). I hope, in this essay, to express and test two observations. The first is that the turn to Barthian and Barthian-like theologies in both Christianity and Judaism helps clear away the fog of binary logic so that we can once again see that the genius of scriptural tradition is not captured in conventional language but in the *difference* between our conventional discourses and the scripturally grounded inquiries that repair them. My second observation is that *Dabru Emet* was a reparative inquiry of this kind, and that *Dabru Emet* therefore complements the Barthian turn in contemporary theology.

I shall first try to articulate these observations in a general way. Then, in conclusion, I shall illustrate them in relation to *Dabru Emet*.

## A General Approach

Who are the Barthians I refer to? I refer, on the one hand, to the Jewish thinkers who first introduced me to Barth: Michael Wyschogrod, followed somewhat later by David Novak, who remains a primary source of my judgments about Barth and the Jews (along now with Randi Rash-

## To Love Tanakh Is Love Enough for the Jews

kover).[4] Consider, for example, these words from Novak's essay in this volume: "My question is . . . *how* Barth thought *like* a Jewish thinker thinks or ought to think *of* the Torah, the object of common concern to both Jews and Christians." While I do not tend to utter phrases like "thinking like a Jewish thinker," I do say something analogous: that Barth thought in ways that complemented a certain Jewish approach to issues of Jewish-Christian theological dialogue.

On the other hand, I also refer to the many Christian thinkers who have extended my education in Barth, especially the Christian postliberals examined in my recent book *Another Reformation: Postliberal Christianity and the Jews*.[5] Prime among these instructors have been Robert Jenson, Hans Frei, George Lindbeck, Stanley Hauerwas, David Ford, Daniel Hardy, and many close students and colleagues of these teachers, including Garret Green.[6] Of course, along the way I was also instructed by the scholars who make Princeton Seminary the name for both Barth scholarship and the dialectics of Barth scholarship: George Hunsinger and Bruce McCormack as well as most of the folks whose essays appear in this volume.

I am using the term "Barthians" in a loose, connotative sense to refer to a broad tendency rather than some strict fidelity to Barth's words. In this sense, Barthians are defined first by what they reject: which, I believe, is something close to what I have labeled the logic of binarism or opposition that informs and is also reinforced by modern conceptualism, colonialism, and so on. As I shall explain in a moment, this logic of binarism is close to the logic of what Barth calls natural theology.

I define the Barthian turn negatively because, in the sense that I am interested in them, Barthians are reparative thinkers, moved to repair what is not (*nichtige*) rather than to make claims about what is. To illustrate the difference, consider these different uses of language:

- *The first we might call "language use in times of peace."* I use this phrase metaphorically, to refer to the way everyday communication works when its underlying language system is relatively undisturbed (so that

---

4. Randi Rashkover, *Revelation and Theopolitics: Barth, Rosenzweig, and the Politics of Praise* (London: T. & T. Clark, 2005).

5. Peter Ochs, *Another Reformation: Postliberal Christianity and the Jews* (Grand Rapids: Baker Academic, 2011).

6. Among some dozens of somewhat younger postliberal "Barthians" I include Eugene Rogers, Bruce Marshall, Kendall Soulen, Scott Bader Saye, Tom Greggs, and many more.

the language itself is "at peace," whether or not it is a time of societal conflict). At such times, the paradigm for language use is dinnertime conversation among close friends or family members. Here, if you ask your tablemates to "please pass the salt," they will not pass you the pepper and they will not stop to ask what you really mean. In times like this, the order of language use seems to correspond to the order of the world: language is "natural language." (Philosophers among you might identify this with language as portrayed in Wittgenstein's *Tractatus*.)

- *The second we might call "language use in times of nonpeace."* I use this phrase to refer to the way both everyday and specialized forms of communication work when *a society's language system is undergoing radical change*. At such times, the rules of conventional systems of language are no longer reliable. These rules may hold in individual cases of communication, but they may also fail: for example, because events are observed that no longer correspond to the vocabulary or even syntax of a given system of natural language; because traumatized or exiled individuals may forget conventional language conventions; or because language communities may be enslaved or uprooted and absorbed into other communities, so that different vocabularies and rules of syntax are hybridized in various ways. In such settings, a given order of language may no longer correspond to the order of the observed world.

The key issue for us is how these two types and contexts of language are portrayed in any theological or philosophic inquiry. I suggest that there are two ways of conducting such inquiries that correspond to the two contexts of language use.

- What I will label "*conventional inquiry*" makes true-or-false judgments about the human or natural worlds as if both the authors and readers of the inquiry shared a single conventional language that enabled them to make direct observations and clear and distinct judgments about whatever can be seen in these worlds. (This is the kind of inquiry Wittgenstein characterized in the *Tractatus*.)
- What I will label "*reparative inquiry*" assumes that its readers share certain conventions of language use but observes that these conventions are no longer fully reliable in some way. Reparative inquirers write to draw their readers' attention to these aspects of disruption or disorder and then recommend certain hypotheses about how various conventions of language use can be modified so that these dis-

*To Love Tanakh Is Love Enough for the Jews*

ruptions can be repaired. Repair does not mean a return to previous conventions but the effort to nurture some new way of extending or transforming the conventions.

As remembered by Raymond Anderson, Barth's inquiry was obsessively reparative (where obsession is a good thing!):

> Barth's lifetime work was driven by the specter of the horrors that he had seen unleashed in Germany, first under Kaiser Wilhelm in world war one and then under the NAZI movement.... Those who knew Barth became increasingly aware of an inner compulsion here. His labor over many years on a vast, comprehensive discourse for the churches was fueled by his dismay at the theological sponginess that had been implicated in liberal Christians' failure to present a clear front against the racist nationalism of NAZI Germany. It is probably recognized that the entire *Church Dogmatics* became in fact a protracted effort to free church teaching from the toils of natural theology. Close observation of the German church tragedy was behind this virtual obsession.[7]

For me, the first virtue of Barthians is that they recognize the difference between the two types and contexts of language use and two types of theological or philosophic inquiry. Their second virtue is that they say NO to theologians and philosophers who confuse these differences. There are several typical ways of confusing the two, and Barthians say NO to all of them:

- *They say NO to those who ignore the difference and treat all theological or philosophic inquiry as if it were conventional*—this is, for example, the way of logical positivists and both religious and nonreligious literalists, who apply conventional standards of truth or falsity even to language use in times of nonpeace. Language use in times of nonpeace is often neither true nor false because the conventions that govern language use are disrupted or in a state of radical change.
- *They say NO to those who deny the difference and treat all inquiry as*

---

7. Raymond Kemp Anderson, *An American Scholar Recalls Karl Barth's Golden Years as a Teacher (1958–1964): The Mature Theologian* (Lewiston, NY: Edwin Mellen Press, 2004), 46–47.

*if it were reparative*: as if no statement even within a community of conventional language use could be trusted to mean what it says, as if language use were always in disorder. This radical skepticism is unwarranted, since reparative inquiry is made in relation to some convention of language use; to claim that all conventions are in doubt is to arrogate to oneself the capacity to make such a judgment independently of any single convention. This is one of the errors of foundationalism or Cartesianism or of radical humanism, which often begin in radical skepticism only to end in radical dogmatism.

- *They say NO to those who acknowledge the difference but then treat one single method of reparative inquiry as if it would apply to all conditions of disrepair whatsoever.* This is the error of dogmatism, which ignores the context-specific character of each reparative inquiry, generalizing the solution to one problem as if it applied to all possible problems. This dogmatic side of foundationalism is often translated in the modern world to a new kind of rationalized religious foundationalism: as religious fanatics universalize their own subjective experience of salvation.

Here are some illustrations of Barthian no-saying:

1. *No to those who treat all language and inquiry as if it were conventional.* Consider the conventionalism of Job's set of friends, sorry listeners whose insistence on conventional wisdom makes them deaf to what is unprecedented in Job's words of misery. Job says to them, "I stand up in the assembly and cry for help. I'm a brother of jackals, and a companion of ostriches" (Job 30:28–29, NRSV) and "Why do you, like God, pursue me, never satisfied with my flesh?" (19:22). Zophar represents the conventionalism of all three: "Should a multitude of words go unanswered, and should one full of talk be vindicated? Should your babble put others to silence, and when you mock, shall no one shame you?" (11:2–3). Illustrating what I consider a Barthian response, David Ford comments: "As readers we already know that the friends' categories are inadequate.... Their conception of wisdom cannot allow for a question that is open ... : whether Job fears God for nothing.... [But] something novel, something not to be exhaustively accounted for by precedence, is going on."[8]

---

8. David Ford, *Christian Wisdom: Desiring God and Learning in Love* (Cambridge: Cambridge University Press, 2007), 126.

In Ford's reading, those who recognize the rules of conventional language alone will fail to hear the cries of those whose voices can be heard only at and beyond the limits of those rules. For God, such cries are not empty, because the rules of meaning extend beyond the limits of convention.

For Randi Rashkover, Barth's commentary on Job gives voice to a full-throated rejection of religious and theological conventionalism: "Barth turns to his interpretation of Job's friends to illustrate this character of falsehood. Unlike Job who trembles in his self-certainty, the friends are zealous defenders of God. Divine apologists, they plunge deeper and deeper into falsehood with every 'right' claim they make. Secure in their self-justification, they hubristically speak for God, and not surprisingly, their defense falls on deaf ears."[9]

Arguing, in her study *Freedom and Law*, that divine lawgiving is a prototypical display of divine freedom, Rashkover adds that

> Recognition of the law is concomitant with recognition of the temporality or historicality of one's claims. The friends by contrast, Barth points out, "preach timeless truths" [*CD* IV/3.1, 457] impervious to change and challenge. But the truth of the law requires a historical self-consciousness of one's claims.... As law, wisdom prohibits the free assertion of eternal truths. Inevitably, the friends' insistence upon the timeless character of their truths only contributes further to their self-alienation and failed communication.... There is, Barth says, no limit or law on their assertions, and therefore, there is no room for anyone else to make a contribution. Truth is closed, and seen from this perspective, all other persons function only as instruments. Either they bolster the certainty of the claimant with their agreement, or they get in the way and must be dismissed or contested in disagreement.[10]

*2. No to those who deny the difference and treat all inquiry as if it were reparative.* This No to radical skepticism complements the preceding No to conventional dogmatism. In Tom Greggs's account of Barth's "theology against religion," Barth's two No's add up to a comparable critique of an entire habit or mode of religious living:

---

9. Randi Rashkover, *Freedom and Law: A Jewish-Christian Apologetics* (New York: Fordham University Press, 2011), 266.

10. Ibid., 266–67. *CD* in this quotation and hereafter refers to Barth's *Church Dogmatics*.

God's own hiddenness means that all our ideas, however pious and religious, are unsuitable and inadequate for comprehension of Him [*CD* II/1, 335], and that there is always infinitely more to God. This is not to say, however, that theology should say nothing. Theology is not to be apathetic but engaged in the dynamic tension between the kataphatic and the apathetic: "We are allowed to view and conceive the inconceivable God in obedience, to proclaim the Ineffable in obedience.... And woe betide us if we rely upon our impotence and omit to praise him!" [*CD* II/1, 204]. However, the very worshipful nature of God determines that there is ever more to the God who is eternally deserving of ever greater praise [*CD* II/1, §33.1], and so Barth describes the task of theology as follows: "We are drawing upon the ocean. We are therefore faced by a task to which there is no end" [*CD* II/1, 406]. This inexhaustible ocean is not religion, but the God who will be the all in all, and can never be captured within the confines of human religiosity. St. Augustine puts this positively when he speaks of God not in terms of the darkness of unknowing, but in terms of the one who is so gloriously mysterious that His "ineffable light beat back our gaze" [*De Trinitate* 15.10].[11]

In Eberhard Busch's words, Barth's double negative is a mark of "God's Beginning with Us."[12]

How do we arrive at the knowing of God? The answer is to be found, in Barth's view, by a reversal of the question. We don't arrive at such knowledge.... That we don't arrive there is, however, not the despairing conclusion of our self-knowledge, leading to the postulate that there must be some other way to arrive at such knowledge.... [It] is for Barth a negative consequence that can be grasped only in the light of the preceding positive statement, namely, that we can know God only as God comes to us. "The beginning of our knowledge of God ... is not a beginning which we make with him. It can be only the beginning which He has made with us" (II/I 213=190).[13]

---

11. Tom Greggs, *Theology against Religion: Constructive Dialogues with Bonhoeffer and Barth* (London: T. & T. Clark, 2011), 221.

12. Eberhard Bush, *The Great Passion: An Introduction to Karl Barth's Theology*, trans. Geoffrey W. Bromiley (Grand Rapids: Eerdmans, 2004), 61.

13. Ibid.

For Busch, this is Barth's reply to Feuerbach: "Revelation for Barth is not something to be postulated in order then to investigate whether or not it might 'exist' somewhere. That the beginning of all knowledge is this beginning that God makes with us is a conclusion that simply does justice to the *reality* that God has already made this beginning with us.... It is grounded in an event that expounds and interprets itself: ... the *Easter event* [with reference to IV/3, 41–44]."[14]

3. *No to those who acknowledge the difference but then treat one single method of reparative inquiry as if it applies to all conditions of disrepair whatsoever (dogmatic dogmatism).* In his essay in this volume, David Novak illustrates a Jewish version of the Barthian critique when he writes of Maimonides's insistence "that we can only say what God does, not what God is" (*Guide* 1:52).[15] In the terms I am using, this means that to describe what God IS is to apply the grammar of our conventional language (that speaks of what is and what is not, what is true and what is false) to the "one who speaks and it is"—that is, to the one whose speech generates being but is not therefore captured by being. If we speak of God's being, we may be fooled into thinking that our speech applies, like God, to all instances of his action. If so, our claims will be dogmatic in a way that exceeds conventional dogmatism, since we would assume that our claims apply to any convention whatsoever.

Restated in these terms, Novak reasons that, for Maimonides, claims of "is" or being display their meaning only with respect to the rules of some conventional language, but we share no such rules with God. To say that we know God in his action means that, yes, God reveals his word to us by way of our natural language conventions but not within the terms of those conventions. Novak explains that Maimonides thereby condemns humanly initiated partnerships with God: as the rabbinic sages say, "whoever partners [*na-meshattef*] the name of God with anything else is uprooted from the [God's] world" (b. Sanhedrin 63a re Exod. 22:19). Nonetheless, the rabbis also speak of God's partnering (*meshattef*) his great name with Israel so that "they might live" in a world that would otherwise swallow them up (y. Ta'anit 2:7/65d). Since we do not share natural language with God, how can the rabbis speak of Israel's partnering with God's name? Novak's response is that God can engage us in his language—displayed in the way he performs his name in the Hebrew language. This performance is glimpsed

---

14. Ibid., 64.
15. David Novak, "How Jewish Was Karl Barth?," p. 20 above.

through the plain sense of spoken and written Hebrew the way the wind is glimpsed through the trees.

God's redeeming work may be understood in a comparable way. As redeemer, God partners with humans, but on his terms, not ours: it is the difference between humanly and divinely initiated acts of repair. To illustrate this difference, Novak cites the Talmudic dictum of Rabbi Yohanan bar Nappaha: "Everywhere you find a statement of God's might [*gevurato*], you also find thereafter a statement of His lowliness [*anavtanuto*]. . . . In the Torah it is written: 'For the Lord your God is God-supreme and Lord-supreme' (Deuteronomy 10:17), but thereafter is written: 'who executes justice for orphans and widows' (10:18)." For Novak, this means, in other words, that God comes down from his pedestal and involves himself intimately with the most vulnerable, the most lowly, of his people. It means that, whereas humans need to practice humility before God so as to continually be aware of the fact that they are not God's equals, God chooses to practice humility so as to show humans he is with us when we are most alone in the world.

Mark Lindsay reads Barth in a comparable way: "Barth . . . is determined that in becoming a necessary object of human speech, God is not thereby objectified. God retains divine self-subjectivity. The way in which Barth ensures that the subjectivity is indeed retained is by recourse to the nature of address, as opposed to the nature of being-in-itself. States Barth, 'the presupposition of the Bible is not that God is but that God spoke. We are directed, not to God-in-himself, but to God communicating himself' (*GD*, 58). There is, of course, a caveat to this, to the effect that God is, in his self-revelation, wholly revealed."[16]

Lindsay adds that, like the Jewish post-Holocaust thinker Eliezer Berkowitz, Barth taught that even in his revelation God is the *hidden* God, the one "who is never so distant as when he is near, the one who, because he is God, can never be object (*GD*, 135)."[17]

4. *And a complementary No to "natural theology."* Could we not redescribe this complement as a declaration of NO to all efforts that reduce theology and philosophy to the form of conventional inquiry alone? You may ask why, what is the connection between naturalism and conven-

---

16. Mark R. Lindsay, *Reading Auschwitz with Barth: The Holocaust as a Problem and Promise for Barthian Theology* (Eugene, OR: Pickwick, 2014), 124. The abbreviation *GD* in this quotation and the next refers to Barth's *Göttingen Dogmatics* (Grand Rapids: Eerdmans, 1991).

17. Ibid., 125.

tionalism? Are they not opposites, as displayed for example in scholastic distinctions between what Augustine called *signa data* and *signa naturalia*, or conventional and natural signs? According to the approach of this essay, the answer is NO: naturalism and conventionalism *appear* to be opposites because the binary logic that generates them *poses* them that way, the way early modern philosophy posed empiricism and rationalism as opposites. But all these opposites are merely the opposing faces of a single twisted body.

What body, what faces? To explain what I mean, I shall offer a brief thought experiment.

Step 1: Imagine, if you will, that we knew only of our own society and our own language and that, for this reason, we were not particularly aware of speaking a language per se; we were aware only that we saw things in the world that we knew how to describe in words. This is what we mean by "conventional language use."

Step 2: Imagine next that someone visited us from another society and, even after apparently learning our manner of speech, used it to describe a world that was not exactly what we seemed to be seeing. Would we not consider our visitor odd, someone who saw things other than how they really were? Imagine that we adopted the term "nature" to describe things as they really are, as we normally see *and* describe them, and that we described this visitor as seeing things in an "unnatural" way.

Step 3: Imagine next that the visitor said, "Oh no, you in this society don't see things as they truly are, because the world that you see was made that way by a great Creator God who both makes things and changes them and teaches you how to modify your own languages so that you can learn to see things in new ways when things get changed!" I do not think the visitor would be received well at all.

Step 4: Imagine next that, on another occasion, we introduced a new assumption into our society: that there are two kinds of language use, "conventional" and "reparative." In such a society we might perceive our language use as specific to some convention, while recognizing that other conventions are possible as well. In this case, language would not be invisible to us and we would not see the world out there as if through a clear window. But where would we locate "nature" in such a society?

While we were trying to answer that question, what if that same visitor came to us with the same story about creation? I believe that, this time, we might welcome the visitor with words like these: "We cannot prove that you are right or that you are wrong. But we can tell you that

89

yours is the first story we have heard that makes sense of our belief that there are both conventional and reparative modes of language use. We could adopt the word 'creation' in place of the word 'nature,' without binding the creation word to any particular convention of language use. We could say that different conventions of language show us the created world in different ways. But we see nothing about which we could say, 'Well, it just is what it is,' since your God could always change it. We could not in fact apply our old notion of 'that which is what it is' to anything other than the God."

This has been my thought experiment for clarifying how conventionalism and naturalism could be described as two aspects of the same belief system, neither of which were compatible with the belief that there is a God who creates the world and changes it. It is also my thought experiment for suggesting how the distinction of conventional and reparative language groups might be applied to Barth's doctrine of creation in *Church Dogmatics* III/1, or in the kind of improvement in III/1 that Ray Anderson reads out of *Barth's Table Talk,* concluding that "Barth is completely misunderstood, when it is assumed that he was somehow downgrading the natural creation or the importance of natural science or ecology.... Whereas the bulk of nature-based speculative religion tends to dualize the world..., incarnation-based revelation takes positively the bodily wholeness of man. This faith can delight in the intrinsic goodness of God's entire creation."[18]

So much, then, for three or four nos. But when Barthians say no to such errors, to what do they say yes? If they offered only one all-inclusive answer to that question, they would be guilty of their own dogmatism (in Novak's terms, they would be too kataphatic). If they failed to say yes, they would be guilty of radical skepticism (in Novak's terms, they would be too apophatic). Those I label "Barthians" claim instead to take a third approach that I identify with the different kinds of yeses and nos that belong specifically to reparative inquiry. I believe that the Barthians' good news about Scripture—speaking of both Jewish and Christian Barthians—is that, among other salvific purposes, Scripture comes to the world to teach the differences between peacetime and nonpeacetime language and between conventional and reparative inquiry and to demonstrate how

---

18. Raymond Kemp Anderson, *Karl Barth's Table Talk: Transcripts of Barth's Conversations with His Students at the Bruderholz Restaurant in Basel during the Years 1958–1964* (Lewiston, NY: Edwin Mellen Press, 2014), 244–45.

## To Love Tanakh Is Love Enough for the Jews

human beings can serve as instruments of reparative inquiry. I say "serve as instruments" because reparative inquiry is completed only by the one who speaks Scripture.

I shall illustrate this third approach through a Jewish postliberal reading of two rabbinic doctrines. The first is the distinction between the plain sense of Scripture (*peshat*) and Scripture's interpreted sense (*derash*). Following the Talmudist David Weiss Halivni, I understand "plain sense" as the way a given verse fits into its broader literary context (the "spread" of the scriptural passage, such as the meaning of "earth" within the specific plot of Genesis 1). The plain sense tends to be relatively clear and relatively the same for all time. But the plain sense does not disclose its performative meaning as instruction to the people Israel in the time and context in which they receive it. This "instruction"—*torah/hora'ah* in Hebrew—is disclosed only through the hard work of interpretation—*derashah*—performed by the community of inquiry of a given time and space. For another time and place, the community of inquiry must again work through the plain sense in search of fresh instruction for this day.

In these terms, the plain sense stands independently of the time and place of its reception, but by itself, the plain sense neither legislates nor dictates; it remains "vague" or incompletely defined until it is interpreted.

In these terms, the interpreted sense indicates how, for a given time and place, the plain sense directs some particular rabbinic community to act in a given way. While rabbinic practice displays many different strategies of *derashah*, including conventional-like forms of discourse, the prototypical work of interpretive sense is doubly reparative: repairing some apparent challenge or disruption in the apparent plain-sense meaning of Scripture that signals a complementary way of repairing some aspect of disrupted conventional life and speech in a contemporary rabbinic community.

By way of illustration, consider Novak's study of Micah 6:8. "It has been told to you, O man [*adam*], what is good [*mah tov*] and what the LORD requires of you [*doresh mimmekha*]." Novak writes that for Barth, revelation is a special event, occurring at a unique time and place, as experienced by a unique people.

> As Barth emphasizes . . . : "We do not know God otherwise than as acting God—we have to understand divine action, and therefore an event [*ein Ereignis*]—not a reality which is, but a reality which occurs [*eine geschehende Wirklichkeit*]." Humans in general, though, are the subjects of only ordinary experience, what regularly occurs anywhere at any time

and place. It is from this ordinary experience that some philosophers try to infer some timeless truth that, in principle, could be found by anyone.... But "what" (*mah*) they have been told is different from what they could have told themselves or could have been told by anyone else but God. Just as those directly addressed by God are unique and not "men as such and in general," and just as the method of this address is unique and not a process of general experience and inference therefrom, so the content of the message being addressed to this people is not "a natural duty incumbent on men generally."[19]

As I read it, the implication is that God cannot speak to Israel by the plain sense alone, for only Israel's space and time-specific *derashah* distinguishes God's word to Israel, per se, from that which "can be found by anyone" who claims to read the written plain sense.

In these terms, the rabbinic distinction of plain and interpreted senses can also be read as a mark of the second rabbinic doctrine: that revelation—*mattan torah*, or the giving of Torah on Sinai—comes to instruct the people Israel how to perceive and act upon the distinction between conventional and reparative conditions of speech and inquiry. Why? Because to act upon this distinction is to anticipate times when they will share in the work of repairing terrible disruptions not only in the conventions of pre-Israelite human nature but also in the conventional discourses of the Torah itself.[20]

---

19. See David Novak, "How Jewish Was Karl Barth?," p. 7 above.

20. One stimulus to my claim is David Weiss Halivni's comment about the difference between Beit Hillel (the classic rabbinic school whose legal interpretations of Scripture tend to take the more compassionate approach to human needs) and Beit Shammai (the school whose interpretations take the more rigorous approach). Halivni comments that Beit Hillel speaks to the frail human condition of each generation, while Beit Shammai anticipates the law for the end day when humanity achieves its intended strength. Halivni's words complement my effort to identify the interpreted sense with the way in which a given generation or community receives the plain sense according to its own capacities. I do not understand this reception to be merely subjective, but to display God's will for them as they are at that time. This move enables me to portray time-specific interpretations as having validity (technically we say being truth-functional) with respect to God's compassionate concern for whatever ails or limits the human community at the time of its study of the law. The move also enables me to reason, conversely, that the interpreted sense belongs most specifically to some finite space-time, which belongs most generally to the time after humanity left the Garden of Eden. The time of Gan Eden is a time of creation, or the eternal plain sense. (See, for example, David Weiss Halivni, *Breaking the Tablets: Jewish Theology after the Shoah* [Lanham, MD: Rowman and Littlefield, 2007], 66.)

## To Love Tanakh Is Love Enough for the Jews

In rabbinic memory, one *locus classicus* of such a time is the *Chorban*, the destruction of the Second Temple that signaled the utter disruption of Israel's conventional readings of Torah. With the destruction of Jerusalem, the cessation of temple service, and the beginnings of *Galut*, the Jewish community inhabited a world whose character made no sense in terms of the scriptural plain sense of God's promises to Israel: there would either be no sense or Israel would have to find another, reparative one. By way of illustration, consider this reparative *derashah* from the Mishnah that is often placed at the head of the texts from *Pirke Avot* ("Ethics of the Fathers") that appear in the daily prayer book: "All Israel have a portion in the world-to-come, as it is written, 'your people shall all be righteous, they shall possess the land forever; they are a shoot of My planting, the work of My hands in whom I shall be glorified' (Isaiah 60:21) [*Mishnah Sanhedrin X:1*]." One must imagine that the historical setting of the midrash is rabbinic reflection on the site of the destroyed temple in Jerusalem, sometime in the early second century. Imagine how a rabbinic sage would read the passage from Isaiah while gazing on the site of that ruin. He would have to read the plain sense of the scriptural text as counterfactual evidence either that the people Israel is no longer Isaiah's people Israel or that God's promise is not fulfilled, or perhaps something even worse. The historical facts run counter to the plain sense. In one brief sentence, the rabbinic midrash restores a meaningful relationship between the word of God and the people of God in history by both subverting the plain sense and reaffirming a "deeper" sense of the Scripture: that the time of the promise is in "the world-to-come," not in this world of destruction. It is in the world-to-come that Israel will possess the land forever and will fulfill their portion as the shoot of God's planting. The "world-to-come" is not an explicit phrase in the Bible. By rereading various biblical tropes as types of the world-to-come, the rabbis uncover a dimension of the divine word that is addressed specifically to the historical context of Israel's life after destruction. The disclosure of this dimension of Scripture heals what would otherwise be a rupture in Israel's relation to God. It heals by uncovering a word (the world-to-come) that coheres with the other words of Scripture but that appears at this time as the "new word" that both repairs apparent contradictions in the scriptural tradition and offers Israel a way to act meaningfully, once again, in a world that would otherwise have lost touch with the scriptural source of meaning.[21]

---

21. I draw this reading from previously published words of mine: Peter Ochs, "Recovering the God of History: Scriptural Life after Death in Judaism and Christianity," in *Jews*

PETER OCHS

## *Dabru Emet*

So goes a Jewish Barthian reading of the distinction between *peshat* and *derash*. Will there be a Barthian reading of *Dabru Emet* as well? I close by restating several claims about *Dabru Emet* and about Barthian readings and then pondering how the latter might indeed be applied to the former. I begin with a question: Did the theological dialogue of *Dabru Emet* display the results of a conventional or a reparative inquiry? Hypothesizing that it displays a reparative inquiry, I then proceed to measure it in terms of reparative tendencies in Barthian theology.

### *Arguments for Reading* Dabru Emet *as Reparative Inquiry*

1. As noted in my brief history of *Dabru Emet*, we claimed to pursue *Dabru Emet* to show gratitude to the work of the Christian scholars and to help correct Jewish misunderstandings of Christianity and Jewish misjudgments today about who really are friends or enemies of the God and Torah we serve. These were reparative goals.

2. We recognized that helping change Jewish perceptions of Christianity also meant helping change at least some of modern Judaism's conventions for talking about and talking to Christians. This meant that we too did not come prepared for the task, but had to spend several years repairing our own discourses before offering public words that might help repair our community's discourses.

3. We recognized that our Christian colleagues and communities faced analogous challenges in changing conventions for talking with and to us and of course in repairing the long heritage of anti-Judaism that was itself part of conventional Christian discourse work.

4. In retrospect, we might see that *Dabru Emet* marked a point of different yet in many ways parallel and complementary change in two broad networks of different religious communities, each undergoing complex processes of change in itself and in relation to the other. If so, *Dabru Emet* was a multiple reparative process.

---

*and Christians, People of God*, ed. Carl E. Braaten and Robert W. Jenson (Grand Rapids: Eerdmans, 2003), 114-47 (123-24).

*To Love Tanakh Is Love Enough for the Jews*

*Barthian Readings of* Dabru Emet *as Reparative Inquiry*

1. *If* Dabru Emet *is reparative inquiry, what guides the repair?* The Word, alone, repairs: "The church does not control that Word as earthly things can be controlled."[22] If so, *Dabru Emet* would serve a reparative purpose only insofar as it was guided by the Word. And what is the Word? In Paul Jones's reading, Barth identified the Word strictly with "Scripture":

> At stake here is the belief that the theologian may not adjourn responsibility for listening to the Word of God as it happens in the Bible. . . . Barth's understanding of scripture's revelatory power demands a theological attitude alert to what God is saying, by way of the human words of scripture, *now*. . . . The Bible alone provides unique witness to God's self-revelation and reconciling action. Thus Barth: "After [a] privileged hearing of the Church confessions, we have to go and tread our own way in the understanding, exposition, and application of Holy Scripture. The confession cannot and will not deprive us of our own responsibility to Scripture."[23]

2. *What in the reparative work of* Dabru Emet *could be said to be guided by the Word, and what not?* In the mid-1990s, when *Dabru Emet* was brewing, Jewish-Christian dialogue was only beginning to turn from several decades of societal, ethical, and legal engagement to focus on theological exchange. We authors of *Dabru Emet* were self-conscious about our effort to place intimate religious belief at the center of our dialogue, and intimate study and response to Torah at the center of our Jewish contribution to the dialogue. While we did not, at the same time, seek scriptural warrants for each statement of *Dabru Emet*, it is reasonable to claim that, throughout this work, we defended and debated our judgments on the grounds of

---

22. Karl Barth, *Anselm: Fides Quaerens Intellectum; Anselm's Proof of the Existence of God in the Context of His Theological Scheme* (Eugene, OR: Wipf and Stock, 1975), 282. For Raymond Anderson, the citation is significant, since "Barth often referred to his own small 1931 book on Anselm . . . as the most seminal among his own writings and, therefore, the most important" (Anderson, *An American Scholar Recalls*, 54). Anselm enabled the younger Barth to discover "a faith-intrinsic approach." Barth explains that he simply put Christ in place of Anselm's Catholic tradition to generate his elemental approach to the divine word (Karl Barth, *English Colloquium*, December 5, 1960, cited in Anderson, 57).

23. Paul Jones, *The Humanity of Christ: Christology in Karl Barth* (London: Bloomsbury T. & T. Clark, 2011), 36.

our individual relationships to Torah and to the communities of rabbinic belief and worship to which we, variously, belonged (these happened to fall across the range of American Jewish traditions, Reform, Reconstructionist, Conservative, and Traditional-Conservative). To the degree that we received the Word in both its plain and interpreted senses, I would argue that our effort fell within the scope of a reparative reasoning based on Torah.

In my contribution to our companion book, *Christianity in Jewish Terms*, I wrote:

> The title of this chapter ["The God of Jews and Christians"] represents the ultimate reason we have compiled a book like this. We speak and write as members of a people pulled apart from the world and, to a degree, from other peoples only because of our relationship to the One we call Creator of the world (*bore olam*), Master of the world (*ribono shel olam*), Almighty (*el shadai*), Holy One blessed be He (*hakadosh barukh hu*), the Place (*hamakom*), the Presence (*hashekhinah*), Merciful—or "womb-like"—Father (*av harachamim*), the name YHVH who cannot be spoken, our God (*elohenu*).[24]

This paragraph's singular focus on divine names was, of course, because that was the topic of my chapter, but the more general point still stands: that *Dabru Emet* was an effort to repair interreligious relations in the name of Torah rather than only in the name of the worldly consequences (social, legal, ethical) of bad relations. As the four of us wrote collectively in our preface, "This is a bold undertaking: to be open to thinking seriously about Christianity, let alone about God and religion in a new way! . . . This is also an effort to help Jews relearn the vocabulary of their own faith and then, within this vocabulary, to help them recognize and understand the main tenets of their neighbors' faiths."[25]

The work of *Dabru Emet* addressed a range of worldly as well as religious issues, but this would complement Barth's claim that "it is a matter of hearing the whole, the real Word of God, and therefore, both the *unveiling* of God and His *veiling* as well as the *veiling* of God in His unveiling. The

---

24. *Christianity in Jewish Terms*, ed. T. Frymer-Kensky, D. Novak, P. Ochs, D. Sandmel, M. Signer (Boulder, CO: Westview Press/Perseus for the Institute for Christian and Jewish Studies, 2000), 49.

25. *Christianity in Jewish Terms*, xiii.

secular form without divine content is not the word of God and the divine content without the secular form is also not the word of God. We can neither stop at the secular form as such, nor can we fly off on this and try to enjoy the divine content alone.... The coincidence of the two is clear to God, not discernible by us."[26] In Bruce McCormack's reading, "The event of the Word occurs only where a synthesis of content and form takes place, but this is a synthesis which no human being can bring about."[27]

3. *But the Word is addressed to its elected community. How could the Word be shared in dialogue?* This question has often been addressed both to the Abrahamic theological dialogue sponsored by the Society for Scriptural Reasoning and to the Jewish-Christian theological dialogue sponsored by the ICJS in support of *Dabru Emet*. Introducing *Christianity in Jewish Terms*, Novak cites Malachi in response to this question:

> "Then shall all those who fear the Lord speak, each to his neighbor, and the Lord shall listen and hear. It shall be written in a book of remembrance before Him, for those who fear the Lord and contemplate His name" (Mal. 3:16). In this text, the prophet speaks of a time when the worshipers of God will communicate in a new way. From an earlier verse, it is clear that the worship of God, which is the basis of this new conversation, is not confined to the Jews: "For from the rising to the setting of the sun My name is great among the nations" (Mal. 1:11).

George Hunsinger's chapter in this volume offers an elaborate, complementary response:

> Just as there is only one covenant, so also is there only one people of God. Karl Barth's doctrine of the one twofold people of God is another signal contribution.... There is only one indivisible people of God, I would contend, and yet everywhere it is riven into factions. The unity of this one people is displayed neither among Jews nor among Christians—nor, to say the least, in the wounded relations between Christians and Jews. Among the Jews, we have divisions of varying degrees and stripes.... Among Christians, the fragmentation is if possible even worse.... Notwithstanding all these sorry divisions, subdivisions, and

---

26. Karl Barth, *Church Dogmatics* I/1 (Edinburgh: T. & T. Clark, 1975), 175.
27. Bruce McCormack, *Karl Barth's Critically Realistic Dialectical Theology: Its Genesis and Development, 1909-1936* (Oxford: Oxford University Press, 1997), 465.

factions, I want to suggest that Jews and Christians, whether separately or together, cannot undo their divine election as the one indivisible people of God.[28]

4. *In such a context, is the Word received in its plain sense (for, if so, I do not see how the communities of Israel and the church can engage in dialogue)? If not, how is it received and with what authority?* As noted above, the work of *Dabru Emet* was carried out in the spirit of Torah and debated in light of its authors' relationships to rabbinic traditions of interpretation. The reparative Word is not displayed to the plain sense alone, but through the way that plain sense is received in the space- and time-specific contexts of its interpretation and performance. Hunsinger has written as much of Barth's understanding of church doctrine: "Doctrines are understood to be hermeneutically based (I/1, 308-11). Doctrines arise from and point back to the interpretation of scripture. Scripture as a whole is interpreted to bring out its essential underlying conceptual patterns as they converge upon and are clarified by the name and narrative of Jesus Christ."[29]

In George Lindbeck's terms, this is the "grammatical" sense of scriptural reading. For Kathryn Greene-McCreight, this sense may be identified with a deeper plain sense: "The polyvalence of the biblical texts means for Barth that a plain sense reading of Scripture must encompass the figural as well as the simple or surface meaning. . . . It is those elements of the story that point beyond themselves that signify no less than the simple, the proper and plain sense of the text."[30]

For Hunsinger, this is what Barth called the operation of "grounding." Given the actuality of what we know in the world at a given time and space, Scripture calls us to consider with respect to what necessary conditions this actuality appears to us.

> "Grounding" is meant to indicate that aspect of the *intellectus fidei* which thinks about relations of necessity, possibility, and actuality. Revelation itself is thought to put the question of these relations to us, and the act

---

28. George Hunsinger, "A Christian Appreciation of Jews and Judaism," pp. 63-64 above.

29. George Hunsinger, *How to Read Karl Barth: The Shape of His Theology* (Oxford: Oxford University Press, 1993), 56. The internal reference is to Barth's *Church Dogmatics*.

30. Kathryn Greene-McCreight, *Ad Litteram: How Augustine, Calvin, and Barth Read the "Plain Sense" of Genesis 1-3* (New York: Peter Lang, 1999), 241.

of theological understanding is precisely the act of taking up that question and attempting to answer it. "What is a necessary and sufficient condition for the possibility of the occurrence of a given actuality?" This question often dominates the pattern of argumentation in the *Church Dogmatics*. A certain actuality is taken as a given (usually on the basis of Holy Scripture). The question is then posed about what makes this actuality possible. What condition or set of conditions had to be met in order for this actuality to have occurred?[31]

For Rashkover, this operation of grounding corresponds, in some ways, to Immanuel Kant's practice of transcendental reflection, except that, along with Franz Rosenzweig, Barth assigns this activity of reflection not to the autonomous rational will but (in Rashkover's words) to the "ethical labor of the elect individual who seeks through her moral behavior to testify to the loving act of the transcendent God,"[32] who gives his Word in love. In the language of Rashkover's more recent *Freedom and Law*, "ethical labor" means acting in response to God's free and loving command: his Word given, at once, as law, wisdom, and love.[33]

Without gainsaying its actual merits, we can say at least that *Dabru Emet* was offered for the sake of such ethical labor.

5. *Is the Word received, then, in times when human language is at peace with itself, or not at peace?* As noted earlier, *Dabru Emet* was a response to crisis. According to the argument of this chapter, crisis marks a time when human language is not at peace and when, therefore, conventional rules of meaning prove inadequate to guide communication and inquiry about the aspects of life that are in crisis. There are, to be sure, degrees of crisis, each degree marking a level of failed conventions of meaning. Barthian scholarship provides resources for identifying the degree of crisis that exhausts the capacities of language conventions per se, and that leads either to utter failures of human life and societal order or to reparative responses from beyond the realm of human language.

In McCormack's words,

> A close examination of central texts in *Romans* II reveals a careful attempt to subject the term "crisis" to a searching *theological* criticism. . . .

---

31. Hunsinger, *How to Read Karl Barth*, 57.
32. Rashkover, *Revelation and Theopolitics*, 3.
33. Rashkover, *Freedom and Law*, 267–71.

In so far as an individual recognizes in the cross of Christ the word of divine judgement, she is placed in crisis. She knows herself to be judged, rejected, reprobate. But to precisely the extent that she understands this word of judgement *in the light of the resurrection of Christ*, she knows herself also to be elect. She knows herself to be placed in the dialectic of reprobation and election, of judgement and grace. Such a crisis is not realized once and for all time in a single event in the life of an individual. It is realized anew with each fresh hearing of the Word of God in the cross and resurrection of Christ. It is thus a permanent crisis. Barth employs the "permanent dialectic of time and eternity" in *Romans* II in order to bear witness to this theological dialectic. The crisis of which Barth speaks in *Romans* II is not only permanent; it is also universal in scope. It is not to be limited to the experience of the individual. The whole of creaturely reality is placed in crisis by the Self-revelation of God in the cross and the resurrection. God Himself is the "absolute crisis . . . for the world of humankind, time, and things." Because God is the absolute crisis of *all* creaturely reality, no particular event or historical situation may be directly identified with the Word of God.[34]

What are the consequences of this absolute crisis for the use of human language? In Rashkover's words, "Revelation assumes no positive, objective form, but only awakens humanity to the crisis in its world and the promise for an unseen world beyond presented exclusively through the negation of the current reality. The word of God does not allow believers to positively testify to God's reality in this world because it does not permit them to apprehend God's reality in terms they can express through language or institutions."[35]

In sum, God's presence marks and introduces the ontological crisis that marks humanity's ultimate reliance on God alone. Humanity is offered a home in creation, and creaturely languages accommodate human life in this creation. But God's presence to humanity marks the limit of that accommodation, the point at which human life is sustained only through God's word and its transforming consequences for human reason and human language. As we have already discussed, God's Word is Scripture, so that crisis marks the moment and character of humanity's dependence on Scripture. But when is scripture Scripture?

---

34. McCormack, *Karl Barth's Critically Realistic Dialectical Theology*, 212.
35. Rashkover, *Revelation and Theopolitics*, 140.

## To Love Tanakh Is Love Enough for the Jews

I have written elsewhere of the people Israel's "meantime end-times," or those moments of crisis in Israel's life that display catastrophic ruptures in Israel's life in the world and, thus, in Israel's relations with God, in Israel's religious discourses, and in Israel's conventions of language use, which include conventional practices of scriptural study, interpretation, and enactment. From one perspective, the account of Israel's meantime end-times contrasts with the Barthian account of crisis, since the latter is universal and all at once, while the former is a periodic phenomenon whose cessation would mark the end of human history per se. From another perspective, the two accounts overlap to the extent that an end-time marks that point at which God's word alone redeems and humanly initiated discourse fails.[36] How shall we accommodate the two perspectives?

Without taking time to explore the matter in detail, I shall suggest that Jewish-Christian theological dialogue may be characterized, for one, as a dialogue between rabbinic and christological eschatologies or between meantime and ontological accounts of the meaning of God's presence in history. In these terms, *Dabru Emet* introduced a practice of Jewish-Christian eschatological dialogue.

### Love That Is Love Enough

We have, of course, offered no definitive account, but rather a set of reasonable suggestions that Barth may be read in ways that complement our effort to distinguish reparative from conventional modes of theological (and philosophic) inquiry and to read *Dabru Emet* as a reparative inquiry that contributes to Jewish-Christian efforts to share the Word in theological dialogue. I have suggested that, if so, a statement like *Dabru Emet* would be deepened by even more attention to the Word as warrant for reparative inquiry.

It is time, finally, for an account of the title of this paper: for the sake of the Jews, love of the Torah/OT is love enough (and most trustworthy in the long run). I mean that Christians who seek to repair a history of Christian anti-Judaism would do better not to profess love of or care for the Jews (since such human efforts and desires are rarely equal to the task of repair) but, instead, to read the Word so deeply that they rediscover in it love of

---

36. Ochs, "Recovering the God of History," 114–47.

Torah/OT. This is what Barth did and the reason why his teachings have, in the long run, nurtured readers who have—it appears—displayed more love of the people Israel as well as their Torah than readers of any other single Christian theologian. Still, in days of spiritual trial since the Shoah, Jews might be encouraged in the same way: to examine the people Israel so deeply that they rediscover love of Torah (deep within this people). That is also love enough. These two loves (in one) would be resource enough for statements like *Dabru Emet*.

> Belief or unbelief in the divine world-governance, whether we do or do not apprehend and confess it, is no longer a matter of the right or wrong development of the idea, but of the right or wrong relationship to this reality to which the idea has reference.[37]

---

37. Karl Barth, *Church Dogmatics* III/3 (Edinburgh: T. & T. Clark, 1960), 177.

# 6

## Karl Barth and the Early Postwar Interfaith Encounters, 1945–1950

VICTORIA J. BARNETT

In the late summer of 1947, an international group of sixty-five Protestants, Catholics, and Jews convened in the Swiss village of Seelisberg to discuss what had just happened in Europe, address the ongoing problem of anti-Semitic violence, and strategize about how they together might build a postwar foundation for greater interreligious understanding.[1] Most of them were not religious leaders, but rather community, governmental, and academic leaders who came from a broad range of organizations, and the meeting included one representative of the Allied occupation authorities. Many of them had worked together before the defeat of Nazi Germany in refugee or advocacy work; others were invited because of their international reputations.

The Seelisberg meeting was the second meeting of the newly founded International Conference of Christians and Jews. It was coorganized by the British Council of Christians and Jews (which had been founded in 1942) and the National Conference of Christians and Jews (NCCJ) in the United States, which had been founded in 1928. Much of the organizational legwork for the conference was done by the Reverend Everett Clinchy, the director of the NCCJ, who spent the early postwar years in Europe working together with the US military and governmental officials as well as with UNESCO (United Nations Educational, Scientific and Cultural Organization) to bring together Protestant, Catholic, and Jewish religious leaders to rebuild the social fabric of postwar Europe along the ideals of American democratic pluralism.[2]

---

1. For more on the Seelisberg meeting, see Victoria J. Barnett, "Seelisberg: An Appreciation," and Christian M. Rutishauser, "The 1947 Seelisberg Conference: The Foundation of the Jewish-Christian Dialogue," in *Studies in Christian-Jewish Relations*, vol. 2/2 (2008), pp. 54–57 and 34–53, respectively.

2. See Victoria J. Barnett, *"Fault Lines": An Analysis of the National Conference of Christians and Jews, 1933–1948* (George Mason University, 2012), pp. 153–54.

103

Clinchy hoped that the Seelisberg meeting would initiate a process in postwar Europe similar to the approaches toward interfaith understanding that had shaped the NCCJ's work in the United States during the 1930s. Originally founded as an office of the ecumenical Protestant Federal Council of Churches in New York, the NCCJ became an independent organization in 1932. In the following decade it created a nationwide, high-profile interfaith network dedicated to the fight against religious prejudice (both anti-Catholic and anti-Semitic) under the broader rubric of advocacy for democratic values.[3] The NCCJ's primary methodology consisted of helping establish a network of local coalitions around the country that could engage not only religious leaders but also civil servants, educators, business leaders, and academic leaders who represented the different faiths and would bring the spirit and values of democratic pluralism to their various spheres of work. These coalitions served as models of interfaith understanding, but the NCCJ did not understand itself as an "interfaith" organization and it deliberately avoided terms like "interfaith dialogue" and programs that focused on theological differences, concentrating instead on the creation of common ground around social and community issues.

This was the lens through which Clinchy viewed the events that had just unfolded in Europe. He and several NCCJ staff members had visited Europe several times between 1933 and 1945; he made a fact-finding trip to Germany to document the rise of anti-Semitism in 1932 (before Hitler came to power), and so he was familiar with many of the individuals and groups throughout Europe who shared the NCCJ's concerns and were reaching across faith lines even before 1945.[4] Clinchy also reached out to prominent political and church leaders to obtain high-profile support for his programs; in fact, in December 1947 he had an audience with Pope Pius XII, who, according to Clinchy, fully supported these international attempts at reconciliation and peace building.[5]

This was Clinchy's goal in Seelisberg. Accordingly, he wanted certain people at the table, including well-known individuals whose names would carry a certain weight in the shattered landscape of postwar Europe and

3. Ibid.
4. See Barnett, *"Fault Lines,"* as well as Barnett, "Track Two Diplomacy, 1933–1939: International Responses from Catholics, Jews, and Ecumenical Protestants to Events in Nazi Germany," *Kirchliche Zeitgeschichte* (Fall 2014).
5. Barnett, *"Fault Lines,"* p. 57. The report of the meeting with Pius XII is in the Everett R. Clinchy Papers, Social Welfare History Archives, University of Minnesota Library: Box 12: "Correspondence 1947–48," folder: September–December 1947.

give his cause greater impact. The Europeans who received invitations to participate in Seelisberg represented a wide range of groups and interests. The list of religiously affiliated invitees included Rabbi Leo Baeck; Gerhard Riegner, the head of the World Jewish Congress; Hans Ornstein of the Swiss Council of Christians and Jews; Pastor Paul Vogt of the Swiss Relief Agency; Adolf Freudenberg, the refugee officer at the ecumenical offices in Geneva—and Karl Barth, who apparently sent a letter of regret that his schedule would not allow him to participate.[6]

There were two main points on the Seelisberg agenda, one short-term and one long-term. The short-term issue was how best to address the alarming continuation of anti-Semitic violence in postwar Europe. The long-term issue was to create in Europe the kinds of community coalitions the NCCJ had created in the United States. Delegates at Seelisberg were assigned to one of five commissions that were asked to recommend a course of action at the conclusion of the conference. Their reports focused on the possible strategies in postwar Europe that might combat anti-Semitism and build democratic coalitions through educational and university reform, civic and social service initiatives, and interfaith and governmental relationships.[7]

The Seelisberg meeting took an unexpected and provocative turn, however, in the report issued by the interfaith representatives, a report titled "The Task of the Churches." It is a brief, powerful document that remains one of the most remarkable interfaith statements in history, both because of the timing and because of the text.[8] It began with a brief introduction that openly addressed the Christian failures during the Holocaust, concluding with the "Ten Points of Seelisberg" written by French Jewish historian Jules Isaac, who consulted beforehand on the text with the French Catholic philosopher Jacques Maritain and Gertrud Luckner, a German Catholic social worker who had been sent to Ravensbrück concentration camp for her assistance to Jews. The "Ten Points of Seelisberg" was a theological document that outlined the fundamental changes in Christian teaching and witness that would be necessary for Jews and

---

6. Everett R. Clinchy Papers, Box 5, Folder: "International Emergency Conference to Combat Antisemitism, Seelisberg, Switzerland 1947," and Box 12: "Correspondence 1947–48."

7. *Reports and Recommendations of the International Conference of Christians and Jews. Seelisberg, 1947* (International Council of Christians and Jews, 1947).

8. The full text can be found at the International Council of Christians and Jews website: http://www.jcrelations.net/An_Address_to_the_Churches__Seelisberg__Switzerland__1947.2370.0.html?id=720&L=3&searchText=seelisberg&searchFilter=*.

Christians to talk to each other in the wake of the Holocaust. These changes included the acknowledgment that Jesus and his disciples were Jewish, the recognition of the Jewish roots of Christianity, the repudiation of anti-Jewish interpretations of Christian Scriptures, the repudiation of using biblical texts to condemn contemporary Jews (i.e., clear repudiations of the deicide charge and supersessionist teachings), and the necessity for a different approach to understanding and teaching the passion narratives. In short, "Ten Points" demanded a thorough reexamination and repudiation of what Jules Isaac later described as the Christian "teaching of contempt" for Jews and their tradition.[9] To a great extent, the dramatic emergence of an unplanned but absolutely necessary theological conversation at Seelisberg was the result of the Jewish delegates' raw emotions in the immediate wake of the Holocaust, beginning with Isaac himself, who had lost his position under the Vichy authorities and whose wife and daughter had been murdered in Auschwitz.

The Seelisberg statement effectively laid the foundation of post-Holocaust theology and post-Holocaust Christian-Jewish dialogue. Theologically and historically, there is a direct line from Seelisberg forward to the Second Vatican Council and *Nostra Aetate*. The pre–Vatican II conversations between Catholics and Jews involved many of those who played a role at Seelisberg and in the conversations that followed, and the theological issues outlined in "Ten Points" were the points of discussion at the council. The Seelisberg meeting opened the door for organized European circles of Christians and Jews to begin to talk and reflect together, including John Oesterreicher, Gertrud Luckner, Karl Thieme, Ernst Ludwig Ehrlich, and Paul Demann. Jules Isaac's book *Jesus and Israel* appeared in 1947, the same year he cofounded the French interfaith organization Amitiés judéo-chrétiennes. The first issue of the *Freiburger Rundbrief* (published by Oesterreicher and Luckner), which became the primary European publication on Jewish-Christian relations, appeared in 1948. In Germany, the Council of Christians and Jews was founded in the early 1950s; the Christian-Jewish dialogues that began in 1961 would become regular features of the national German *Kirchtentag* meetings. The latter was one place where Karl Barth's theological perspectives became incorporated into Christian-Jewish relations, largely through the engagement of his student Friedrich-Wilhelm Marquardt, who himself became a leader in this area.

---

9. Jules Isaac, *The Teaching of Contempt: Christian Roots of Anti-Semitism* (McGraw-Hill, 1964).

In other words, the years between 1945 and 1950 were a remarkable transition period during which a new theological conversation between Jews and Christians began. The concrete commitment at Seelisberg to address and combat Christian anti-Semitism soon shifted to broader discussions about Christian-Jewish relations and the rethinking of Christian teachings about Judaism. If one were to map the historical trajectories of related developments, such as the different denominational statements about Christian-Jewish dialogue,[10] the historical research about the churches and the Holocaust, and the subsequent conferences about the Holocaust and the churches that began in the United States during the 1970s,[11] one would see both continuities and breaks in the agenda set in Seelisberg. The continuities came as different generations of scholars continued to address the theological challenges posed in the Seelisberg text; the breaks came as new historical research offered a more complex and often more critical portrait of the role played by Christian churches and teachings in the Holocaust.

In many respects, however, Seelisberg and the other early Jewish-Christian encounters during that era were not entirely new conversations, but a new phase in the relationship between individuals throughout Europe who had actively tried to help Jews during the twelve years of Nazi terror or were already thinking theologically about the Jewish-Christian relationship. There is growing interest among scholars in examining the historical and theological role played by many of these people both during the Holocaust and in its aftermath. John Connelly's recent book *From Enemy to Brother*[12] documents many of these continuities and the theological trajectories that began before 1933 and found new directions after 1945. Connelly looks particularly at the "border crossers"—Jewish converts to Christianity who, instead of repudiating Judaism, incorporated their knowledge and appreciation of it into their adopted Christian tradition, ultimately leading to changes in Christian theology. In addition to such theological pioneers, there were Jewish and Christian activists in Europe and the United States—such as the NCCJ—who were working together during this period to address anti-Semitism and help its victims.[13]

    10. These statements, beginning with the 1947 Seelisberg declaration, can be found at the International Council of Christians and Jews website: www.jcrelations.net.
    11. This was the Annual Scholars' Conference on the Holocaust and the Churches, founded by Dr. Franklin Littell; see their website at http://ascconf.org/.
    12. John Connelly, *From Enemy to Brother: The Revolution in Catholic Teaching on the Jews, 1933–1965* (Harvard University Press, 2012).
    13. See Barnett, "Track Two Diplomacy."

These continuities were evident in Seelisberg, for all those invited to that conference had a track record of some kind, in terms of either their engagement on behalf of the Jews through refugee or resistance activities or their record of theological reflection on this issue. Both factors influenced the decision to invite Karl Barth. Several of the faith representatives who were consulted on the guest list and attended had in fact worked closely with Barth during the war years: the ecumenical refugee officer Adolf Freudenberg; Rabbi Zwi Taubes of Zurich; Pastor Pierre Visseur of Geneva (secretary of the International Conference of Christians and Jews); and Professor Erich Bickel, Hans Ornstein, and Gertrud Kurz of the Swiss Council of Christians and Jews.

Karl Barth was invited to Seelisberg partly because he was Karl Barth. Not surprisingly, the organizers of Seelisberg hoped to have the leading Protestant European theologian lend prestige to this important meeting. But Barth was also invited because of his record of outspoken opposition to the Nazi regime, particularly during the late 1930s, as well as because of his assistance during the war to resistance and rescue organizations. Especially in the Jewish community in Switzerland, Barth was well known not so much for his theology but for his outspoken calls for the defeat of the Nazi regime. After his return to Switzerland in 1935, Barth noted that while in Germany his opposition had been "for the sake of the preservation of the true church and the just state, I had to persevere in my opposition to National Socialism even after I had returned to Switzerland."[14] That decision made him one of the most outspoken Christian theologians of the late 1930s and, especially as war became imminent, set him at odds with church and ecumenical leaders and theologians who still hoped that war with Nazi Germany could be averted and were made uneasy by Barth's militant language. Barth's open letters to the churches of Europe and his call to arms were described by others in the ecumenical movement as "crusade theology" (by Willem Visser 't Hooft) and "general staff verdicts" (by Eduard Thurneysen).[15] When Barth wrote his 1938 letter to Czech theologian Josef Hromádka in which he stated that every Czech who fought the Nazis would be fighting "for the Church of Jesus Christ," he was accused of being a warmonger; even Confessing Church

---

14. Eberhard Busch, ed., *Karl Barth: His Life from Letters and Autobiographical Texts* (Eerdmans, 1994), p. 271.

15. See Klemens von Klemperer, *The German Resistance: The Search for Allies Abroad* (Oxford University Press, 1992), pp. 143 and 149.

## Karl Barth and the Early Postwar Interfaith Encounters

leaders in Germany wrote a letter criticizing it, accusing him of acting not as a theologian but as a politician.[16]

In the eyes of European Jews and many others, however, Karl Barth had been on the right side of history and was one of the very few Christians who had spoken out so bluntly against Nazi Germany. In addition, the Swiss Jewish community was well aware of his engagement and advocacy for refugees and rescue groups. The most prominent instance was with respect to the so-called Auschwitz Protocol, a document smuggled into Switzerland in the spring of 1944 by two Slovakian Jews that described in great detail what was happening in the death camps. The document was translated by George Mantello, a Hungarian Jew working in the Salvadorian consulate in Geneva, and passed on to international church leaders and diplomats, with a cover letter signed by Karl Barth, Paul Vogt, Emil Brunner, and Willem Visser 't Hooft, in the hopes that this would galvanize international attention.[17]

In addition, Barth had been politically and financially supportive of some of the rescue networks in Nazi Germany. His connections stemmed from relationships that went back to the religious socialist circles of the 1920s, particularly his friendship with Gertrud Staewen, a social worker who by the late 1930s was connected to several resistance groups, including the Kaufmann circle, a small resistance and rescue group that helped forge false papers for Jews in Berlin and passes to help them reach Switzerland.[18] Staewen compiled a list of people (both Jews and "non-Aryan" Christians) seeking Swiss visas and sent this to Adolf Freudenberg in Geneva.[19] Barth stayed in regular touch with Staewen, sending money secretly into Nazi Germany to support her work and urging Swiss officials to issue more visas.[20] When the Kaufmann group was discovered by the Gestapo in 1943,

---

16. See Friedrich-Wilhelm Marquardt, "Theological and Political Motivations of Karl Barth in the Church Struggle," in *Theological Audacities: Selected Essays* (Pickwick, 2010), pp. 190–91.

17. See Alfred Wetzler, *Escape from Hell: The True Story of the Auschwitz Protocol* (Berghahn Books, 2007).

18. See Victoria Barnett, *For the Soul of the People* (Oxford University Press, 1992), pp. 150–51; Katrin Rudolph, *Hilfe beim Sprung ins Nichts* (Metropol, 2005), pp. 105–6, 185; and Marlies Flesch-Thebesius, *Zu den Außenseitern gestellt: Die Geschichte der Gertrud Staewen 1894–1987* (Wichern Verlag, 2004), pp. 198–229.

19. See Flesch-Thebesius, *Zu den Außenseitern gestellt*, pp. 198–212.

20. On Barth's work with the Swiss Aid Committee, see also Busch, *Karl Barth*, p. 325. See also Adolf Freudenberg, *Rettet sie doch! Franzosen und die Genfer Ökumene im Dienste der Verfolgten des Dritten Reiches* (EVZ-Verlag, 1969).

most in the group were arrested and Franz Kaufmann was murdered in Sachsenhausen.[21] Cioma Schönhaus, the Jewish artist who had worked with the group, forging false papers for Jews, escaped to Switzerland with Barth's help and lived with Barth for several years.[22] Barth also had ties to the French Protestant CIMADE organization (Comité inter-mouvements auprès des évacués), which viewed Barth as a theologian of resistance, particularly after his October 1940 letter to the French Protestant churches that urged the "spiritual necessity" of ongoing resistance.[23] On at least one occasion in spring 1942, CIMADE activist Suzanne de Dietrich tried to arrange for him to meet with the French youth organization associated with CIMADE.[24]

And then there was his theology of Israel, the affirmation of the Jewishness of Jesus, and his painstaking examination of the relationship between Judaism and Christianity that shaped his theological work. This, too, was why they wanted Barth in Seelisberg. Much of the energy that went into and came out of Seelisberg was theological, focused on the very questions that were at the heart of Barth's theology. The pioneers of Jewish-Christian dialogue, both Protestant and Catholic, had read him and referenced him and reached out to him even before 1945. As early as the mid-1930s, Dietrich von Hildebrand and the dissenting circles of Austrian Catholics who would later become leading proponents of *Nostra Aetate* were circulating Karl Barth's work privately.[25] In 1938 the Catholic activists Karl Thieme and John Oesterreicher, exiled in Paris, reached out to Jacques Maritain, Karl Barth, and others about creating a group that would push the Vatican to speak out about the Nazi anti-Jewish measures, and Barth attended at least one meeting of the group.[26]

In his 1986 book *The New Encounter*, the Catholic thinker John Oesterreicher paid tribute to Barth's influence when he wrote: "With Karl Barth, the great theologian of the twentieth century, I would like to say: 'The Bible . . . is a Jewish book; it cannot be read, understood, or interpreted unless we enter into the speech, the thought, and the history of the Jews

---

21. Barnett, *For the Soul of the People*, pp. 150-51, 186-87.

22. Robert P. Ericksen, "Cioma Schönhaus and the Kaufmann Circle" (paper presented at "Lessons and Legacies," 2010).

23. From Uta Gerdes, *Ökumenische Solidarität mit christlichen und jüdischen Verfolgten: Die CIMADE in Vichy-Frankreich 1940-1944* (Vandenhoeck & Ruprecht, 2005), p. 240.

24. Ibid., p. 238n108.

25. Connelly, *From Enemy to Brother*, p. 102.

26. Ibid., p. 157.

in complete openness, unless we are ready to become Jews with the Jews. Thus we are asked to take a stand toward the continued existence of the Jews as a proof that God is and works through history whether we affirm it or intend to howl against it with the wolves.'"[27] In the early pages of the *Freiburger Rundbrief*, Karl Thieme explored the relationship between what he described as the old and the new Israel and based much of his thinking on Barth's exegesis of Paul's letter to the Romans, which referred to the Jews as the *Stamm Abrahams*.[28]

Yet Seelisberg was only the beginning of a difficult and complicated dialogue that continues until today, precisely because it was a dialogue between two traditions that shared both common roots and a bitterly painful history. Barth, like so many others, found himself called to address the theological complications of his theology of Israel that, in the wake of the Holocaust, were impossible to resolve.[29]

Two discussion evenings in January and March 1950 between Barth and Emunah, a group of young Swiss Jews, illustrate the ongoing differences. The Emunah group had requested the meetings after Barth had given a radio address entitled "The Jewish Question and Its Christian Answer."[30] According to a report published in the *Freiburger Rundbrief*, the group posed eleven questions to Barth about the Christian understanding of Judaism and the theological relationship between Christians and Jews, including the mission to convert the Jews.[31] Barth said that he continued to see evangelization as part of Christian mission but emphasized that he distinguished it from the mission to other non-Christians (similarly to how this issue was subsequently framed in *Nostra Aetate*). Barth (as quoted in the report) stated that "The goal for Jews as well as for Christians is the same, only the path is different. To use a comparison, the Jews go up the mountain, whereas the Christians go down," and he noted that there was

27. John Oesterreicher, *The New Encounter* (Philosophical Library of New York, 1986), p. 338. Oesterreicher was quoting from *Church Dogmatics* I/2 (T. & T. Clark, 1956), pp. 510–11.

28. Connelly, *From Enemy to Brother*, pp. 220 and 260.

29. For a thorough analysis of these issues with respect to Barth's theology, see Mark Lindsay, *Reading Auschwitz with Barth: The Holocaust as Problem and Promise for Barthian Theology* (Pickwick, 2014).

30. Eberhard Busch writes that this radio address was "a simplified version of a passage from Church Dogmatics III, 3." Busch, *Karl Barth*, p. 368.

31. "Jüdische Jugend befragt Karl Barth," *Freiburger Rundbrief* 2, no. 7 (1949/1950): 20. The *Freiburger Rundbrief* report was a summary of an article about the meeting published in *Israelitisches Wochenblatt für die Schweiz*, no. 15 (Zurich 1950): 26–27.

no reason for mission, "for the entire Old Testament strives toward one point, toward its fulfillment in Jesus Christ. The Jew must independently recognize that Old and New Testament constitute a unity." This description of the Jewish-Christian relationship, however, was not welcomed by the Jewish participants. As the report continues: "Precisely on this point in the discussion it became very clear how fundamentally the religious views of Jews and Christians are divergent, ruling out a deep understanding of the other side. One speaker observed here that the core for Christians consisted of 'being redeemed' (*Erlöst-Sein*) and the core for Jews of 'being obligated' (*Verpflichtet-Sein*)."

The last question posed by the group concerned anti-Semitism: What did the church have to say to the Jews of the world in that historical moment? Barth (according to this account) replied: "For all its repudiation of anti-Semitism Israel should nonetheless be somewhat proud of it, for it is proof of its election and its preeminent mission." "The reply from the Jewish side was that from a Protestant theological standpoint that may all well be true, but the *reality* in its full gruesomeness didn't allow this kind of fatal statement. On this point *other* factors needed to be taken into consideration. To which Professor Barth replied: 'The theological aspect is the entire point. The issue is how we understand it from God.'"

For his part, notes Eberhard Busch, Barth later wrote of this conversation that "I have never felt myself so much on Jordan's bank as in that closely packed hotel room." Busch continues: "Barth felt that here he could 'only confirm' to his Jewish conversation partners 'that the messiah has already come, the law has already been fulfilled, morality is only an act of gratitude, and so on.'"[32]

Both the report in the *Freiburger Rundbrief* and Barth's own account revealed the deep differences and pain that characterized such conversations in the wake of the Holocaust, even those in which Jews and Christians were honestly seeking to understand one another. Despite Barth's comment, the "theological aspect" was not the entire point, nor could theology per se address the theological roots of Christian complicity and culpability in the Holocaust. History had altered such theological conversations. For that reason, Seelisberg is more relevant than Barmen for our understanding of Barth in that postwar context. Much of the examination of Barth's attitudes toward Judaism and Jews revolves around his reactions

32. Eberhard Busch, *Unter dem Bogen des einen Bundes: Karl Barth und die Juden 1933-1945* (Neukirchener, 1996), pp. 368-69.

to the German church struggle, particularly in the early years of National Socialism, and to the debates between the *Deutsche Christen* and the Confessing Church—the 1934 Barmen confession of faith being Barth's most prominent stand in these debates. Yet the postwar conversation with the Emunah group—like the Seelisberg meeting itself—took him outside the internal Christian conversations into true interreligious engagement and, more importantly, confronted him (and other Christians) with the broader issues of the role of Christianity in the Holocaust.

These issues about the role of Christianity in the persecution of the Jews were related to the demographics of the Holocaust. In the countries of western Europe, including Germany, the Jewish population was a fraction of a percent, and a significant portion of that fraction consisted of assimilated Jews: people who had either converted to Christianity or were secular. But the vast majority of Jews murdered in the Holocaust, and the vast majority of Jewish survivors, came from eastern Europe. Before the Holocaust, the largest Jewish communities in Europe were in Poland, with about 3,000,000 Jews (9.5 percent of Poland's population); the European part of the Soviet Union, with 2,525,000 (3.4 percent); and Romania, with 756,000 (4.2 percent). The Jewish population in the three Baltic states totaled about 255,000: 95,600 in Latvia, 155,000 in Lithuania, and 4,560 in Estonia.[33]

In many parts of eastern Europe a particularly strong amalgamation of Christianity, fascism, ethnocentrism, and violent anti-Semitism had taken place before 1933. The most striking examples of this were the Iron Guard in Romania and the role of Josef Tiso in Yugoslavia.[34] During the Holocaust significant sectors of the Jewish populations in eastern Europe were not murdered by German troops or in death camps but by local collaborators. The Seelisberg declaration itself illustrated the degree to which Christian

---

33. See "Jewish Population of Europe in 1933: Population Data by Country," Holocaust Encyclopedia, United States Holocaust Memorial Museum, accessed April 19, 2017, http://www.ushmm.org/wlc/en/article.php?ModuleId=10005161.

34. See Paul Shapiro, "Faith, Murder, Resurrection: The Iron Guard and the Romanian Orthodox Church," in *Antisemitism, Christian Ambivalence, and the Holocaust*, ed. Kevin Spicer (Indiana University Press, 2007), pp. 136–73; James Ward, *Priest, Politician, Collaborator: Jozef Tiso and the Making of Fascist Slovakia* (Cornell University Press, 2013); Ionut Biliuta, "Sanctifying, Judging, or Recovering the Past? Post-1990s Understanding of Romanian Fascism in Christian Orthodox Environments," in *European Review of History* (2014), and "Fascism as Political Religion: A Critical Survey," *Studia Universitatis Petru Maior* (2008).

anti-Semitism was a primary concern of the Jewish community, and although Seelisberg represented an attempt to reach across these divisions and provoke a new, deeper dialogue, in the broader Jewish community considerable distrust and skepticism about this new Jewish-Christian relationship remained.

The American Jewish rabbi and author Arthur Cohen expressed this skepticism in his scathing essay about one of the early attempts at Jewish-Christian reconciliation, John Oesterreicher's journal the *Bridge*, published in the 1950s. In his essay, titled "The One-Way Bridge," Cohen wrote:

> It is not easy to read *The Bridge* without irritation. . . . Throughout there runs the multifibered cord of Olympian condescension, Christian reverence for mysterious Israel, and pious indignation at Jewish stubbornness. . . . We can but ask if Rome, for all its love for Israel, is as well contrite for what it did not do for Israel. The speeches of random cardinals were nothing against the fury of the past decades. . . . This is our single plea: that the Church of Rome make confession for its profound and unforgettable diffidence. There is excommunication for heresy. Is there no excommunication for murderers? If there is none, one might at least insist that there be contrition for having countenanced murder.[35]

In another essay, Cohen wrote of the Protestant churches: "The consequence of the de-Judaizing of Christian theology could not be more evident than in the pitiful inability of the Protestant . . . churches to oppose German national Socialism. . . . Only Dietrich Bonhoeffer in Germany and Karl Barth at its borders inveighed against the capitulation of Church to State."[36]

Notably, Cohen acknowledged the clarity of both Bonhoeffer and Barth about the German churches' response to Nazism, but as his writings illustrated, the *Deutsche Christen* were seen not as an aberration but as an example of the much deeper problem within Christianity itself that extended far beyond the struggles of the churches in Nazi Germany, and thus the focus of both historiography and post-Holocaust interfaith dialogue was necessarily broader than the limited scope of the *Kirchenkampf*. For

---

35. In Arthur Cohen, *The Myth of the Judeo-Christian Tradition: And Other Dissenting Essays* (Schocken Books, 1971), pp. 118–19.

36. Cohen, "Theological Enmity and Judeo-Christian Humanism: A Dialectic of the Supernatural and the Natural," in *The Myth of the Judeo-Christian Tradition*, pp. 199–200.

these reasons, Barmen and the German church struggle were not items of discussion at Seelisberg. The story of the Confessing Church, the Barmen Declaration, and postwar texts such as the 1945 Stuttgart declaration of guilt had meaning for Protestants, and they had some meaning ecumenically, although less than one might think in the grand scheme of things in postwar Europe. But the German church issues played a minor role in the broader postwar Jewish-Christian encounters, in part due to the strong representation of Catholic thinkers in these encounters, and in part because the Barmen and Stuttgart documents were completely silent about what had happened to the Jews.[37]

Thus, Barth's invitation to Seelisberg was primarily due not to his role in the Protestant *Kirchenkampf* but to his theological work on Christians and Jews. However, in the context of his response to the German Protestant issues, he did tackle these broader concerns, particularly in his clear condemnations of the ethnocentric versions of Christianity being promulgated in Germany during the 1920s and 1930s by theologians such as Paul Althaus and Emanuel Hirsch, and his insistence on acknowledging the Jewish roots of Christianity. While these texts were made within the German context and of course directed primarily at the *Deutsche Christen* after 1933, this was the issue that connected the Christo-fascism in parts of the eastern churches and the German form of this ideology propagated by the *Deutsche Christen*. A closer examination of Barth's significance in the broader context of the debates during the 1920s and 1930s among European Christians, in east and west, about the theological intersections of Christianity, anti-Semitism, and ethno-fascism, remains an important and underresearched area.

Finally, there is a special challenge that arises in any examination of a figure such as Karl Barth in light of the history before 1945 and the ways in which Jews and Christians addressed this history afterward: the theological texts must be read in light of the history, and vice versa. In understanding how Barth (and others) responded to the language not just of religion but of ideology in addressing the contentious theological issues of that era, one must be able to grasp the theological subtexts of historical documents and the historical subtexts or context of the theological ones. Like Bonhoeffer, Barth has been judged historically by his theological texts, which are examined in order to situate him more clearly against

---

37. See Barnett, *For the Soul of the People*, and "Barmen, the Ecumenical Movement, and the Jews: The Missing Thesis," *Ecumenical Review* 61, no. 1 (2009): 17–23.

the backdrop of the Christian relationship to Judaism and of course the Holocaust.[38]

To understand the theological and historical complexities of Barth's relationship to Judaism and the Jewish people, however, it is also important to reflect on the nature of interreligious dialogue, especially those exchanges (such as Seelisberg) that were initiated to repair ruptured relationships and deal with histories of violent hatred. Intrinsic to these kinds of conversations is the reality that there are emotions and perspectives that will never be felt or comprehended by both parties equally, even with the best of intentions. There may be a healing that over time can cover the rupture, but it does not close it or erase it, and there must be the recognition from the beginning that there are things that cannot be resolved. This was what Barth and his Emunah Jewish conversation partners discovered in 1950.

As I have written elsewhere,[39] every interreligious conversation always entails three concurrent conversations constantly interacting with one other: the direct dialogue with the dialogue partner; the internal dialogues that each partner has with his/her respective traditions as the interreligious dialogue raises questions and challenges and provokes new insights; and the external dialogue in which the partners, individually or together, address the main outside issues that frame their conversation. In Seelisberg, these external issues were the Holocaust and the interreligious challenges in its wake.

When the process of interreligious dialogue works, the religions involved can be revised and transformed, but only in conversation with the others. The true transformation of a religious tradition is not the product of a purely internal process of reform, but of reforms provoked by the engagement with others outside the tradition: in the case of Seelisberg, the product of honest conversation with history, with Judaism, and with Jews. This lesson—that interpretations of crucial texts and self-understandings of religious identity, relationship, and theology can and must change as a result of historical events and relationships—remains a crucial one for other interreligious relationships today.

---

38. See especially Wolfgang Gerlach's *And the Witnesses Were Silent: The Confessing Church and the Jews* (University of Nebraska Press, 2000). The German edition of this work includes a section that is highly critical of Barth in comparison to Bonhoeffer: *Als die Zeugen schwiegen: Bekennende Kirche und die Juden* (Institut Kirche und Judentum, 1987), pp. 403–24.

39. See Barnett, *"Fault Lines,"* pp. 12–14, 17–18, 38, 166–67.

## Karl Barth and the Early Postwar Interfaith Encounters

Between 1945 and 1950, Karl Barth and others became part of such a process. It was a development that came relatively late in Barth's career. He had already produced a significant body of theological work, and so he was less engaged in these conversations in revising his own thought and served far more as a point of reference for others who were wrestling with these issues. The Seelisberg moment was soon subsumed under other issues such as the Cold War. Yet, an examination of Barth in conjunction with the other figures of his times in the Jewish-Christian relationship, as they engaged with the burning questions after the Holocaust and with Barth's writings, may also give us new insights into his theological writings as well as into his remarkable and complex life and times.

# 7

## The Divine Vocation and Destiny of Israel in World History

Thomas F. Torrance

The people of Israel are charged with a divine destiny not of their own choosing. They are called to fulfill a definite function in God's saving purpose for all peoples. Far from having only a temporary significance that ended with the rise of the church, Israel continues to play an all-important role, if often a hidden one, in the mysterious decisions of God—decisions that will not be fully manifest until his kingdom comes at the end-time. God does not go back on his unique covenant with Israel, nor does he change his mind about his special gifts to them, nor does he revoke his calling of Israel to fulfill a universal mission. The permanent significance of Israel is central not only to the Old Testament but also to the New. Israel's mission is made clear, for example, in important chapters of Saint Paul's epistles, most notably Romans 9–11 and Ephesians 2.

My main theme is that the people of Israel have been given a vicarious mission to carry out. Their mission is of vital importance not only for the church but also for all humankind. From the very beginning of Israel's history, God established an intimate communion with them—a communion that contained within itself God's saving purpose for the entire human race. After a long spiritual and historical ordeal—the ordeal of Israel's struggle with God—God's universal saving purpose became embodied, finally and fully, in the human existence of Jesus Christ. Not only did the eternal Word of God become incarnate in him—the Word by whom all were created and in whom all have their being. In a decisive manner he also gathered up in himself the whole history of Israel in its ever-deepening communion with God. Through his death, resurrection, and ascension, he fans this communion out in an expansive movement toward the coming world community or *oikoumene* (Heb. 2:5), the all-embracing people of God.

## The Divine Vocation and Destiny of Israel in World History

The place of Israel in salvation history remains central to the inner logic of God's kingdom and his people. Under the constraint of God's Spirit, the church acknowledged the Old Testament as Holy Scripture. In doing so it sealed for itself Israel's irrevocable place in God's universal saving plan. The apostolic community could not but see itself as incorporated within the one people of God. Through Christ they were "grafted into the trunk" of Israel, the elect people of the covenant promises and the divine oracles.

That is surely how we must continue to regard the Jews as our brothers and sisters today. They belong in the profoundest sense to the one *ecclesia* of God. Within themselves they continue to hold the secret of the unity of humankind in God's redemptive purpose for the world. They stand as the appointed instrument of God's self-communication and his self-commitment to the human race. As such, Israel constitutes the critical center of human history. They represent God's will "to gather together into one the scattered children of God" (John 11:52). That is their peculiar destiny and status when seen as a people (*laos*) and not merely as a nation (*ethnos*). Israel is the people who, through their relation to God and his universal purpose, are called to transcend ethnic divisions and open up the way toward the one undivided kingdom of God among human beings.

Strange as it may seem from a theological perspective, this is not a destiny to which the people of Israel have ever been fully reconciled. A deep-seated tension has often existed between their spiritual destiny and their ethnic actuality. This tension has not been helped by the long tradition of Christian anti-Semitism and anti-Judaism. Especially deplorable is the widespread Christian belief that Israel was replaced by the church as the people of God—a belief in sharp conflict with both Testaments, the New as well as the Old.

It is of the utmost importance that Christians today should recover the apostolic perspective. Jews and Christians belong together as the one internally diversified people of God. The church cannot break with Israel without breaking from the center of God's redemptive plan to re-create and reunify all humankind. Nor can Israel break with the nations, or turn fundamentally against them, without breaking with its divine vocation.

Schism between Christians and Jews is the deepest schism of all. It is the root cause of all other tragic divisions that have arisen in the one indivisible people of God. Rebellion against God's reconciling purpose, as ordained to take place through Israel, cannot but have dire consequences, no matter where the rebellion may break out. It cannot but generate further fragmentation among the peoples and nations of the earth.

Nationalism in the form of group egoism or ethnic sin is the poisonous root of all racism. In modern times racism and anti-Semitism go together. Behind all anti-Semitism lurks a perverted animosity against God. It is an animosity against the pathway God has ordained among the nations for the salvation of the human race. Anti-Semitism is a rebellion against the peculiar vocation and destiny of Israel, especially against its vicarious mission. For that very reason it is also at the same time a deep-seated rebellion against Christ and his own vicarious mission. In other words, anti-Semitism is a manifestation of what the New Testament calls "anti-Christ." Of course, we can only dare to speak this way on the basis of faith in Christ. There is much here that baffles us. Nevertheless, three points about Israel's vocation and destiny surely need to be stressed.

1. *Israel is the unique partner of divine revelation.* What ultimately stamps the people of Israel as so distinctive is that they are chosen from among all others for a special purpose. They are chosen to be God's instrument in mediating divine revelation and reconciliation to humankind. To use Jeremiah's analogy, in the hands of the divine potter, Israel is at once molded, broken down, and reshaped through the ordeal of its experiences with God. All that Israel endured in history, especially at the spiritual level, was not merely for its own sake, but finally for the sake of the world.

The role for which Israel was elected was agonizingly difficult. Chosen to be the earthen vessel of divine revelation, Israel had to suffer from its flame as no other people has ever had to suffer. Through divine initiative and providence, Israel became the people where God's revelation of himself was impressed into the clay of humanity. Through the responses this revelation evoked, it was translated into basic patterns of human understanding and speech. In this way God's self-revelation became available to all human beings and all ages. The Word of God struggled with the ways of Israel—with its patterns of life and thought and worship. It broke through barriers of naturalistic and pagan convention that hindered knowledge of the living God. Through a complex historical process—whether of assent or dissent, obedience or disobedience, apostasy or reform—God used Israel's responses as instruments for an ever-deepening penetration into its existence. In this way God's Word was communicated and made intelligible to humankind.

This mediation of divine revelation and reconciliation did not always go smoothly. The Old Testament Scriptures do not hide stories of Israel's continual disobedience and rebellion. Nevertheless, the people's obstinate behavior was fashioned into an essential component of their vicarious mission. What Israel represented was human nature in its stubborn estrangement from God, that is, humanity's sinful existence. It was precisely with this difficult people that God bound himself forever in a covenant, in a partnership of steadfast love. Although God's very intimacy with Israel intensified their refusal of him, that did not rob God's faithfulness of its effect. The people may have been unfaithful to God, but God remained faithful to them. Divine faithfulness did not exclude judgment for the sake of grace. Through the trials and tribulations of judgment, God's people would finally be reaffirmed and restored in the fullness of his love.

In a profound sense, Israel underwent what it did in our place and for our sakes. Israel's vicarious role in judgment and grace prepared the way for the coming of Christ. In him that role was taken up and fulfilled in an unprecedented way. In his atoning passion—the passion of God incarnate—a reconciling sacrifice was offered on behalf of Israel and all other peoples. Thus Israel had and continues to have an inner organic bond with Jesus Christ not shared by any other people. It is in virtue of that bond, as consummated in his crucifixion and resurrection, that Israel's historical experiences of abandonment—"My God, my God, why hast thou forsaken me?" (Ps. 21:1)—not least in the pogroms and extermination camps of modern Europe, point ahead to its own promised future in resurrection and reaffirmation in the fullness of the divine covenant.

2. *Israel is the only people with messianic promise.* As gentiles we were "without Christ," Saint Paul reminds us, "being aliens from the commonwealth of Israel, and strangers from the covenants of promise, having no hope, and without God in the world" (Eph. 2:11). All these privileges belong to Israel (Rom. 9:4–5). Therefore, gentiles are with God, they have Christ, they are included in the covenantal promises, they have hope—they are saved—only as they are incorporated into Israel, the one people of God. For gentiles, how does that happen? According to Saint Paul, only through union with Christ. We gentiles, who were far away, have been brought near through the shedding of Christ's blood (Eph. 2:12–19). As Saint Paul sees it, through the sacrifice of Christ on the cross, the old barrier has come down—the barrier that was erected around the holy precincts of the temple to keep out all gentiles, unbelievers, and excommunicated people. They were prevented from joining with faithful Jews as they drew near to God in worship and sacrifice. That is the barrier that comes down in Christ, together with the legal ordinances that gave rise to it.

It is on that ground, Saint Paul claimed, that gentiles are no longer to be regarded by Jews as foreigners or strangers, but as fellow citizens with God's people. They too are now included within the scope of the ancient promises. The covenantal relation between God and Israel remains in force, but now as the core of a wider communion. In Christ the gentile church is called to remain faithful to Israel, even as Israel is called to extend its covenantal blessings to gentiles, who were previously excluded. The tragedy of schism at this point is the deepest tragedy in the history of the covenant.

3. *Israel will have a central place in the consummation of all things.* As we have suggested, Israel will have a basic part in the reunion of the fragmented gentile church. It is not too much to say that the whole future of ecumenism and evangelism depends on the relation of Jews to Jesus Christ as the messianic Savior and King. Only through the double witness of Jews and gentiles to Christ will the gospel finally be extended to cover all the peoples of the earth. Only then will the scattered children of God be gathered into one compact people.

To that end Israel will have a basic part to play in the relation of the church to world humanity. Ultimately, of course, the salvation and renewing of humankind depend on the reconciling, resurrecting power of Christ himself. Nevertheless, if the actual unification of world humanity is to come about, it must involve at its very center the reconciliation of Jew and gentile in Christ. And how is that to take place? It can only occur through the fulfillment of Israel's vicarious role, which remains entirely in force because God's covenant with Israel is not annulled.

Let us recall the unceasing struggle in historic Israel between its divine calling to be God's people and its worldly aspiration to be a nation like any other. Insofar as Israel simply behaves like others, its vicarious function does not become manifest. On the other hand, the closer the covenant bonds between Israel and God are drawn, the more intense its relationship with God becomes. Israel's very existence becomes implicated all the more in the mediation of divine revelation and salvation beyond itself. At certain points Israel seems forced into a position where it manifests our estranged human nature, our human self-centeredness and self-will. Paradoxically, God uses that very state of affairs to fulfill his self-giving through his covenant with Israel. From a Christian standpoint, that is precisely how we are to understand Israel's strange rejection of its own Messiah. God bends this very rejection to further the reconciliation of the world to himself. He bends it to create a space in Christ for gentiles to be grafted into the covenant.

What does all this have to say to us now? What do the people of Israel mean for the Christian church today? One thing at least is clear: we must acknowledge both our immense debt to Israel and our abject shame for what Christian peoples have done to Israel. The time has come for the whole church of Christ to recognize far more profoundly and sincerely than it has that the church stands in debt to Israel. For it could not exist as church except as it is grafted on to the stock of Israel, which occurs, in a sense, at Israel's expense. Nevertheless, Israel remains the servant of the Lord with a vicarious function to fulfill *even for the Christian church*. Without heeding Israel or listening to its witness, the Christian church cannot properly understand its own existence or mission.

The church today cannot relate sincerely to Israel without acknowledging the immensity of its guilt toward Israel. It is called to confess its sin of rejecting and persecuting Israel throughout the Christian centuries. It cannot brush off the abominable horror of the mass extermination of Jews in modern times simply by putting it down to the Nazis. This unspeakable horror had its poisonous roots in many centuries of anti-Semitism fostered by the Christian church. It is a horror that discloses a deep-seated enmity that must constantly be dug out. It must be submitted to the flame of divine judgment in the cross of Jesus Christ. In faithfulness to the God of Israel and the Father of our Lord Jesus Christ, the Christian church can never be the same after the Holocaust. The church's understanding of divine revelation and salvation, mediated through Israel, must be affected by the cry *"Eli, Eli, lama sabachthani?"* For Christian faith it is a cry of anguish in which Israel and Jesus Christ are forever forged together in a new and quite irreversible way. The Christian *ecclesia* and the Jewish *ecclesia* are now harnessed together in the mysterious judgments of God for witness, service, and mission. They are joined in the accelerating rush of world events toward the end-time, when Christ himself will come to take up his reign and make all things new.

Now let us consider three things we Christians may learn today from and through Israel.

1. *Israel can help us understand Jesus.* In modern times immense effort has been devoted by Christian scholars to what has been called "the quest of the historical Jesus." This Jesus has proved to be tantalizingly elusive to our historical-critical reconstructions. Now it is becoming more and more evident that our constant problem arises because our very approach to Jesus gentilizes him and obscures him, so that he keeps vanishing from our "observations." Behind this lie the many, many centuries of ethnic and cultural conditioning of Christianity.

All we seem finally to do is to construct a picture of Jesus that fits into our Western cultural preconceptions. We need to strip away the gentile patterns of thought and behavior that we have foisted on "the historical

Jesus" if he is to disclose himself to our inquiry as he really was and is. But how can we manage to do that without the help of the Jews, our religious brothers and sisters, themselves? How can we see Jesus, the Jew from Bethlehem, Nazareth, and Jerusalem, without the use of Jewish eyes?

I recall an experience I had many years ago while working with a Jewish scholar. I found that he himself could discern things in the New Testament that I could not see and that took me some time to see even with his help. I could not see them because I was looking through the lenses of gentile spectacles, which distorted what was there. I had to learn to take off the spectacles I did not even know I was wearing.

That common study with my Jewish friend taught me the kind of cooperation between Christians and Jews that we desperately need to enable us to discard the unconscious anti-Semitism and anti-Judaism embedded in our culture. It puts blinkers on our eyes, preventing us from seeing Jesus as he is actually mediated to us in and through Israel. We need to go to school with the people of Israel, as it were, in order to share with them the training they were given by God. It is a training that took place through many, many centuries until there emerged a matrix of understanding, thought, and worship. That matrix was prepared in Israel for the proper reception of God's ultimate self-revelation in Jesus Christ.

Recall the second commandment, by which Jews were forbidden to conceive of God by using images. In this vein Martin Buber used to speak of the Hellenic habit of "thinking with the eyes." He placed that in contrast to a Hebraic way of thinking, which was oriented more to the ear. It is notable that quantum physics has had to cope with what is inherently invisible. It has had to find appropriate ways of thinking in terms of imageless relations and structures. This is where the Jewish mind, as perhaps seen in someone like Einstein, has evidently had the advantage, through ingrained habits of thought that go back through the discipline of many, many generations in learning to think imagelessly of God.

I believe that biblical scholarship today can reap immense benefits from a rigorous scientific approach of this kind, pioneered by Jews. It is an approach that operates with imageless ways of thought. This applies above all to the quest for the historical Jesus, which for more than 150 years has been dominated by the observationalism and phenomenalism of Western culture. It breaks down again and again. The artificial images and constructs we use, in seeking to understand and interpret Jesus and the gospel, are quite alien to the essential nature of God's revelation of himself in and through Israel.

2. *Israel can help us understand the atonement.* With the atonement

## The Divine Vocation and Destiny of Israel in World History

we enter "the holy of holies" of the Christian faith. The atonement represents the awesome and unfathomable mystery of God incarnate racked in anguish while in Gethsemane and on the cross. There he is under the immeasurable weight of the world's sin and his own judgment upon it.

Throughout history the church's doctrine of atonement has constantly disintegrated. The atoning sacrifice offered by Christ has a range and a depth that defy formal articulation. Were it not for the evangelical record of that last night, when, through a reconstruction of the Passover rite, Jesus inaugurated the new covenant in his body and blood, the church would be completely bewildered. Quite evidently, doctrinal formulation of the atonement needs to be recast again and again. Otherwise its infinite truth in God is obstructed from disclosing its deeper aspects to us. But what is so distressing to us is that an adequately coherent outline of its essential pattern keeps eluding us. Is it not here also that Israel may help Christian understanding?

Let us recall the ancient rite enjoined by the Torah (Leviticus) for the annual renewal of the covenant on the Day of Atonement. On that day all Israel assembled before God. It was the only day of the year when the high priest might pass through the veil in the tabernacle and enter the holy of holies. There he made intercession and received the divine peace.

That rite has haunted the soul and memory of Israel ever since ancient times. Yom Kippur is still the most solemn and poignant observance in the Jewish liturgical year. Two goats were taken from the flock and presented before the Lord for a sin offering. One goat was killed and offered in holocaust on the altar as an atoning sacrifice for the people in expiation of their sins. Its blood was sprinkled before the mercy seat of the divine presence. At the same time, it was also an act in atoning consecration of the very holy place itself. The other goat was made a living sacrifice. The high priest laid his hands on it, confessing over it all the iniquities, transgressions, and sins of Israel. He then sent it away in utter rejection into the wilderness. It was released alive as a "scapegoat," bearing and bearing away the guilt of the people. Each half of that mysterious ritual was incomplete without the other. How much Israel had to learn from the fact that both sacrifices were required—the sacrifice by blood and the living sacrifice—in liturgical witness to an atonement for sin that God himself alone could provide.

It is significant that both aspects of that atoning rite are reflected in Isaiah's account of the "Suffering Servant" who bears a vicarious affliction (Isa. 53). On the one hand, we have the utter rejection of One despised and driven away as an unclean outcast on whom the iniquity of all has been laid. On the other hand, we have the sacrificial death, under judgment, of the Righteous

One whose soul was made an offering for sin. In bearing the sin of many, he made intercession for the transgressors. It is also significant that both of these aspects of atonement, not least as they were personalized through the Suffering Servant, are reflected at remarkable points in the Gospel presentation of the vicarious life and mission of Jesus, the Son of Man.

Jesus's life proceeded from his baptism in the river Jordan and his struggle with the evil one in the wilderness to his lonely death upon the cross. He was the Lamb of God who bore and bore away the sin of the world along with the curse of its guilt. At the same time, he was ridiculed and disowned by his brothers and sisters, becoming the outcast of humanity. Apart from the matrix of atoning significance fostered through Israel's liturgy of sacrifice, the death of Jesus would remain a bewildering enigma.

In light of the matrix of meaning established in Israel through Passover, Leviticus, and Isaiah, Jesus's death was seen as an atoning sacrifice. It was effected in his person as the incarnate Son. His blood was shed to bring about the removal of sin and so restoration to God. His atoning sacrifice was not only perfected once and for all at Calvary. It was also a living sacrifice, one that would avail eternally for all humankind. Through the very fact that he remains an outcast from Israel, repudiated by his own, the despised and rejected of men and women, Jesus, the anointed Servant of the Lord, continues on this path. He continues to bear the contempt and antagonism of the human heart to God. He vanquishes it in the atoning love of God as embodied in himself. It is in this way that Jesus Christ is the messianic Savior of Jews and gentiles alike. Through his death on the cross, he remains offensive to Jews and foolish in his weakness to gentiles.

However, when we consider the actual history of the world since New Testament times, we find the twofold meaning of the atoning sacrifice of Christ not only unfolding itself but also constantly splitting apart. It splits apart through the widening schism between the Christian *ecclesia* and the Jewish *ecclesia*. The Christian *ecclesia* went out into history from the resurrection side of the cross with the message of universal salvation and reconciliation. The Jewish *ecclesia* went out from the shadow side of the cross to be scattered among the nations, where Jews were despised and rejected. They were the butt of humanity's taunts, the scapegoat for all its ills, bearing mute and unwilling witness to humankind's antagonism toward God as embodied in its antagonism toward the Jews. It thereby attested the ineradicable reality of God for humankind.

I believe that the sufferings of the Jews can serve to remind Christians that the Jew of Calvary is still despised and rejected. Their suffering can teach

## The Divine Vocation and Destiny of Israel in World History

us a deeper understanding of the Suffering Servant with whom Jesus identified in his own vicarious passion. But the Jews also need Christians to help them understand something of the finality of what took place in the crucifixion of Jesus and of the hope he brings for the coming of the promised future.

Only as Israel penetrates into the mystery of its own most harrowing suffering through contemplating the crucifixion of Jesus—who is not only the greatest of the Hebrew prophets, as Buber called him, but the very Holy One, the Redeemer of Israel, become incarnate—and only as the Christian church acknowledges as never before not only its own guilt but also the depth and continuity of Israel's divine calling in the Christian era, together with the representative character of their rejection by the world but for the sake of the world, can Christians and Jews help each other to understand in a new way the atoning and living sacrifice that God himself has provided for all humanity in Jesus Christ. Then Jews and Christians may advance together toward the fulfillment of God's redemptive purpose not only for them both but also for the whole human race.

3. *Israel can help us understand the interaction of God with the world.* Throughout history we have witnessed something extraordinary: the very existence of the Jews and their miraculous persistence in existence against all the forces that have sought their complete eradication. I believe their persistence bears incontestable witness not only to the living God, with whom the Jews have been uniquely and intimately bound up, but also to the saving purpose of God for the human race. It is a purpose ordained by God and mediated in and through Israel. The Jews have always presented us with what John Macmurray used to call "the clue to history." From the perspective of the reconciliation of Jews and Christians in Jesus Christ, which we have already discussed, we cannot help but understand this in the light of the death and resurrection of Jesus Christ. The promised future entails the redemption and resurrection not only of the people of Israel, but also of all humankind.

Jesus Christ will come again to take up his kingdom and reign in divine peace. He will reign over all peoples and nations in a renewal of the whole creation. This renewal will far surpass anything that we can conceive in terms of prior human experience and history. No one knows exactly what God will do in the future. We can never anticipate God, as Jesus warned us. When God acts, he always takes us by surprise in breathtaking events. We may believe, however, that the living God of Israel and of Jesus Christ will act, and act decisively, in human history. He will fulfill his universal purpose of love and peace.

# 8

## Light from Saint Paul on Christian-Jewish Relations

C. E. B. Cranfield

In this short essay I shall try to draw out what seem to me the main implications for Christian-Jewish relations today of Paul's teaching as I understand it. For the sake of clarity I shall number my sections

1. We may start from Paul's strikingly emphatic and solemn declaration of his grief in Romans 9:1–5 ("I speak the truth in Christ, I do not lie—my conscience bears me witness in the Holy Spirit—*when I declare* that I have great grief and continual anguish in my heart. For I would pray that I might be accursed *and cut off* from Christ on behalf of my brethren, my kinsfolk according to the flesh").[1] It attests his clear recognition that the central point at issue between Christians (whether Jewish or gentile) and non-Christian Jews is of transcendent importance. The fact that the great majority of his fellow Jews reject he who is, Paul is convinced, the true Messiah of Israel, is proper cause for deep anguish. The first point with regard to Christian-Jewish relations to be learned from Paul is, we submit, that we should recognize with full frankness the reality of the chasm that separates us and not indulge in any attempt to paper it over.

2. But the same passage shows something else: Paul's equally clear recognition that the unbelieving Jews are still his "brethren," still "Israelites" (note the present tense, *eisin*, in v. 4), still fellow members of the people of God's choice. If we would be true to Paul's teaching, we must surely repudiate altogether the notion, which is very widespread among Christians and has often been expressed by theologians (including—God

---

1. I hope I may be forgiven both for using in the quotations from Romans my own translation from *A Critical and Exegetical Commentary on the Epistle to the Romans* (Edinburgh, vol. 1, ³1980, and vol. 2, ²1981)—for giving me permission to do this I have to thank T. & T. Clark, Ltd.—and also for referring the reader to that commentary for the detailed exegesis, which is the basis of much of what I shall say here.

forgive him—the present writer), that the Jewish people, having rejected Jesus Christ, has been dispossessed of its election and simply replaced by God by a new Israel, namely, the Christian church. The whole of Romans 11 bears this out, set as it is under the sign of verse 2a, "God has not cast off his people whom he foreknew."[2] Addressing the gentiles among the Roman Christians, Paul says concerning the at-present unbelieving Jews in verses 28–29, "As regards *the progress of* the gospel they are enemies for your sake, but as regards the election they are beloved for the sake of the fathers, for the gifts and the call of God are irrevocable." We may compare Romans 3:3–4 ("What then? If some have failed to respond with faith, shall their lack of faith render God's faithfulness ineffective? God forbid. We confess rather that God is true, and all men liars").

Paul does indeed recognize that "not all who are of Israel are Israel" in the sense of standing in a positive relationship to the accomplishment of God's purpose, but that does not mean that only part of Israel is the elect people of God. All Jews, "all who are of Israel" (Rom. 9:6), are members of God's elect people, members of that community that is Jesus Christ's environment, all without exception witnesses to God's grace and faithfulness, but not all of them are Israel in the narrower sense of being the company of relatively understanding, willing, grateful witnesses to that grace and faithfulness. Barth was surely right to see in Romans 9–11 the recognition that the people of God exists in two forms in history: on the one hand, as the believing element of the people in Old Testament times, the Israel within Israel, and (continuous with it) the church consisting of both believing Jews and believing Gentiles, and, on the other hand, that bulk of Israel that is not the inner Israel and (continuous with it) the still-unbelieving Jews.[3] While it is only in its existence in one of these forms that the people of God bears a testimony to Jesus Christ that is positive, conscious, voluntary, and joyful, even in its existence in the other it cannot help bearing witness to him, and its witness, though negative, unconscious, involuntary, and joyless, is in its own peculiar way impressively eloquent.

3. In Romans 10:1 Paul declares that the desire of his heart and his prayer to God for his unbelieving fellow Jews are "that they may be saved,"

---

2. The relative clause should not be taken as limiting the reference of "his people" to those members who are objects of God's secret election (*pace* Calvin), for in verse 1, in the light of 10:21, "his people" must surely denote the people of Israel as a whole, and it is unnatural to give it a different sense in verse 2.

3. Reference may be made to the section on God's election of grace in *Church Dogmatics* II/2 (Edinburgh: T. & T. Clark, 1957), pp. 1–506, as a whole.

and his declaration indicates a continuing duty of the Christian church, a duty that includes seriously and wholeheartedly willing, earnestly and faithfully praying for, and therefore also persistently but at the same time humbly, graciously, and in a truly brotherly fashion working for[4] the salvation of the Jews. It would seem to be an indication of the feebleness of faith and absence of serious engagement with Holy Scripture that appear to be characteristic of present-day British church life that one so seldom hears in public worship any specific prayer for the salvation of non-Christian Jews.

4. In the following verse, the last four words of which give expression to very grave criticism, Paul pays to his still-unbelieving kinsmen a most notable tribute: "I bear them witness that they have zeal for God." Both "zeal" and "for God" are significant. He acknowledges that their zeal has the right object: it is zeal for the one true God. And he acknowledges that it is indeed zeal. It is a double acknowledgment that the church ought always to remember. It should both encourage a brotherly and open attitude toward the Jews on the church's part and also contribute to a salutary disturbance of Christian self-complacency (for, of how much of the churches' own membership could it be stated with equal confidence that the object of its worship is really the living God and not one or another of the various idols of an acquisitive, spendthrift, corrupt society, and, even where the churches' members are concerned with the true God, how much of their concern could be described with any accuracy by so strong a term as "zeal"?).

5. We take a look next at the last words of Romans 10:2. The meaning of the words "yet not according to knowledge" is that, in spite of the earnestness of the still-unbelieving Jews' zeal and the fact that their zeal is really zeal for the true God, it contains a grievous flaw — it is "not according to knowledge." That does not mean that the persons concerned do not know God; they certainly do know him (cf. v. 19). But they will not know him as he really wants to be known, as he really is. There is an incomprehension at the heart of their knowledge, and a stubborn disobedience in the center of their dedicated and meticulous obedience (cf. Mark 4:12). Paul goes on in verse 3 to explain that their ignorance consists in their failure to acknowledge God's righteousness, that is, the status of righteousness before him that he himself offers as a gift, and — what is the other side of this failure — their obstinate determination to establish their own righteousness, that

---

4. Cf., e.g., Rom. 11:13-14, also Acts 13:14ff.; 14:1; 17:1-3, 10, 17; 18:4-5; 19:8; 21:39-40; 22:1ff.; 28:17ff.

is, their claim to be counted righteous before God by virtue of their own deserts. This is indeed a failure to know God as he really is—in his mercy and faithfulness and in the seriousness of his claims. The disobedience that results from this ignorance is their refusal to "submit to the righteousness of God," that is, to humble themselves to accept it as an undeserved gift of God's mercy.

6. The meaning of the last four words of Romans 10:2 and the following verse can be properly seen only in the light of their context. From 9:30–32a we learn that Israel, that is, the great majority of the people of Israel, failed to attain to the law of righteousness "because *they pursued it* not on the basis of faith but as on the basis of works." They misunderstood that law God had given them in his graciousness. Instead of recognizing the seriousness of its claims upon them and so allowing themselves to be led to put their trust in God's forgiving mercy and to respond to it by giving themselves to him in thankfulness and humility (that is, of pursuing it "on the basis of faith"), they had cherished the illusion that they could so adequately fulfill its commandments as to put God in their debt (that is, they had pursued it "as on the basis of works"). From verses 32b and 33 we learn the christological dimension of Israel's ignorance and disobedience. "They stumbled against the stone of stumbling, even as it is written, 'Behold, I lay in Zion a stone of stumbling and a rock of offense, and he who believes on him shall not be put to shame.'" Verses 30–33 as a whole indicate the intimate and essentially positive relation between the law and Christ, which is clinched by the words "For Christ is the end of the law" in 10:4, in which (in spite of many recent confident assertions to the contrary) "end" (Greek *telos*) must surely have the sense of "goal," "substance," "innermost meaning." Israel has failed to recognize its Messiah because it has failed truly to come to grips with its own law, and it can never understand its law aright until it recognizes and accepts him who is the very substance and inmost meaning of the law. So the Messiah, who has been given for Israel's and the world's salvation, can only be, so long as Israel's stubborn perverseness persists, the occasion of Israel's undoing.

7. The guilt of Israel is rendered abundantly clear by Romans 9:30–10:13; it is guilty because it has failed to heed properly its own law for which in its uncomprehending way it has been so zealous. But the fact that it has been given the law, the goal and inmost substance of which is Jesus Christ, does not by itself constitute such a full opportunity to invoke the name of the Lord in the sense of Romans 10:12 and 13 as would render Israel altogether and unquestionably without excuse. For that fullness of

opportunity to have been given, it was necessary that the message that the divine promises have now been fulfilled should have been proclaimed by messengers duly commissioned by God himself. So, before going on in Romans 11 to give the assurance that, all human ignorance and disobedience notwithstanding, God has not cast off his chosen people, Paul is concerned to drive home in 10:14–21 with final, incontrovertible decisiveness the fact that still-unbelieving Israel is altogether without excuse by showing that such a proclamation has indeed taken place. Paul will have it clear beyond any shadow of doubt that the salvation of Jews no less than that of gentiles is a matter of sheer mercy, without the least handhold for human merit.

8. Jesus Christ, who is the occasion of the deep and grievous division between Jews and Christians that may not be concealed, is also the One who unites them. He, who is the acknowledged Savior and Lord of all who believe in him, is himself a Jew, the *Jew* par excellence. The supreme privilege and dignity of the Jews is the fact that he is, so far as his human nature is concerned, a member of their race (cf. Rom. 9:5), and this, their surpassing dignity, can never be taken away from them. To despise them is to despise and dishonor him, in whom alone there is salvation for men. The Jewishness of Jesus of Nazareth is the final and irrevocable condemnation of every form of anti-Semitism, whether it be blatant and brutal or subtle and even more or less unconscious, and the unbroken bond between believing Christian and unbelieving Jew.

9. Closely related to this bond between Christian and Jew that Jesus Christ himself is in his own person is the bond consisting of the Old Testament that bears witness to him. If the church heeds Saint Paul, it will recognize that truly to believe in Jesus is to believe in him according to the fullness of the Old Testament's attestation of him, which certainly includes believing in him as the Messiah of Israel. It will recognize too, surely, that statements representing Christ and the Old Testament law as opposed to each other (common though they have been in recent decades among New Testament scholars) are mistaken and should be repudiated, and that the law should be seen as an essential part of the Old Testament's testimony to Christ, by which church and synagogue are bound together. It will recognize that, though at present a veil does indeed lie on the Jews' hearts, when they hear or read the law, it is nevertheless true that in all their engagement with the law, they are, objectively though unconsciously, having to do with Jesus Christ himself, who is its substance and meaning and who is speaking to them through it, and it will look forward with ea-

gerness to the time when their hearts will turn to him and the veil will be taken away (cf. 2 Cor. 3:14–16).[5]

10. If Christians and Jews are united by their special relatedness to Christ and by their common commitment to, and engagement with, the Old Testament, they are also further united by the special clarity with which by reason of these things their sinfulness is made manifest and by the specially serious character their sinfulness possesses. According to Romans 5:12–21, sin was already present and active in the world before the giving of the law, but it was as yet nowhere absolutely clearly visible and sharply defined. If sin was ever to be decisively defeated and sinners forgiven in a way that is worthy of the altogether good, merciful, and faithful God, sin had first to be made to increase somewhere in the sense of being rendered clearly manifest. So the law was given "in order that in one people (for their own sake and also for the sake of all others) sin might be known as sin. But when the advent of the law makes sin increase in the sense of becoming manifest as sin, it also makes it increase in the sense of being made more sinful, since the law by showing men that what they are doing is contrary to God's will gives to their continuing to do it the character of conscious and wilful disobedience."[6]

It is in Israel and in the church, where God's grace and God's commandments are most fully known, that human sin is most exceedingly sinful. Nowhere else can it be so hateful. The same evil that, when perpetrated outside Israel and the church, is monstrous is, when perpetrated within Israel or the church, immeasurably more monstrous. "You only have I known of all the families of the earth; therefore I will *visit* upon you all your iniquities"—such is the warning of Amos 3:2, and similar is the significance of Luke 12:48: "And to whomsoever much is given, of him shall much be required."

It is in this context that we should, I think, look at 1 Thessalonians 2:15–16, where Paul says the unbelieving Jews (according to the English Revised Version) "both killed the Lord Jesus and the prophets, and drove out us, and please not God, and are contrary to all men; forbidding us to speak to the Gentiles that they may be saved; to fill up their sins alway: but the wrath is come upon them to the uttermost." The most difficult part of this is at the end. It is frequently understood as a declaration that there is

---

5. With regard to the substance of this paragraph, reference may be made to Cranfield, *Epistle to the Romans*, especially pp. 845–70.

6. Cranfield, *Epistle to the Romans*, p. 293.

now no hope for the unbelieving Jews. So in the New English Bible the original is rendered "and now retribution has overtaken them for good and all." But, if this "for good and all" really were an accurate representation of the sense of the Greek, it would be necessary to assume a very drastic change in Paul's thought with regard to the situation of the Jewish people between the writing of 1 Thessalonians 2 and the writing of Romans 11, and, while such a change may be conceivable, it seems to us more likely, in view of what Paul says elsewhere, that the meaning of this sentence is that God's wrath has already come upon the Jews to the uttermost—in the event of the cross. In the first words of verse 15 Paul is not forgetting the part played by the Romans, but is underlining the special guilt of God's chosen people. In the event of the cross, the disobedience of God's people reached its hideous climax, and God revealed it in its true character with final and absolute clarity. And in that special guilt of the Jews, the Christian church should see itself as having a share. For is it not itself, in spite of all its overwhelming privileges, continually putting Christ to shame by its unfaithfulness and willful disobedience? While the judgment of the cross is, of course, God's judgment on all men without exception, it is the sinfulness of Christians and Jews that is most starkly revealed by it.[7]

11. Paradoxically, in view of what has been said above, and yet perhaps after all not altogether surprisingly, church and synagogue are united also in proneness to self-righteousness and complacency. In Romans 2 Paul apostrophizes the typical Jew who is sure of his own moral superiority over the gentiles. Much of what he says could be applied to very many Christians. But this proneness to self-complacency common to Jews and Christians—though in a good many it has been, and is, to a considerable degree, counteracted by serious engagement with Holy Scripture—is so obvious a matter, particularly to observers from outside, that it need not be dwelt on here.

12. But the fact that Jesus Christ and the Old Testament, though it is over them that they are so deeply and grievously divided, nevertheless bind Christians and Jews together means that they are also bound together in hope. The importance of the place hope has in the life of believers, according to Paul, is clear enough from such passages as Romans 5:4–5; 8:17–39; 12:12; 15:4, 13. Romans 11 shows that he saw the existence of the

---

7. I am grateful to the editor of *Irish Biblical Studies* for allowing me to use in this paragraph some phraseology from my "A Study of 1 Thessalonians 2," *Irish Biblical Studies* 1 (1979): 215ff.

still-unbelieving Jews also as set by the mercy of God under the sign of hope. To his own question, "Has God cast off his people?," he gives the firm reply, "God has not cast off his people whom he foreknew" (Rom. 11:1–2); and he assures the Roman gentile Christians that God can graft in again the branches of the cultivated olive tree that have been broken off (vv. 23 and 24). But his hope for his non-Christian fellow countrymen does not ignore the need for faith in Christ (v. 23 includes the words "if they do not remain in their unbelief"). The salvation of "all Israel" mentioned in the course of verses 25–27 would seem to be envisaged as an eschatological event, the coming of the Deliverer out of Zion probably being understood by Paul with reference to the parousia of Christ. The relentless concentration of the composite Old Testament quotation in verses 26–27 on God's forgiveness and on Israel's need of it dashes all Israel's illusory hopes of establishing a claim on God on the basis of its merit. There is hope for Jews as for Christians because for both alike the last word is with God's mercy on sinners.

13. Finally, we must say something about the services that Jews and Christians do, as a matter of fact, whether consciously or unconsciously, render each other, and also about those further services that they may or may not, but that we hope they will, render each other.

To each of the two communities the very existence of the other continuing through the centuries is a valuable challenge to examine again and again itself, its own foundations and present life. That we ought to show each other not (as we have too often done) hatred, contempt, and cruelty but brotherly affection, respect, and kindness should surely be absolutely clear without having to be said. It surely also should be generally agreed that the temptation of blurring differences for the sake of easier and more comfortable relationships ought to be firmly resisted and that we ought to express to each other what we believe as clearly as possible with the utmost frankness and sincerity.

We shall suggest first a service additional to the services already mentioned (that rendered by our very existence and that indicated in number 3 above), which the church and individual Christians can and surely ought to render the Jews. We owe it to them always faithfully to try to recall them to the Law, the Prophets, and the Writings, whenever they seem to us to have forgotten them or to be in serious danger of forgetting them. We certainly have to do this very humbly indeed in view of all that we gentile Christians have on our consciences in relation to them. We dare not forget the monstrous barbarities perpetrated by the Nazis and by many collaborators belonging to other nations; the shameful silence of those who did not wish to know what was being done in their midst; the disgraceful failure of those in power in Western democracies to promptly do what they could to save many more Jews from the Holocaust; the long, long record of Christian persecution of Jews that preceded the hideous horror of the Hitler days; and the continuing shame of the existence of anti-Semitism today, whether in cruder or in more subtle forms. But we would only be increasing that burden if we allowed it to inhibit us now and in the future from speaking frankly. And we need to be very specially on our guard against the insidious temptation (often below the level of conscious decision) to make amends for our own sins at others' expense by a sentimental and uncritical commitment to the Israeli state's aspirations, which takes little or no account of the rights of the Palestinians. To succumb to this temptation would assuredly be to add yet more to the great pile of wrongs already inflicted on the Jews by Christians.

We certainly do owe them the clear challenge to examine their national, and particularly their political national, aspirations, critically in the light of the Law and the Prophets and the Writings. Are the scriptural foundations of those aspirations as firm and sure as is often assumed? Even the question whether they are wholly illusory ought to be honestly faced. Are there perhaps serious spiritual dangers in Zionism? Is it possible that a good many Jews in their present preoccupation with political national goals and in their determination to attain them—sometimes, it seems, at any cost—are in danger of losing their own souls? If Jews commit injustice against people whose families God has allowed, in *some* cases for very many centuries, to dwell in the land once given to Israel and if—O that the suspicions might be proved ungrounded!—they quite often descend to gross inhumanity, are they not trampling upon the Law and the Prophets?

With regard to the service the Jews constantly render to Christians, we may add that their very survival until now, in spite of all they have suffered, is a particularly cogent evidence of the reality and faithfulness of God, a precious testimony presented to us for which we should be thankful.

But there is a further service they can do for us, and which we should desire to receive from them, and indeed urgently implore them to render us. They should recall us to a proper engagement with the Old Testament— in fact, they should do us the same service we suggested that we owe to them. Thereby they would be conferring upon us immeasurable benefits, for the church today suffers grievous damage from the various forms of Marcionism that afflict it, and where the church fails to draw nourishment and instruction from the Old Testament, it is, not surprisingly, stunted and enfeebled. Serious engagement with the Old Testament is necessary if the church is to sustain anything approaching an adequate Christology, a proper Trinitarian doctrine, an adequate soteriology, and a satisfactory doctrine of creation, to mention just four examples. But our imploring the Jews to try to recall us to the Old Testament should surely include the earnest entreaty that they should never cease from pointing out to us with the utmost forthrightness and rigor our daily-repeated failures to judge ourselves by the standards of goodness that we and they together possess in the Law, the Prophets, and the Writings—our persistent hypocrisy, our double standards, our despicable self-righteousness and complacency, our deliberate flouting of God's commandments, our inhumanity, our godlessness. They are in a specially good position to be perceptive, penetrating critics of the church and of individual Christians. If they do criticize us in the light of those Scriptures that we hold in common and bring their criticism home to us relentlessly and fearlessly, they will put us forever in their debt.

# 9

## From Anti-Semitism to Theological Dialogue

HANS KÜNG

### The Afflictions of the Past

The sufferings of the Jewish people begin with Jesus himself.[1] Jesus was a man—that has always been more or less stressed by Christians, who were less prepared to admit, however, that Jesus was a *Jewish* man—a genuine Jew. As such he was far too often alien to Christians *and* to Jews.

### *Jesus the Jew*

Jesus was a Jew, a member of that small, poor, politically impotent people on the fringe of the Roman Empire. He was active among Jews and for Jews. His mother Mary, his father Joseph, his family, and his disciples were Jews. His name was Jewish (in Hebrew, Jeshua—a late form of Iehoshua, "Yahweh is help"). His Bible, his divine service, and his prayers were Jewish. In the existing situation it was impossible for him to conceive of proclamation among the gentiles. His message was for the Jewish people, but for the entire Jewish people, without any exception.

That is the basic situation: without Judaism there would be no Christianity. The Bible of the early Christians was the Old Testament. The New Testament writings became the Bible by attachment to the Old Testament. The gospel of Jesus Christ wholly (and quite consciously) presupposes the Torah and the Prophets. In both Testaments the same God of grace and justice is speaking, even according to the Christian conception of things.

---

1. These observations form part of a complex of problems presented in my introduction to Christianity.

This special relationship is the reason why I do not consciously treat Judaism in the early chapters of my forthcoming book on Christianity—those deal with the non-Christian religions. Christianity does not enjoy this unique relationship with Buddhism, Hinduism, and Confucianism, not even with Islam (influenced by Christianity), but only with Judaism. It is a relationship of the origins, and several common structures and values result from it. In that case we have to ask why, despite its universal monotheism, not Judaism but the new movement emanating from Jesus—Christianity—became a universal religion of mankind.

Enmity between very close relatives can be very bitter. One of the most tragic events in the history of the last two thousand years has been the enmity that existed between Jews and Christians almost from the start. It was reciprocal, as so often happens between an old and a new religious movement. Of course, the young Christian community at first seemed no more than a special religious orientation within Judaism, one that acknowledged and practiced a special religious constitution but otherwise upheld the connection with Jewish national society. But the process of detachment from the Jewish national community was based inwardly on an acknowledgment of Jesus. It was very soon dissolved by the formation of a gentile Christianity without the law. Before long the gentile Christians were in the overwhelming majority and their theology lost its real attachment to Judaism. After a few centuries the process concluded with the destruction of Jerusalem and the end of the temple cult. Hence, in the course of a dramatic historical process, the church of Jews became a church of Jews and gentiles, and finally a church of gentiles.

Those Jews who did not wish to acknowledge Jesus were inimical to the young church. They ejected the Christians from the national community and persecuted them, as the story of the Pharisee Saul shows (who nevertheless as the apostle Paul always held to the specially chosen status of the people of Israel). It was probably by the second century that the cursing of the "heretics and Nazarites" was included in the main daily rabbinical prayer ("Shmone 'Esra'"). In short, the separation took place quite early on. The intellectual dispute was increasingly reduced to a continual struggle to find texts for or against the fulfillment in Jesus of the biblical prophecies.

HANS KÜNG

*A History of Blood and Tears*

What happened after that was largely a history of blood and tears. The Christians who later won control of state power soon forgot the Jewish and gentile persecutions they had suffered. Initially Christian enmity toward the Jews was not racially but religiously conditioned. More exactly, one should speak of anti-Judaism instead of anti-Semitism. Even the Arabs are Semites. In the Constantinian imperial church the pre-Christian and gentile anti-Judaism was adopted with "Christian" emphases. And though subsequently there were instances of fruitful collaboration between Christians and Jews, the position of the Jews became much more sensitive, especially after the high Middle Ages. There were massacres of Jews in western Europe during the first two Crusades and pogroms in Palestine. Then came the annihilation of three hundred Jewish communities in the German Empire in 1348–1349 and the expulsion of Jews from England (1290), France (1394), Spain (1492), and Portugal (1497). And later there were the vile anti-Jewish speeches of the old Luther, persecutions of Jews after the Reformation, and pogroms in eastern Europe. During this period the church certainly made more martyrs than it produced in its own ranks. All that seems incomprehensible for a present-day Christian.

Not the Reformation, but humanism (Reuchlin, Scaliger), Pietism (Zinzendorf), and especially the tolerance of the Enlightenment (the Declaration of the Rights of Man of the French Revolution) prepared the way for a change and in part produced it. The full assimilation of the European Jews in the period of emancipation only succeeded in part, however, and most fully in America. It would be presumptuous to record yet again the century-long, despicable history of the suffering and death of the Jewish people that culminated in the Nazi mass hysteria and murders that disposed of a third of all Jewry. The regret in the Vatican II declaration—which, like a corresponding declaration of the World Council of Churches, is more a beginning than an end—was extremely weak and vague in view of this vile history. It has been all but blocked by the Roman curia, which nevertheless got very heated about Hochhuth's highly problematic *The Representative*—as before, out of political opportunism and not fully suppressed anti-Jewish feelings, the Vatican refuses diplomatic recognition to the state of Israel.

In view of this situation, which is by no means resolved, and a recalcitrant anti-Judaism in Rome and Moscow, but unfortunately also in New York and elsewhere, I must state quite clearly that Nazi anti-Judaism was the work of godless anti-Christian criminals; but without the almost two-thousand-year-long prehistory of "Christian" anti-Judaism that also prevented Christians in Germany from a convinced and energetic resistance on a broad front, it would not have been possible!

Even though some Christians were also persecuted and yet others—especially in the Netherlands, France, and Denmark—effectively helped the Jews, if we are to grasp the question of guilt proficiently, the following must be taken into account. None of the anti-Jewish measures of the Nazis—distinctive clothing, exclusion from professions, the Nuremberg "laws" forbidding mixed marriages, expulsions, the concentration camps, massacres, gruesome funeral pyres—was new. All that already existed in the so-called Christian Middle Ages (the fourth great Lateran Council was in 1215) and in the period of the "Christian" Reformation. What was new was the racial grounding of these measures—prepared by the French Count Arthur Gobineau and the Anglo-German Houston Stewart Chamberlain, and then carried through in Nazi Germany with cruelly exact organization, technical perfection, and a terrible industrialization of death. After Auschwitz there is nothing to extenuate: Christianity cannot evade a full avowal of its guilt.

## Possibilities for the Future

The latest, most frightful catastrophe of the Jewish people and the unexpected, for Christians, revival of the state of Israel—the most important event in Jewish history since the destruction of Jerusalem and the temple—shattered "Christian" anti-Jewish theology: that pseudotheology that falsely interpreted the Old Testament salvation history of the Jewish people as a New Testament history of divine condemnation, and overlooked the continuing choice of the Jewish people accepted by the New Testament, and referred to itself exclusively as the "New Israel." With the Second Vatican Council a consciousness of this won a place in the Catholic Church as well. The idea of a collective guilt for the death of Jesus on the part of the Jewish people then or today was expressly rejected by the council. The ancient widespread prejudices—Jews are "money-grubbers," "well-poisoners," "Christ-murderers," "God-killers," "cursed and condemned to wander"—no one dares any longer to put forward seriously. The psychological motives operative in anti-Judaism—group enmity, fear of foreign bodies, the scapegoat mentality, a counterideal, disorientation of personality structure, mass hysteria—are now increasingly acknowledged. The implicit or explicit excuses, that "The Jews make mistakes as well"; "You have to understand everything in its historical context"; "It wasn't the church itself"; "You have to choose the lesser evil"—these are now obsolete. People recognize that the Jews form a community of fate that is in many respects mysterious and astonishingly persistent: a race and not a race, a linguistic community and yet not a linguistic community, a state and not a state, a people and not a people, a community of destiny whose religious secret for the believing Jew as for the believing Christian is a special vocation of this "people of God" among the peoples of the earth. The fact that in this perspective the return of the Jews to their "promised land"—with cruel sacrifices for the Arab Palestinians who have been there for centuries—also has a religious significance for many Jews is something that Christians should at least be aware of.

Whatever Christians (also those of Arab origins—who need our understanding) may think of the state of Israel, it is true that a church that, as often in the past, preaches love and yet sows hatred, proclaims life and yet spreads death cannot invoke Jesus of Nazareth as its founder.

Jesus was a Jew, and all anti-Semitism is treachery toward Jesus himself. The church too often stood between Jesus and Israel. It prevented Israel from acknowledging Jesus. It is time for Christians not only to preach "conversion" to the Jews, but to "convert" themselves to an encounter that has hardly taken place, not only to a humanitarian but also to a theological dialogue with the Jews, which could serve not "mission" and capitulation but understanding, mutual help, cooperation, and—indirectly perhaps—even a growing understanding between Jews, Christians, *and* Muslims, who of course (who could forget it?) by their own origins are as closely joined to the Jews as they are to the Christians. All this should take place through a common faith in God the Creator and the resurrection of the dead in acknowledgment of Abraham and Jesus, who both have an important place in the Qur'an. The prerequisites for a genuine dialogue between Christians and Jews, to whom Christianity, Islam, and mankind as a whole owe the incomparable gift of a firm belief in one God, are at present (despite all the foregoing) as good as nonexistent. An unconditional recognition of the religious autonomy of our admittedly rigorous and exacting Jewish partners is a presupposition of that.

1. In Christianity, and especially in German and English or American exegesis, long before the Hitler period there was a new openness to the Old Testament's autonomy and accordance with the New Testament. The

significance of the rabbis for an understanding of the New Testament was also recognized. And in comparison with the Greek-Hellenistic world, people had begun to emphasize the strong aspects of Hebrew thought—the greater degree of historical dynamics; a holistic orientation; a faithful and positive attitude to world, body, and life; hunger and thirst for justice; an orientation to the coming kingdom of God. All that contributed to the desuetude of the Neoplatonic, neo-Aristotelian, and neo-Scholastic encrustation of Christianity. For the official Catholic Church, the declaration on the Jews of the Second Vatican Council was "the discovery or rediscovery of Judaism and the Jews in their own right as in their significance for the Church" (J. Oesterreicher).

2. The spiritual situation of Judaism has changed considerably, especially since the founding of the state of Israel. There has been a decreasing influence of casuistic and legalistic piety, especially among the younger generation, and an increasing importance of the Old Testament in contradistinction to the earlier universal emphasis on the Talmud. Great Jewish minds of our century—women like Simone Weil and Edith Stein, men like Hermann Cohen, Martin Buber, Franz Rosenzweig, Leo Baeck, Max Brod, Hans-Joachim Schoeps, and more indirectly Sigmund Freud, Albert Einstein, Franz Kafka, and Ernst Bloch—brought what was uniquely Jewish nearer to Christians. Hence the way was open for the present common scientific Jewish-Christian research into the Old Testament, the rabbis, and the beginnings of work on the New Testament (as a witness to the Jewish history of faith). It has also meant a more vital and more fundamental design of divine service on both sides that reveals a visible relationship reaching far beyond literary criticism and philology. There is no question: from the basis of his Judaism a Jew can discover aspects of the New Testament that as often as not escape the Christian. In spite of numerous restrictions and difficulties, the consciousness of a common and not only humanitarian but also theological Jewish-Christian basis is in the making. From the Jewish side as well there is a demand for "a Jewish theology of Christianity and a Christian theology of Judaism" (J. Petuchowski). In any case, theological dialogue between Christians and Jews is shown to be much more difficult than that between separated Christians, which at least has a common basis in the Bible. The conflict between Christians and Jews, on the other hand, goes right through the Bible and splits it into two Testaments, of which one group prefers the first and the other the second. And is it ever possible to evade the particular point of controversy? Precisely he who appears to unite Jews and Christians separates them most fundamentally: Jesus the

Jew from Nazareth. Can Jews and Christians ever reach an understanding about him? What is in question seems to be much more than "two modes of belief" (M. Buber). That the Jews should surrender their unbelief in regard to Jesus seems just as unlikely as that the Christians should abandon their belief in him. For if they did so, the Jews would no longer be Jews, or the Christians Christians.

## Dialogue about Jesus

The dispute seems unsolvable. Has Jewish-Christian dialogue about Jesus of Nazareth any meaning at all? But one might just as well ask: Wouldn't both sides gain something if in answer to a Christian readiness to reach understanding, on the Jewish side mistrust, skepticism, and malice in regard to the figure of Jesus could be reduced, and instead it was possible to extend a historically objective judgment, genuine understanding, and perhaps even a valuation of the person of Jesus? Recent progress cannot be ignored. A long list of authors and works on Jesus of Nazareth has been published in the last few years in the state of Israel. Of course, many Jews would accept at least the "Jesus of culture" while rejecting the "Jesus of religion." The cultural significance of Jesus is also acknowledged. Surely, too, it is very difficult for a modern Jew fully to take part in Western culture without continually coming into contact with Jesus, even though only in the great works of Bach, Handel, Mozart, Beethoven, Bruckner, and Western art in general.

But there is still the question of the religious significance of Jesus. Christians have acknowledged the religious significance of Judaism. Surely, then, Jews have also to face the problem of the religious meaning of Jesus, the last of the Jewish prophets. Even in the nineteenth century there was a respectable Jewish tradition that tried to take Jesus seriously as a genuine Jew, and even as a major witness to faith. At the turn of the century, Max Nordau, the faithful colleague of the founder of the Zionist movement, Theodor Herzl, wrote: "Jesus is the soul of our soul, just as he is the flesh of our flesh. Who then would wish to exclude him from the Jewish people?" In the first half of the twentieth century came the first thorough studies of the figure of Jesus from the Jewish side, the various publications of Claude G. Montefiore, and the best-known Jewish book on Jesus by Joseph Klausner, which on account of its use of material from the Talmud and from midrash may be thought of as the beginning of modern Hebrew research into the life of Jesus. The important Jewish thinker Martin Buber stresses the word of Jesus as that of the "great brother" who deserves "a major place in the history of faith of Israel," which can be "reduced to no conventional category." The Jewish researcher into Jesus's life, David Flusser, points out that Jesus is a Jew addressing the Jews. A Jew can learn from him how he should pray, fast, and love his neighbor, what is the meaning of the Sabbath, the kingdom of God, and the Law. It was along this line that Schalom Ben-Chorin wrote in his recent book *Our Brother Jesus: The Nazarene from a Jewish Viewpoint*: "Jesus is certainly a central character of Jewish history and faith-history, but he is also a piece of our present history and our future, and no different from the prophets of the Hebrew Bible—whom we should not look on in the light of the past alone."

That reveals the beginnings of a Jewish recognition of the Jewish Jesus, as Ben-Chorin puts it: "I note his brotherly hand, which grasps mine, and follow him." But he goes on: "It is *not* the hand of the Messiah—that wounded hand, in whose lines the most profound suffering is engraved.... The belief of Jesus unites us, but belief in Jesus separates us." But surely it is that wounded hand that we need to interpret, to explain more profoundly.

It is not impossible that in the future more Jews will manage to recognize Jesus as a great Jew and witness to faith—as indeed a great prophet or teacher of Israel. The Gospels have a special fascination for some Jews. They show a Jew the possibilities lying within the Jewish faith itself. And surely Jesus is to be understood precisely as an individual symbol of Jewish history. The Jewish painter Marc Chagall always portrayed the suffering of his people in the image of the Crucified. Perhaps we ought to put it like this: surely the history of this people and its God, this people of tears and life, of lamentation and trust, culminates in the one figure of Jesus and his history as a spectacular sign of the crucified and resurrected Israel.

And still one provocative question will remain: Who is Jesus? More than a prophet? More than the Law? The Messiah? A Messiah crucified in the name of the Law? Must discussion end quite unconditionally at this point? It is probably here that a Jew could help a Christian to conduct dialogue about Jesus not yet again "from above," but "from below." That would mean that we today also see Jesus from the perspective of the Jewish contemporaries of Jesus. Even Jesus's disciples had at first to start from the Jewish man Jesus of Nazareth and not from an already proclaimed Messiah or Son of God. Only thus could they pose the question of the relation of Jesus to God. And that relation consisted for them—at a later date as well— not in a mere identification with God, as though Jesus were God the Father.

Perhaps Jews could help Christians to understand more proficiently the central New Testament pronouncements about Jesus and particularly his special titles, which enjoy an eminently Hebraic background.

As always, if we start from the Jewish man Jesus of Nazareth, we find we can go quite a long way with an unprejudiced Jew. Finally the ultimate decision for or against Jesus looks rather different than we might expect from the viewpoint of the long contestation between Christians and Jews. In this regard, all we should do initially is to strive for openness so that the unavoidable—Christian or Jewish—preunderstanding does not become prejudice. It is not neutrality that is wanted but objectivity in the service of truth. In a time of basic reorientation of the relationship between Christians and Jews, we have to stay open to all future possibilities.

—Translated by JOHN MAXWELL

# 10

## Toward Ending Enmity

ELLEN T. CHARRY

Perhaps the longest-running theological controversy in history is that between Judaism and Christianity. Each claims that it and only it worships the creator of heaven and earth truly. Adherents of each claim to be the exclusive people of God. While individuals within each community might disagree with that exclusivity, and Christians and Jews are friends, colleagues, spouses, and so on, these exclusive claims drove history to disastrous results for Jews once Christianity was legalized.

While the historical record alone warrants serious Christian reexamination of its scriptures and its doctrinal positions that impact Jews and Judaism, to attend to Christianity's moral integrity this paper will argue that there are theological reasons for each tradition to rethink its theological assessment of the other for the sake of its own theological well-being. On the Christian side, there are residual traces of both Marcionism and Manichaeism that a fully positive embrace of Judaism could quiet. On the Jewish side is the problem of theological neglect of "the other" that a positive embrace of Christianity would address.

Marcionism is what Kendall Soulen has helpfully called "Israel forgetfulness" or "structural supersessionism" (Soulen 1997). It is the idea that God's history with Israel is irrelevant to the Christian narrative construed as creation-fall-redemption-consummation. The four moments of this narrative reveal the problem. The movement from fall to redemption made by the creeds completely ignores God's life with Israel, as if the exodus from

---

I am indebted to Kendall Soulen and Christopher Leighton for criticizing a prior draft of this paper.

Egypt were the signature reason for depending on the goodness of God that Jesus proclaimed.[1]

Manichaeism is moral dualism. It claims that evil and good are reified in opposing categories sometimes characterized as forces of light and forces of darkness, into which classes of people are categorized.

Jewish theological neglect of the other is problematic because it localizes and tribalizes God.

The purpose of this paper is to suggest that by becoming theological friends, Judaism and Christianity could not only end the enmity that has characterized their relationship but also address all three theological (read "dogmatic" in the technical sense of the word) problems. Since that is a radical proposal that quite upends theological history, it will be necessary to identify where the theological problems lie on both sides of the divide and then identify how each enables the other to address its own problem(s). Since the Christian side of the argument is better developed and more consequential than the Jewish side, most of the effort here will address the question of Christian Israelology.

### Envision Friendship

Before venturing into the substance of the matter, it will help to identify the framework for a different relationship: friendship. Perhaps the most important treatise on friendship is Cicero's dialogue with Laelius (Cicero 1967). Cicero defines friendship as a relationship between people that involves complete sympathy suffused with good will and affection for others in the relationship. It can only obtain between honorable people who trust one another. We must believe that the person will not turn against us and be committed to not turning against the person. While friendship requires virtue, it should further improve one's character by pulling up the best in us, especially kindness and generosity. Because friends are called to challenge one another, it is also necessary to receive criticism for the sake of one's own well-being. Thus, long-term friendships are difficult to sustain and sometimes must be ended, for example, when a friend ex-

---

1. That Marcionism survived its progenitor's formal condemnation is also illustrated by the fact that the creeds jump from creation to redemption in Christ without considering God's redemptive work in the exodus or any other element of Old Testament history. Perhaps if the creed had read "I believe in God the Father almighty, maker of heaven and earth who delivered Israel from Egypt..." things might have been different.

ceeds the limits of friendship by asking one to become involved in evil. Friendship is demanding, but it gives us hope for ourselves and provides opportunity to practice loving effectively that is both deeply rewarding and self-enhancing.

In the twelfth century, a monk in northern England offered a Christian rendition of Cicero's work, titling it *On Spiritual Friendship*. In setting out to propose friendship in place of enmity, we do well to heed his advice.

> First, there should be a mutual caring; friends should pray for each other, blush and rejoice for one another, each should weep over the other's lapse as though it were his own, and look on his friend's progress as his own. In whatever ways he can, he should encourage the timid, support the weak, console the sorrowful and restrain the hot-tempered. Moreover, he must respect the eyes and ears of his friend, and never presume to wound them with an unseemly act or an unfitting word. A becoming reserve is friendship's best companion: take reserve away from friendship and you deprive it of its greatest ornament. How often has a sign from my friend damped down or quenched the smouldering fire of anger, already on the point of flaring out! How many times have his graver features checked the undignified remark already on the tip of my tongue! How often when I have needlessly dissolved into laughter, or fallen into idle chatter has his arrival restored me to a proper gravity! Besides, if there is something that needs saying, it comes better from a friend and leaves a deeper mark. A recommendation must carry real weight when the giver is known to be loyal and yet not given to flattery. Therefore between friends sound advice should be given confidently, candidly and freely. Mutual admonishment is an integral part of friendship; it should be kindly and not roughly given, and patiently, not resentfully, received. For believe me, there is no scourge of friendships like flattery and complaisance, the characteristic vices of the light-minded and smooth-tongued, those who say what's sure to please and never what is true. So let there be no hesitation between friends, none of the pretence that is so utterly incompatible with friendship. One owes a friend the truth; without it the word friendship has no meaning. (Rievaulx 1993, 187)

Perhaps one must squint to imagine that Judaism and Christianity might become friends. How are those who have been enemies for two millennia to become spiritual friends? It will be necessary for both parties to admit their own insufficiency and that they need the other in order to become their best theological self, that is, to worship God truly, and that, without the other, they falter in that goal. Each must admit in the other's presence that they can and must beat their swords into plowshares and their spears into pruning hooks (Isa. 2:4) to be obedient to God and become who God intends them to become. Isaiah's imagery is most apt here because becoming friends after being enemies means acknowledging that both parties are putting their hands to a common plow and that each needs to be lovingly "pruned" by the other for the sake of their common work of worshiping God truly for the well-being of creation that is their common mission.

I begin with the observation that strong stable relationships are founded on an exchange of gifts. Each party to the relationship must feel both respected and empowered by the relationship. Among other criteria, each must come to appreciate the other's self-definition. Further, each must experience being genuinely helped, enriched, or enhanced by the other's contribution to their well-being. That is, there must honestly be a mutually beneficial exchange of gifts between the partners. As Proverbs puts it, "Everyone is a friend to a giver of gifts" (19:6). To receive gifts requires understanding that each party needs help beyond what their own resources can supply. That is challenging for Christianity and Judaism, which have both seen themselves as complete in themselves, although Christians have generally recognized that they must define themselves in relationship at least to Jewish Scripture if not to the Judaism that emerged from it. Having identified the framework for a fresh conversation, I turn to the substance of the matter at hand.

## Christian Israelology

Israelology runs rarely recognized throughout Christian theology. Christianity's doctrine of Israel is an essential ingredient of ecclesiology that asks who is the people of God or who is Israel.[2] A doctrine of Israel, whether intentionally stated or silently assumed, is unavoidable when considering

---

2. By "Israelology" I mean the Christian doctrine of Israel, the church's theological teaching on the place of Jews and Judaism in the divine economy. "Israelology" is not related to the third Jewish commonwealth, the current sovereign state of Israel as a homeland for the Jewish people.

the doctrine of election if for no other reason than that before the church there was no question but that the Jewish people was Israel, that is, the Israel of God. With Paul of Tarsus that assumption was quite undone, and subsequent Christian theologians were saddled with the problem of how to understand non-Christian Jews who did not bow before Jesus. Here I touch on Paul, Augustine, Aquinas, and Karl Barth.

*Reading Paul's Israelology*

Substantial rethinking about Paul's Israelology has taken place over the past five decades, and it will provide theologians with fresh insights into Christianity's greatest mind for the future (Davies 1955; Dunn 2008; Gager 1983; Gaston 1987; Sanders 1977, 1985; Stendahl 1963; Stowers 1994; Watson 2007; Wright 2005). But standard Christian Israelology that shaped the relationship between Judaism and Christianity was driven by a contemptuous view of Judaism that it derived from Paul.

Christianity's success is partly, perhaps largely, the result of Jewish resistance to its message as crafted by Paul. The Gospels of Matthew and John assume that Jesus's protest aimed at Judaism and constituted an internal reform movement (Matt. 10:6; 15:24; though cf. 28:19; John 8:12–59; though cf. 4:22). However, we face a different situation when turning to Paul. What Paul calls the hardening of Israel (Rom. 11:7) has been read by the church as Israel's disobedience to God, but here I will argue that it is in fact obedience to God in service to the redemption of the world.

Paul repeatedly met resistance to his gospel from Jews and eventually turned to gentiles (Acts 13:46; 18:6; 2 Cor. 11:24). By eliminating food taboos and the requirement of circumcision for entrance into "the household of God" (Eph. 2:19), Paul rendered his message rather more appealing to gentiles, especially males. To make a theological case for turning outward, Paul redefined "Israel" as those Jews and gentiles who profess Christ so that Jesus followers, not the Jewish people, are now what we might call "the people of God," although Paul did not employ that phrase. The church is now the "Israel of God" (Gal. 6:16).[3] The chief argument for this redefi-

---

3. The phrase "Israel of God" is a *hapax*. Although the grammar of the verse in which the phrase occurs is ambiguous so that the referent of the phrase is debated, I concur with most scholars that the term refers not to the Jewish people but to the "new creation" of Jews and gentiles now faithful to Christ (Cowan 2010).

nition is in Romans 9–11, forcefully in chapter 9, although the theological moves are implied in numerous other parts of the Pauline corpus, most shockingly at Galatians 4:22–31.

At Romans 9:4–5 Paul notes the exalted theological heritage of the Israelites. Yet in the next two verses he undercuts any advantage that identity may now carry by denying that all Jews are Abraham's true descendants. "Not all Israelites truly belong to Israel, and not all of Abraham's children are his true descendants" (Rom. 9:6–7). Some are not. Jewish Israel is not synonymous with the Israel of God on the basis of birth, although Jews retain that pedigree. Rather, "it is through Isaac" (redefined as the ancestor of the gentiles) that the promise is fulfilled (Gen. 21:12).[4] Paul introduces Isaac in order to use the story of the birth of twins to his wife Rebecca (Gen. 25) to support his (Paul's) rejection of ethnic Israel as the Israel of God in order to make room for gentiles as heirs of the promises to Abraham.[5] So it is through gentiles (Gal. 4:28) "that descendants shall be named for you [Abraham]" (Gen. 21:12). Christ fulfills the promise to Abraham found at Genesis 12:3 (26:4), a point Paul makes explicitly at Galatians 3:16 by identifying Christ as the one descendant of Abraham, implying that those who are of Christ are the proper inheritors of the promises.

Paul does not stop here, however, but goes on to redefine the people of God by reversing Genesis's consistent reversal of the conventional preference for the elder over the younger sibling so that the younger is regularly favored (Abel over Cain, Isaac over Ishmael, Jacob over Esau, Rachel over Leah, Perez over Zerah, Joseph over his older brothers, and Ephraim over Manasseh) that constituted Israel's/Judaism's pedigree. Paul constructs an idiosyncratic counter-counter-genealogy through the patriarchs in Romans 9:6–13. In Paul's reversal of Scripture's reversal, Isaac becomes the progenitor of the gentiles while Esau becomes the progenitor of Jews, in flagrant violation of the text (comparable to the reversal of identity of Sarah and Hagar at Gal. 5).

Genesis identifies Esau as the ancestor of the Edomites eight times (25:30; 32:3; 36:1; 36:8; 36:9; 36:19; 36:32; 36:42), but Paul ignores all these texts. Not only does he identify the Jews who resist Christ with Esau, but he goes out of his way at Romans 9:13 to suggest to his gentile listeners that such Jews are hated by God by smuggling in Malachi 1:2b–3a as if it were

---

4. If Paul were consistent in his reversal of Genesis's reversals, that would make Ishmael the ancestor of the Jews, but he never says that.

5. For how this imagery plays out in Augustine's theology, see Charry 2012.

in Genesis 25. Although it may be no more than a rhetorical flourish, it is gratuitously inflammatory. The insertion of the Malachi phrase may be hyperbole on Paul's part, but inserting the hatred motif in addition to the enemy motif of Romans 11:28 has had devastating effects on subsequent Israelology. Although Jews are recognized by God on account of their ancestors (Rom 9:4-5 and 11:28), that did not protect them from Christian wrath when Christians read Paul's Israelology as God's simple rejection of non-Christian Jews.

This gerrymandering of biblical texts that were undoubtedly more familiar to Jews than they would have been to pagans is humiliating and infuriating to Jews of his day (and probably our own) because the Edomites were among Israel's Canaanite enemies. There was serious bad blood between the two nations (2 Sam. 8:13-14; 1 Kings 11:17; 2 Kings 8:21; 14:7; 16:6). Paul is again telling gentiles that his kinfolk are objects of God's wrath just as John 8 has Jesus tell his readers that Jews are not Abraham's children or the children of God. Romans 9:19-22 cites Isaiah and Jeremiah as foretelling the dissolution of Israel as the people of God that Paul is now proclaiming. Paul was telling Romans who had political control of Palestine that Jewish religion was now routed for their sake. It invites Schadenfreude on both counts.

Galatians 3 implies replacing torah (i.e., Judaism) with Christ (v. 16) in fulfillment of God's promise to Abraham for the families of the earth. Ephesians 2:13-16 asserts that with the coming of Christ the people of God became those Jews and gentiles bonded together by faith in Christ, not those gentiles and Jews who adhere to torah. Even if Paul would have permitted Jewish Jesus followers to practice torah (which he never says), that no longer has any theological value; it is at best a nostalgic sop. Yet, this is unlikely because permitting Christian Jews to adhere to torah violates the Pauline insistence on one new community (Eph. 2:14) and his polemic against the "circumcision party" in Galatians 6.

What is one to make of Paul's hermeneutical redefinition of the Israel of God not as Jews and gentiles who join them by accepting Jewish custom and practice but as Jews and gentiles who cling to Christ? First, one can say that Paul is a consummate, clever, and perhaps wily exegete scouring Scripture for ways it can serve his *ex post facto* hermeneutic: Christ has changed everything; Scripture and Judaism must now be reread through this event (Keck 1993).

Second, as what I will anachronistically call a dogmatician, Paul is a Jewish theologian who anticipates later Christian dogmatic issues in important ways so that we can appreciate what comes later by asking how his thought deals with all three dogmatic problems I identified at the outset: Marcionism (Israel forgetfulness), Manichaeism (moral dualism), and theological neglect of the other.

Paul, of course, does not engage in Israel forgetfulness. Israel's life with God, gerrymandered as Paul reads it, is the foundation of his gospel, the basis on which the church is God's field, God's building (1 Cor. 3:9). God has not started over again with Christ Jesus, as one might be able to say was the case with Noah or perhaps the calling of Abraham. While Christ effects a transformation of the Israel of God, the church is not the inauguration of an unprecedented relationship with humanity. Paul insists on continuity with the prior form of the Israel of God. There is only one God, who is God of Jews and gentiles alike.

As for the question of moral dualism, in comparison with the Gospel of John that has the aroma of the Manichaean division that pits those who walk in the light against those who walk in darkness, Paul has no clear categorization of people lining up for or against God in Christ. This may, however, reflect a difference in their contexts. Paul writes *in media res*. He is in constant conversation with Jews, making his case to them and hoping they will be persuaded of his argument. By the time or place of John's Gospel, positions have hardened; anger is high. Paul's use of the images of vessels of wrath and mercy taken from Jeremiah 18 sits ready to be used in a Manichaean manner, and so the images later become in the tradition.

To address the last point: in a word, as a Jewish theologian, Paul definitively smashes theological neglect right between the eyes, killing it with a single blow.

*Augustine's Proto-Israelology*

Early Christian writers welcomed Christianity's replacement of Judaism as the people of God in order to defeat Judaism, whose authenticity threatened the church's claims. At least twenty-six Christian polemics against "the Jews" in the patristic age alone made this case. Barnabas, Justin, Melito, Tertullian, Pseudo-Cyprian, Eusebius of Caesarea, John Chrysostom, Cyril of Alexandria, and Prudentius are among the authors. But it was Augustine of Hippo who not only wrote *Tractatus adversus Judaeos* but in other writings crafted elements of what could have become a coherent and positive Israelology, although he never brought these themes together to do that. At the same time, Augustine consistently christologizes the Older Testament and is notorious for sustaining anti-Jewish rhetoric in his exegesis (Byassee 2007).

Augustine did not develop a doctrine of Israel, but his doctrine of election was strongly influenced by his reading of Romans 9 (Fredriksen 2008), although he did tweak it in important ways, perhaps the most important of which was to remove it from the setting of the relationship between Jews and gentiles and to set it in the context of the almost exclusively gentile church of his day. The elect are not Jews and gentiles who follow Christ, as they were for Paul, but those individuals whom God inscrutably elects within the body of Christ to identify the church as a mixed body of the elect and the nonelect, the visible and the invisible church.

Although he did not engage the issue of the place of the Jews in the economy of salvation in his doctrine of election, Augustine was forced to consider it in the course of pursuing other concerns. In his anti-Manichaean response to Faustus (Augustine 2007), Augustine applies both the curse and the mark of Cain to the Jews. And in his extensive sermon on Psalm 59 (Ps. 58 LXX), he identifies a positive ongoing role for Judaism apart from the church, although he does not develop the idea to stand on its own (Augustine 2001).

In the *Answer to Faustus* (12.11), Augustine allegorizes the first biblically recorded murder to be about Christians and Jews. Abel symbolizes Christ and Cain symbolizes the Jews who handed Christ over to the Romans. Jews bear both the debilitating curse and the protective mark of Cain (Gen. 4:11–15). On one hand, Cain is condemned to be cursed by the ground to futile manual labor and to be a wandering fugitive. This symbolism has flourished in Christian theology as justifying Jewish exile that demonstrated divinely decreed eternal earthly punishment of Jews as Christians triumphantly interpreted it. This theme echoes all down the line. On the other hand, at Cain's request, God puts a protective mark on him, threatening vengeance against anyone who would seek to kill him. From this double inheritance Augustine reads that the church is to protect Jewish life, not minimally but in its fullness, despite Jews' eternal punishment and subordination to Christians (Fredriksen 2008, 267). This is the theological basis of repeated attempts by both bishops and princes to protect Jews from mob violence in the Middle Ages, although Augustine's own deeply anti-Jewish rhetoric roused anti-Judaism long after him. Yet further, Augustine recognized the Jews' "crime" (handing Christ over to the Romans) as a blessing of sorts, although he cannot manage that word, because that death enabled the salvation of the gentiles (Fredriksen 2008, 266–67, citing *Answer to Faustus* 12.11).

The second prong of Augustine's tweak of Romans 9, also in *Answer to Faustus* (12.23), is respect for Jewish faithfulness to Scripture and Jewish practices. "For what else is that people today but a certain library for Christians, which holds the law and the prophets as a witness to the claim of the Church that we reverence" (12.23). Although the Jews are cursed by God and the church, Augustine nevertheless points to them as forwarding the church's self-understanding in spite of themselves. Even though they are wrong, Jews do witness to God sincerely because they authenticate Scripture for the church. Thus, by confirming its sacred books, Jews do play a positive role in the church's self-understanding, although outside the church where the economy of salvation holds sway.

Augustine reinforces this position in his comments on Psalm 59 (Masoretic Text; Ps. 58 in LXX), preached over two days about a dozen years later (Augustine 2001). The complainant in this typical lament seeks God's punishment of his enemies, yet in the middle of the poem inserts, "Slay them not, lest my people forget" (Ps 59:11 RSV), echoing the psalm's superscript, "Do Not Destroy." Augustine is brought up short by these phrases. While engaging in typical invective against the deicidal Jews, the words "slay them not" stick in his throat, forcing him to think through how the church ought to view Jews. Augustine applied Jesus's injunction to love enemies at this point. Although they are Christ's enemies, "slay them not" directs Christians to protect them or at least not to molest them. Amidst a comment on Psalm 59:10, he adverts to Romans 9:22–23 on the vessels of wrath and mercy following Paul's line that the Jews are the vessels of wrath. For Augustine, the enemies of the protagonist of the psalm are, of course, Jews, while the complainant is a Christian! Augustine is an avid christologizer of the Older Testament. This is, of course, a deep-seated form of Marcionism in itself. Yet despite his Israel forgetfulness, the reality of Jewish existence tugs at him here.

> How does this prayer apply to them: Do not kill them, let them never forget your law? Do not slay those enemies of mine who slew me. Let the Jewish race survive. It has been conquered by the Romans, to be sure; its city has been destroyed, certainly; the Jews are debarred from their own city, yes; but there are still Jews. So many provinces have been subjugated by the Romans, and who can tell any longer which nation is which, now that they are all within the Roman Empire? They have

all become Romans, and all are called Romans. Yet the Jews remain distinct, marked with their sign; they have not been so conquered as to be absorbed by their conquerors. It was on Cain, and, significantly, after he had slain his brother, that God put a mark, to prevent anyone killing him. This [mark] is the sign that the Jews bear today. They preserve tenaciously the remnants of their law; they practice circumcision, observe the Sabbath, slaughter the paschal lamb, and eat unleavened bread. The Jews abide; they have not been killed, for they are necessary to Gentile believers. Why? So that God may give us proof of his mercy by his dealings with our enemies. (Exposition 1 of Psalm 58:21)

Augustine's final conclusion is that in these ways Jews serve the church. He talks about Jewish service to the church as spiritual and moral, although the point was misused when it was advantageous for Christians to impose civil and economic disabilities on Jews (see Fredriksen 2008, 272–77). There can be no doubt that with the rest of the Christian tradition Augustine preferred the conversion of the Jews, but in these materials he provides a theological rationale for the existence of non-Christian Jews.

Thus we have three elements of Augustine's proto-Israelology: (1) by having handed Christ over to the Romans for crucifixion, Jews enabled the death of Christ to be the mechanism of the redemption of gentiles; (2) by carrying the books, Jews authenticate the Christian claim to worship God; (3) by preserving Jewish life, the church is enabled to enact God's command to love one's enemies.

Although his christological hermeneutic eclipses Israel, he realizes that Jews witness to the authenticity of the Hebrew Bible that assures that Christianity can trace itself back to creation itself. The Jews authenticate Christ as sent by God. Further, the existence of the Jews, disobedient though their faithfulness to God may be judged to be by Christians, illustrates God's mercy, and the church must learn to practice that mercy toward them as well. Much later, Barth would follow Augustine on these last two points, insisting that the Older Testament is essential for Christian self-understanding and that the existence of the Jewish people testifies to divine mercy.

Given Augustine's inestimable hegemony over subsequent Western theology, the potential of his positive spin on Israelology was perhaps grudgingly recognized but never appreciated. Instead, deeply rutted anti-Jewish rhetoric sometimes deteriorating into anti-Semitism blossomed in the Middle Ages with repercussions far beyond: the "wandering Jew," the morally depraved Jew, the greedy Jewish banker, the hypocritical Pharisee, the spiritually decrepit Jew, the power-hungry Jew, the self-righteous Jew, the legalistic Jew, and so on lived at least into the mid-twentieth century.

At the same time, much as he struggled against Manichaeism, Augustine was not finally able to extirpate it from his own doctrine of election that subsequently controlled the Western church. In book 1 of *To Simplician* (396), Augustine responds to Simplician's questions about Romans 9. To protect the absolute and arbitrary power of God, the bishop calls upon Paul's reversal of the Jacob and Esau identity to argue that the election of Jacob and the rejection of Esau have nothing to do with their merits. Their destinies were determined before they were born. God's hatred of Esau was not unkind at all, he says, because neither he nor his brother deserved anything better. Indeed, in sermon 159B, on Romans 11:32–36, Augustine explains that since all are under sin and all deserve divine wrath, no one deserves mercy. That Romans 11:32 says that "God has imprisoned all in disobedience so that he may be merciful to all" must then mean that God's rejection of the vessels of wrath is an expression of grace. Rejection of Esau is a merciful act of tough love on God's part, an act of mercy in disguise.[6] God justly hated Esau, and that unto his well-being, so that the Esaus of this world will come to better, deeper self-knowledge because of God's rejection of them and thereby grow in wisdom, that is, toward God. "So then, let this be what we sinners tell ourselves, let this be how we acknowledge[,] in the penalties that overtake us[,] both our own wrongdoing and the justice of our God. In this way, you see, we shall be found worthy to discover the mercy of God in the very penalties themselves" (Augustine 1997, 148).

Jacob was loved without merit; he too deserved the wrath of God but escaped it. Esau got only what they both deserved. Election is not a reward for obedience to divine law or faith, hope, love, wisdom, or any other vir-

---

6. "See that punishment can be the work of caring or kindness, from the example of children, from that kind of thing which nobody can hate. So someone sees his son going the way of pride, setting himself up against his father, claiming more for himself than is proper, wanting to let his life trickle away in trifling pleasures, wanting to squander what he does not yet possess. And there he is, when he's behaving like this, cheerful, laughing, blithely enjoying himself. His father, though, brings him to heel with a rebuke, with punishment, with a whip; he wipes the grin off his face, reduces him to tears. He has apparently deprived him of what is good, and brought what is evil upon him—see what he has deprived him of: enjoyment; see what he has brought on him: groans. And yet if he had left that enjoyment unpunished, he would have been cruel; because he has reduced him to tears, he is shown to be caring and kind" (Augustine 1997, 149).

tue. It does not hinge on God's knowing in advance that Jacob would be good and Esau bad. In fact, the literal sense of the texts does not support this. Here Augustine calls in Romans 9:16 for support: "So it depends not on human will or exertion, but on God who shows mercy." It is not a good will or bad that God anticipates in advance that influences his mercy. It is not that all are called but few respond, "for the effectiveness of God's mercy cannot be in the power of man to frustrate" (Augustine 1958/397, 395). Again, Augustine is concerned only to protect the absolute power of God and the complete powerlessness of humanity in comparison.

That Augustine insists on God's arbitrary division of people into vessels of wrath and vessels of mercy sustains the very Manichaean thread that he wanted to destroy. Augustine formally assigns those categories within the church not between Jews and Christians but to individual Christians, but there can be little doubt that he considered Jews to be vessels of wrath along with unassuming Christians. According to Augustine, one has to be in the church to be among the elect, although being there does not assure election; human agency is annulled here. Barth's Israelology will sustain that Manichaean thread that categorizes Christians in light, Jews in darkness, even though for him, as for Paul, the division of humanity into Jew and Christian is vulnerable to human agency, since Jews can convert. For Augustine, neither the vessels of wrath nor the vessels of mercy have any agency in the matter of their status.

## Aquinas on the Jews

Augustine had more or less stumbled upon the question of the role of the Jews in the divine economy in the course of his struggle against Manichaeism. Aquinas carried that struggle forward. Given that Aquinas lived at the center of the medieval church's rigorous evangelization program that was particularly harsh on Jews, he took a notably moderate position regarding their civil status and public treatment of them.

Although he did not offer a doctrine of Israel, Aquinas did consider the conundrum posed by the fact that Christ suffered and died in order to bring salvation to the gentiles. Even if Jews were complicit in the death of Christ, Aquinas realized that they should not be excoriated for it because they were serving God's will for Christ. To resolve the dilemma, he held that although God willed the death of Christ, he did not will that particular action of the Jews that handed Christ over; that was their own evil desire

(Hood 1995, 69–70). Aquinas works hard to comply with church teaching regarding the deicide charge, knowing that hating Jews for their role in that did not really fit the doctrinal need for Christ to be executed in order to fulfill his redemptive calling.

## Barth's Israelology

Karl Barth was perhaps the first theologian since Paul to specify an Israelology, building on and restructuring doctrinal elements put in place by his predecessors, notably Paul and Augustine. Indeed, he was the first theologian since Paul to find an enduring place for Israel within the divine economy, that is, within the covenant of grace.

While that is a stellar achievement in itself, it remains an ambiguous accomplishment because, according to him, enduring Jewish existence witnesses to God's negative judgment on humanity. In Barth's hands, while the church represents God's election of faithful humanity, Israel represents God's judgment on faithless humanity. Although both are taken up into Christ—the only elected and rejected person—Israel remains the rejected form of the people of God that is passing away while the church is that celebrated form of the people of God that is coming. Here is the last hurrah of Christian triumphalism. Here, the relationship between Israel and the church represents the forces of good and evil pitted against one another in terms of Christianity's great theological argument against Judaism. Although together Israel and the church constitute God's covenant people, the categorization retains a trace of Manichaean dualism that was unable to recognize good and evil inextricably intertwined in every human heart (as rabbinic Judaism did), be it Christian, Jewish, or other.

Barth set his Israelology in the doctrine of election of the community placed within the doctrine of God, making electing grace constitutive of the identity of God. God is God by being committed to humanity. The Israelology came as an exegesis of Romans 9–11 in *Church Dogmatics* (hereafter *CD* II/2 §34). Here Barth jumps back over both Calvin and Augustine to Paul's depiction of the two categories of vessels as symbolizing Christ-resistant Jews and Christ-embracing gentiles and Jews, rather than as an invisible division among Christians as Augustine and Calvin had depicted it. Barth's modification of the Hegelian dialectic, like that of his contemporary Franz Rosenzweig, did not resolve the poles of the opposition into a synthesis that would itself become a thesis to be overturned but remained

*Toward Ending Enmity*

an awkward union of the two into a seemingly enduring enmity that retains the judgment and mercy of God applied to Jews and Christians, respectively. In Barth's case, the law-gospel binary that he inherited from Luther fit nicely into the Hegelian binary. The enduringly resistant Jewish people and the church triumphant become the two persistent forms of one divided community of God that Barth labeled the "dead Israel" of the synagogue and the "living Israel" of the church that would be *aufgehoben* into one undivided entity if only the Jews would at long last Christianize (*CD* II/2, 205).

Barth's great innovation, of course, was to place the standard dichotomy between Israel and the church within the covenant, that has been the theological category favored by Reformed theology since the "federal theology" of the seventeenth century. He is the first Christian theologian to do this, and, working from Romans 11, he understands Israel's ambiguous election to rejection that is passing away as an act of divine grace (*CD* II/2, 267–305). This echoes Augustine's reading of Romans 11:32 in sermon 159B. By locating non-Christian Israel within God's one covenant with humanity, Barth shut the door on "Israel forgetfulness," although the result is ambivalent.

While he had not been Israel forgetful, Paul had paved the way for Israel forgetfulness with the Adam-Christ dichotomy (Rom. 5; 1 Cor. 15) that elides the entire history of Israel prior to the incarnation; that elision is immortalized in the creeds. To be sure, Barth challenges that elision to secure an enduring covenantal place for Israel post-*Christus*, including his strong opposition to the Aryanization of Christ that was established in biblical scholarship of the nineteenth and twentieth centuries (Gerdmar 2009). That is, for better or worse, Barth's doctrine of election follows the Jew-Christian opposition of Romans 9–11, not the Adam-Christ dichotomy of 1 Corinthians 15.

By locating both election and rejection within the covenant, Barth effectively replaced Calvin's doctrine of double predestination that had proven so fearsome to tender souls. Calvin focused on Romans 9:20–23 in 3.23.1 of the *Institutes*, where he defended his doctrine of reprobation against five specific criticisms of it by relying on several of Augustine's works. Augustine's doctrine of election held close to Romans 9–11, although he Christianized it to be not about Jews and gentiles but about Christians only. Barth jumps back over this Christianization to stay closer to Romans and perhaps to find an enduring place for Christ-resistant Jews in the divine economy, although he does not say that. In correcting Calvin, Barth had several goals in mind. Although he did not argue strongly for introjecting God's Yes and No into the self-concept of every Christian—which could have broken the back of Manichaeism—he did follow Calvinism's humiliation/crucifixion and exaltation/resurrection of Christ dynamic (see questions 27 and 28 of the Westminster Shorter Catechism [1647] in *CD* II/2 §34, 198, and in the doctrine of reconciliation [*CD* IV/1 §§59–60 and IV/2 §64]). In portraying Christ as the one who is both humiliated as Lord and exalted as servant, in whom the election of all takes place, Barth undermined the arbitrariness of the Augustinian-Calvinist doctrine of election. Christ represents all who are simultaneous recipients of God's Yes and God's No, and that includes Israel and the church.

Another reason for returning the vessels of wrath and mercy of Romans 9 to non-Christian Jews and Christians is that doing so further undermines the individualism of the Augustinian-Calvinist doctrine of election (*CD* II/2, 195–96). There are not individual Christians who are elected while others are arbitrarily rejected, but rather two forms of the one covenant people of God signifying both election and rejection, both of which are taken up into Christ. It is a pedagogical tool. The theme is further developed in *CD* IV/1 and 2.

The humiliation-exaltation dynamic that undergirds the Israelology of §34 recurs as a major motif in the doctrine of reconciliation. The humbling obedience of Christ, iconicized as the servant lord (IV/1, §59, completed in 1953), recapitulates the Israelology of §34 basically untouched. Similarly, the exaltation of Christ, the lordly servant (IV/2, §64), reinforces the church triumphant of §34. This substantially reshapes not only the Augustinian-Calvinist doctrine of election that was, I think, foremost in Barth's mind, but it also reshapes Christian Israelology by giving the Jewish people a permanent and necessary, albeit negative, role in salvation history that has the positive side effect of displaying divine grace as Augustine had noted. Jews witness to sin and God's wrath against it by resisting Christ in service to the well-being of the church, that is, for its admonition. Barth, of course, weakens that permanent status of dishonor by identifying it with the community that is passing away. What he means by "passing away" is ambiguous. Perhaps he still blindly hopes that "the Jews" will yet convert, even with the stench of the extermination camps in everyone's nostrils.[7] I find use of the phrase "passing away" in 1942 regrettable.

---

7. While some have tried to distance Christianity from the Holocaust by considering Nazism an example of neo-paganism, recent scholarship is showing the dissociation of Christian theology from Nazism to be untenable (Fischer 2014; Gerdmar 2009).

## Toward Ending Enmity

If the Jewish form of the covenant that is "passing away" still holds out for the conversion of the Jews in significant numbers, it undermines the point of locating those elected for rejection within the covenant of grace-judgment. Conversion speeds the liquidation of the Jewish people, after all. Barth is finally ambivalent about the place of the Jews in the divine economy. On one hand, he wants them to become obedient by Christianizing that would resolve the dialectic. On the other, he needs them to remain Jews as a placeholder for human disobedience in order to sustain his dialectic. The great tragedy here is that actual people are sacrificed at the altar of intellectual elegance.

Barth revisits his Israelology briefly in IV/3.2, published in 1959, and sustains the position he took in §34 and in §59. He rejects special "missions to the Jews" not because he has changed his mind about the passing away of dead Israel in the divine economy, but because he is now more realistic about their resistance to conversion, although that does not quite make sense to me. Missions to the Jews, Barth now thinks, are apparently pointless:

> The Gentile Christian community of every age and land is a guest in the house of Israel. It assumes the election and calling of Israel. It lives in fellowship with the King of Israel. How, then, can we try to hold missions to Israel? It is not the Swiss or the German or the Indian or the Japanese awakened to faith in Jesus Christ, but the Jew, even the unbelieving Jew, so miraculously preserved, as we must say, through the many calamities of his history, who as such is the natural historical monument to the love and faithfulness of God, who in concrete form is the epitome of the man freely chosen and blessed by God, who as a living commentary on the Old Testament is the only convincing proof of God outside the Bible. What have we to teach him that he does not already know, that we have not rather to learn from him? . . .
>
> [H]owever, there is the shattering fact that at the decisive moment the same Israel denied its election and calling, that when the hour struck it did not know the fullness and goal of its history, that when it eventuated it did not receive the promised consolation, that when it was fulfilled it did not believe the Word of God spoken to it by Moses and the prophets, that when its King appeared among it He was despised and rejected and delivered up to the gentiles . . . the Synagogue became and was and still is the organisation of a group of men which hastens towards a future that is empty now that He has come who should come,

> which is still without consolation, which clings to a Word of God that is still unfulfilled. Necessarily, therefore, the Jew who is uniquely blessed offers the picture of an existence which, characterized by the rejection of its Messiah and therefore of its salvation and mission, is dreadfully empty of grace and blessing.... What object is there here for missionary activity? What we have to see, and sympathetically to fear, is the judgment of God in His love....
>
> The Church must live with the Synagogue, not, as fools say in their hearts, as with another religion or confession, but as with the root from which it has itself sprung. But it cannot and will not live with it in the only way possible. For the penetrating pain of this hurt it should not seek false alleviation, even though it may be faithfully at work in all other branches of its ministry. The recurrent Jewish question is the question of Christ and the Church which has not been and cannot be answered by any of its ministries. It stands as an unresolved problem, and therefore as the shadow behind and above all its activity in foreign missions. (Barth, CD IV/3, 877-78)

Barth's vessels of wrath and the vessels of mercy have survived the Nazis intact. He rests assured in the beauty of his dialectic that hangs in the air like an elegant hologram. Yet inconsistencies in his Israelology remain. Again, if Jews and Judaism stand as a witness to human sin and God's judgment against it, why should they pass away? Converted Jews would move from the No to the Yes column, and the binary would collapse, the dialectic would fail.

To conclude, it is evident that while Barth decisively shut the door against Israel forgetfulness, he nevertheless sustained residual moral dualism by reifying Israel and the church as symbols of evil and goodness, darkness and light, death and life, despair and hope, or whatever additional oppositions serve the pedagogical purpose. For Barth, Israel's election to rejection is of grace, as it was for Augustine. This teaching is essentially a reprise of Augustine's position in sermon 159B that even those rejected by God are objects of divine mercy, and they should be content.

There is a difference between Augustine and Barth, however. For Augustine the elect and reprobate are invisible to the naked eye, hidden as they are within the church. Barth sets the opposing factions in broad daylight, as had Paul. Further, since Jews can move from the No to the Yes side of the opposition, their condemnation ends up being their own doing.

## Jewish Theology of the Other

For its part, Judaism never formulated a doctrine of Christianity; it thought it never needed to. Such theological autonomy is problematic, however. There is a high price to pay for the theological neglect of "the other," especially of Christianity, which emerged from its womb. Unless Judaism makes theological sense of "the other," how is it to make sense of the universality of God, of Isaiah's vision that the nations shall stream to the Lord's house in Jerusalem (Isa. 2), and that God is the God of the Ninevites?

The theological challenge for Judaism is posed not only by many Scripture passages but also by the basic liturgical unit of Jewish life: "Blessed are you, Lord our God, sovereign of the universe." Unless and until Jews understand how God's love reaches to the ends of the earth, its blessings hang in the air, just as do Christian claims to worship God if God is disassociated from the God of the Jews. While Christians may ask Jews how they understand them (Christians) to be children of God, that challenge is brought to Jewish attention from within Judaism itself because Jews claim to worship the maker of heaven and earth, as the *baruch sh'amar* (Birnbaum 1949, 51) in Judaism's daily morning office plainly says.

While theological neglect of others (i.e., xenophobia) may be understandable for historical reasons, it is theologically problematic because it localizes God, inviting either the suspicion that if God is God of Jews only, there might be other gods for other nations and peoples, or, if Jews really want to claim that God is God of Jews only and there is no other God, then God is a limited God and not the master of the universe.[8] That the Jews survived as a people apart despite being received with social and legal and moral scorn by the host cultures in which they lived has certainly testified to the presence of God in history, and for many suffices to justify their suffering. Yet, Scripture, liturgy, and Judaism's doctrine of God press Judaism's mission in the world beyond mere survival to that of bringing God to the nations. Xenophobia obviates that mission.

The proposal here is that appreciating, nay, embracing Christ overcomes Judaism's theological neglect of the other. By recognizing that in Christ God has enabled Jews and Judaism to bring God to the world, Judaism will awaken from its theological insouciance and fulfill its calling to

---

8. Xenophobia (as translated by Jules Harlow [Harlow 1972, 461]) is specifically mentioned in the central congregational confession of sin recited several times throughout the Yom Kippur liturgies.

be "a light to the nations that [God's] salvation may reach to the end of the earth" (Isa. 49:6 [42:6]).

At this point, some will turn to the Noachian covenant that established criteria for granting civilized status to non-Jews. It may have been devised to permit commerce with non-Jews who might otherwise have been be considered off-limits to Jews. This gesture toward non-Jews is noteworthy, but it is not adequate to Judaism's theological need to be able to claim that God is the sovereign of the universe. Noachian status is a civil, not a theological, status. For Jews to be able to speak the blessing that constitutes the core of their liturgical life, they must be able to account for God's relationship to non-Jews. The Noachian laws do not do that. Christianity as well as Islam does fill that need. Here the concern is with Christianity, primarily because Jewish flesh and blood in Jesus of Nazareth is Judaism's gift to the world.

Befriending Christ and his body, the church, will address Jewish exclusiveness that implies that God's embrace applies to Jews only. Unless and until Jews can look beyond (but not forget) the sting of persecution and fully appreciate that through Jesus Christ God does truly bless the families of the earth, Judaism will fail to exercise the full scope of its election. That is, within the framework of spiritual friendship, Judaism is invited to find its destiny not only in the survival of the Jewish people, necessary as that is as witnessing to God, but also by advancing God's desire that the nations come to know, love, and enjoy God alongside, but not necessarily as, Jews.

## Groping toward Friendship

I have argued that both Judaism and Christianity face theological problems that are entwined with their seemingly interminable theological controversy with each other. Now I argue that they can address those problems by exchanging gifts and thereby becoming friends. Simply acknowledging that neither tradition can address these particular theological problems with internal resources alone and that the other can enable them to do that is itself a radical qualification of the presumed theological autonomy of both traditions and a step toward friendship that enables both to fulfill their common mission of advancing the recognition of God in the world, that is, to enable people to know, love, and enjoy God. If indeed the wall of hostility between Jews and gentiles has come down as Ephesians 2:14 puts it, fresh thinking is in order for both communities to translate that normative judgment into a concrete fact on the ground. That reality, however, will not look like the community that Christians envisioned in which Jews would become Christians.[9] I consider first Christianity's gift to Judaism and then Judaism's gift to Christianity.

## Christianity's Gift to Judaism

Although Jesus of Nazareth remains Judaism's great gift to the world, it is now to be recognized that Jesus Christ is also Christianity's great gift to Judaism. Isaiah's words are too apposite not to recall here:

> For as rain and snow fall from the heavens
>     And return not again, but water the earth,
> Bringing forth life and giving growth,
>     Seed for sowing and bread for eating,
> So is my word that goes forth from my mouth;
>     It will not return to me empty,
> But it will accomplish that which I have purposed,
>     And prosper in that for which I sent it.
>                         (Isa. 55:10–11, Book of Common Prayer, 87)

As redeemer of the world, Christ cuts through Jewish theological insouciance because he is the means that God employs to bring the nations to himself. He and the whole body of Christ are the primary means by which God is known beyond Israel. In this perspective, Jews can appreciate and perhaps even celebrate that God claimed gentiles for himself by revealing himself to them through the life, death, resurrection, and ascension of one of them. They will then thank and praise God that gentiles can now know

---

9. Both Jewish and Christian Scripture enshrine the idea that the world will be converted to its way. Isa. 45:23 reads: "By myself I have sworn, from my mouth has gone forth in righteousness a word that shall not return: 'To me every knee shall bow, every tongue shall swear.'" This verse appears in the ninth-century prayer "Alenu," which concludes every Jewish worship service. It was paraphrased by Paul at Phil. 2:10, "so that at the name of Jesus every knee should bend, in heaven and on earth and under the earth." Thus, Jewish eschatology enshrines the conversion of all to the Jewish way while Christian eschatology enshrines the conversion of all to the Christian way. In honesty, it is not ours to know what God will effect. But we do know that both traditions agree that all are to bend the knee before the God of Israel. This, of course, includes Muslims, who, with Jews and Christians, bow before the God of Abraham, that is, the God of Israel and Jesus Christ.

love and enjoy God through Jesus Christ, enabling them to proclaim every Jewish blessing with integrity.

Further, Jews will not only celebrate along with Christians but will themselves embrace Christ as their ambassador. Christ is Israel's redeemer in the sense that he enables God's embrace of gentiles, even of Israel's enemies; he fulfills Israel's biblical mandate to bring God to the world on behalf of Judaism itself. Jews may still welcome gentiles into the Jewish people through traditional conversion to Judaism (including *t'vilah*, Jewish baptism) if they wish to be in solidarity with Jews, but their Christian confession is the sufficient condition for their belonging to the God of Israel as the church.

## Judaism's Gift to Christianity

For their part, to banish the ghosts of Marcion and Mani who threaten to sever the church from the maker of heaven and earth and from the goodness of creation, Christians can fully embrace the faithfulness of non-Christian Israel that enables them to know God in Christ. When Christians deny that Jewish faithfulness to God through Judaism is indeed faithfulness to God, they endanger the church's own authenticity and faithfulness, fraught as the latter is with rebellion against God. Christians need the eternal people of God to exist not theoretically but physically, in order to be secure in their faith, because without them they cannot claim that in Jesus Christ they worship the maker of heaven and earth and not some phantasm of Christian imagination.

To do this, Christians will want to acknowledge that the Jewish people, the eternal people, is the Israel of God and that Jews do not need to be baptized into the body of Christ to worship God truly, although some may wish to do that to be in solidarity with Christians. Christians have no need to evangelize Jews because Christ ministers to them in a different way outside the church.

Yet further, and perhaps most jarringly, Christians will offer thanks and praise to God that in the first century a very few Jews, led by Caiaphas and assisted by Judah (a.k.a. Judas), were involved in Christ's death, which was needed to prevent a bloodbath in Israel by the Romans who wanted to quell the restiveness among the populace that Jesus and his friends had provoked (John 18). That that death was interpreted as establishing gentiles' relationship with the maker of heaven and earth by the forgiveness of sins is a rather different but by no means incidental matter. These Jewish leaders not only saved Jewish lives at the time but, perhaps unawares, were used by God over the longer term to enable gentiles to experience God's love (by the forgiveness of their sins) and embrace him. Through Christ, Judaism advances the universal recognition of God perhaps in spite of itself. How wondrous are God's ways. The church has simply been wrong, quite wrong, to curse Caiaphas and his colleagues and Judah, indeed all Jews (!), for identifying Jesus to the police. They are rather to be thanked, praised, and esteemed because by Jesus's death other Jewish lives were saved and God gained access to gentile hearts in a way that their conversion to Judaism would have precluded. Their role in Christ's execution was obedience to God, even if no one recognized that at the time.

Finally, the Jewish diaspora, classically depicted as a sign of God's curse on the Jewish people (the curse of Cain), is actually a blessing because by living among Christians Jews proclaim their gift of Christian integrity and continuously remind Christians of the grace of the God of Israel under whom they stand. Conversely, of course, by living among Christians, Jews are reminded that Christ fulfills their calling to be a light to the nations so that they can celebrate the words of Isaiah paraphrased by that Jerusalemite Simeon as he held the child Jesus in his arms:

"Master, now you are dismissing your servant in peace,
    according to your word;
for my eyes have seen your salvation,
    which you have prepared in the presence of all peoples,
a light for revelation to the Gentiles
    and for glory to your people Israel." (Luke 2:29–32)

In this rethinking, gentile Christians will acknowledge that Jews do need Christ, but not for the reason gentile Christians do. Gentiles need the forgiveness of God made available in Christ to be persuaded of God's love for them, that they might embrace and follow him. Jews are already in that relationship. They do not need Christ to be persuaded of God's love for them. Nor do they need Christ to find relief from the guilt of personal sin.

Gentiles need Jesus Christ to come to know the Father, while Jews (who, on the Day of Atonement, address "our Father our Ruler") need him in order to embrace gentiles; this distinction identifies two ways in which Christ atones for sin. Christianity has relied upon sacramental baptism, confession of sin, the penitential system, and faith in Christ's atoning death to find relief from the guilt of personal sins. But that focus obscures the fact that forgiveness is an expression of love that endears the forgiver to the forgiven, which is the goal of the gift. Judaism does not need that gift, for it knows of God's love through its election. Further, Judaism has well-developed penitential mechanisms that reassure Jews of God's ongoing mercy. These include the month of Elul, the Day of Atonement, penitential prayers throughout the year, fasting, almsgiving, and death that is understood to atone for sin. Jews do not need Christ to experience God's grace but in order to embrace their enemies.

On the Jewish side of things, Judaism's theological neglect of the other (xenophobia) is a form of disobedience to God. It is a corporate sin mentioned in the central congregational confession of sin recited several times throughout the Yom Kippur liturgies (Harlow 1972, 461). Seen through the eyes of Jewish-Christian friendship, it is a sin for which Christ atones. Thus we can say that Christ atones for the sins of both gentiles and Jews, although not in the same way.

To conclude, if Christianity and Judaism become friends, it not only would address some theological issues within each tradition but their friendship would also stand as a beacon to all communities at enmity with one another to the effect that from blood and tears can flow a genuinely new creation that that radical Jew, Paul, envisioned: a new creation, a community of former enemies entrusted with the ministry of reconciliation to be broadcast to the ends of the earth.

## Bibliography

Augustine. 1958/397. *To Simplician—on Various Questions*. Book 1. Translated by J. H. S. Burleigh. In *Augustine: Earlier Writings*, edited by J. H. S. Burleigh, pp. 370-406. Philadelphia: Westminster.

Augustine. 1997. Sermon 159B. Translated by E. Hill. In *Sermons Discovered Since 1990*, edited by F. Dolbeau, vol. III/11, pp. 146-63. Hyde Park, NY: New City Press.

Augustine. 2001. Expositions 1 & 2 of Psalm 58. In *Expositions of the Psalms: 51-72*, edited by John E. Rotelle, OSB. *Works of Saint Augustine: A Translation for the 21st Century*, vol. 3/17, pp. 148-77. Hyde Park, NY: New City Press.

*Augustine. 2007. Answer to Faustus, a Manichean. Translated by R. Teske. Works of Saint Augustine: A Translation for the 21st Century, vol. 1/20. Hyde Park, NY: New City Press.*

Birnbaum, P., ed. 1949. *Daily Prayer Book*. New York: Hebrew Publishing Company.

Byassee, J. 2007. *Praise Seeking Understanding: Reading the Psalms with Augustine*. Grand Rapids: Eerdmans.

Charry, E. T. 2012. "Rebekah's Twins: Augustine on Election in Genesis." In *Genesis and Christian Theology*, edited by Nathan MacDonald, Mark W. Elliott, and Grant Macaskill, pp. 267–86. Grand Rapids: Eerdmans.

Cicero. 1967. *On Old Age, On Friendship*. Translated by H. G. Edinger. Indianapolis: Bobbs-Merrill.

Cowan, C. 2010. "Context Is Everything: 'The Israel of God' in Galatians 6:16." *Southern Baptist Journal of Theology* 14 (3): 78–85.

Davies, W. D. 1955. *Paul and Rabbinic Judaism*. London: SPCK.

Dunn, J. D. G. 2008. *The New Perspective on Paul*. Rev. ed. Grand Rapids: Eerdmans.

Fischer, L. 2014. "Karl Barth's letter to Friedrich-Wilhelm Marquardt (5 September 1967): 'I am decidedly not a philosemite.'" Jewish/Non-Jewish Relations: Between Exclusion and Embrace (an online teaching resource). https://jnjr.div.ed.ac.uk/primary-sources/contemporary/karl-barths-letter-to-friedrich-wilhelm-marquardt-5-september-1967-i-am-decidedly-not-a-philosemite/

Fredriksen, P. 2008. *Augustine and the Jews: A Christian Defense of Jews and Judaism*. New York: Doubleday.

Gager, J. G. 1983. *The Origins of Anti-Semitism: Attitudes toward Judaism in Pagan and Christian Antiquity*. New York: Oxford University Press.

Gaston, L. 1987. *Paul and the Torah*. Vancouver: University of British Columbia Press.

Gerdmar, A. 2009. *Roots of Theological Anti-Semitism: German Biblical Interpretation and the Jews, from Herder and Semler to Kittel and Bultmann*. Leiden and Boston: Brill.

Harlow, J., ed. 1972. *Makhzor for Rosh Hashanah and Yom Kippur: A Prayer Book for the Days of Awe*. New York: Rabbinical Assembly.

Hood, J. Y. B. 1995. *Aquinas and the Jews*. Philadelphia: University of Pennsylvania Press.

Keck, L. E. 1993. "Paul as Thinker." *Interpretation*, 47 (1): 27–38.

Rievaulx, A. O. 1993. "Selections from *On Spiritual Friendship*." Translated by P. Matarasso. In *Cistercian World: Monastic Writings of the Twelfth Century*, edited by P. Matarasso, pp. 169–90. London: Penguin Books.

Sanders, E. P. 1977. *Paul and Palestinian Judaism: A Comparison of Patterns of Religion*. Philadelphia: Fortress.

———. 1985. *Paul, the Law, and the Jewish People*. Philadelphia: Fortress.

Soulen, R. K. 1997. "Karl Barth and the Future of the God of Israel." *Pro Ecclesia* 6 (4): 413–28.

Stendahl, K. 1963. "The Apostle Paul and the Introspective Conscience of the West." *Harvard Theological Review* 56: 199–215.

Stowers, S. 1994. *Rereading Romans*. New Haven: Yale University Press.

Watson, F. 2007. *Paul, Judaism, and the Gentiles: Beyond the New Perspective*. Rev. and expanded ed. Grand Rapids: Eerdmans.

Wright, N. T. 2005. *Paul: In Fresh Perspective*. Minneapolis: Fortress.

APPENDIX
# *Dabru Emet*

A Jewish Statement on Christians and Christianity

The Jewish-Christian relationship has, throughout its history, been a turbulent one. Recognizing the growing degree of acceptance and tolerance on the part of Christians toward Jews, leaders of the Jewish community felt that these positive changes deserved a public and considered response. Published in 2000 as a full-page spread in the *New York Times,* the *Baltimore Sun,* and other newspapers, *Dabru Emet* sought to put on public record the most current Jewish perspectives on Christianity.

**Jews and Christians worship the same God.**

Before the rise of Christianity, Jews were the only worshippers of the God of Israel. But Christians also worship the God of Abraham, Isaac, and Jacob; creator of heaven and earth. While Christian worship is not a viable religious choice for Jews, as Jewish theologians we rejoice that, through Christianity, hundreds of millions of people have entered into relationship with the God of Israel.

**Jews and Christians seek authority from the same book—the Bible (what Jews call "Tanakh" and Christians call the "Old Testament").**

Turning to it for religious orientation, spiritual enrichment, and communal education, we each take away similar lessons: God created and sustains the universe; God established a covenant with the people Israel, God's revealed word guides Israel to a life of righteousness; and God will ultimately redeem Israel and the whole world. Yet, Jews and Christians interpret the Bible differently on many points. Such differences must always be respected.

**Christians can respect the claim of the Jewish people upon the land of Israel.**

The most important event for Jews since the Holocaust has been the re-establishment of a Jewish state in the Promised Land. As members of a biblically based religion, Christians appreciate that Israel was promised—and given—to Jews as the physical center of the covenant between them and God. Many Christians support the State of Israel for reasons far more profound than mere politics. As Jews, we applaud this support. We also recognize that Jewish tradition mandates justice for all non-Jews who reside in a Jewish state.

**Jews and Christians accept the moral principles of Torah.**

Central to the moral principles of Torah is the inalienable sanctity and dignity of every human being. All of us were created in the image of God. This shared moral emphasis can be the basis of an improved relationship between our two communities. It can also be the basis of a powerful witness to all humanity for improving the lives of our fellow human beings and for standing against the immoralities and idolatries that harm and degrade us. Such witness is especially needed after the unprecedented horrors of the past century.

**Nazism was not a Christian phenomenon.**

Without the long history of Christian anti-Judaism and Christian violence against Jews, Nazi ideology could not have taken hold nor could it have been carried out. Too many Christians participated in, or were sympathetic to, Nazi atrocities against Jews. Other Christians did not protest sufficiently against these atrocities. But Nazism itself was not an inevitable outcome of Christianity. If the Nazi extermination of the Jews had been fully successful, it would have turned its murderous rage more directly to Christians. We recognize with gratitude those Christians who risked or sacrificed their lives to save Jews during the Nazi regime. With that in mind, we encourage the continuation of recent efforts in Christian theology to repudiate unequivocally contempt of Judaism and the Jewish people. We applaud those Christians who reject this teaching of contempt, and we do not blame them for the sins committed by their ancestors.

**The humanly irreconcilable difference between Jews and Christians will not be settled until God redeems the entire world as promised in Scripture.**

Christians know and serve God through Jesus Christ and the Christian tradition. Jews know and serve God through Torah and the Jewish tradition. That difference will not be settled by one community insisting that it has interpreted Scripture more accurately than the other; nor by exercising political power over the other. Jews can respect Christians' faithfulness to their revelation just as we expect Christians to respect our faithfulness to our revelation. Neither Jew nor Christian should be pressed into affirming the teaching of the other community.

**A new relationship between Jews and Christians will not weaken Jewish practice.**

An improved relationship will not accelerate the cultural and religious assimilation that Jews rightly fear. It will not change traditional Jewish forms of worship, nor increase intermarriage between Jews and non-Jews, nor persuade more Jews to convert to Christianity, nor create a false blending of Judaism and Christianity. We respect Christianity as a faith that originated within Judaism and that still has significant contacts with it. We do not see it as an extension of Judaism. Only if we cherish our own traditions can we pursue this relationship with integrity.

**Jews and Christians must work together for justice and peace.**

Jews and Christians, each in their own way, recognize the unredeemed state of the world as reflected in the persistence of persecution, poverty, and human degradation and misery. Although justice and peace are finally

APPENDIX

God's, our joint efforts, together with those of other faith communities, will help bring the kingdom of God for which we hope and long. Separately and together, we must work to bring justice and peace to our world. In this enterprise, we are guided by the vision of the prophets of Israel:

> It shall come to pass in the end of days that the mountain of the Lord's house shall be established at the top of the mountains and be exalted above the hills, and the nations shall flow unto it . . . and many peoples shall go and say, "Come ye and let us go up to the mountain of the Lord to the house of the God of Jacob and He will teach us of His ways and we will walk in his paths." (Isaiah 2:2–3)

TIKVA FRYMER-KENSKY,
*University of Chicago*

DAVID NOVAK,
*University of Toronto*

PETER OCHS,
*University of Virginia*

MICHAEL SIGNER,
*University of Notre Dame*

*Contributors*

**David Novak** holds the J. Richard and Dorothy Shiff Chair of Jewish Studies as Professor of Religion and Philosophy in the University of Toronto. He is the distinguished 2017 Gifford Lecturer. Among his many books are *The Election of Israel: The Idea of the Chosen People* (Cambridge University Press, 1996) and *Talking with Christians* (Eerdmans, 2005).

**Eberhard Busch** served as Karl Barth's assistant and for thirty years as Professor of Systematic Theology in Göttingen. His many books include *Karl Barth: His Life from Letters and Autobiographical Texts* (Fortress, 1976) and *Karl Barth and the Pietists* (InterVarsity, 2004). He is internationally esteemed as the dean of Barth studies.

**George Hunsinger** is McCord Professor of Systematic Theology at Princeton Theological Seminary. He was the 2010 recipient of the Karl Barth Prize awarded by the Union of Evangelical Churches in Germany. Among his books are *How to Read Karl Barth: The Shape of His Theology* (Oxford University Press, 1991), *Reading Barth with Charity* (Baker Academic, 2015), and *The Beatitudes* (Paulist, 2015). In 2006 he founded the National Religious Campaign against Torture.

**Peter Ochs** holds the Edgar M. Bronfman Chair of Modern Judaic Studies at the University of Virginia. He is a leading exponent of the Scriptural Reasoning movement. Among his many works are *Another Reformation: Postliberal Christianity and the Jews* (Brazos, 2011) and *Peirce, Pragmatism, and the Logic of Scripture* (Cambridge University Press, 1998).

CONTRIBUTORS

**Victoria J. Barnett** is director of the Programs on Ethics, Religion, and the Holocaust at the United States Holocaust Memorial Museum. She is a general editor of Dietrich Bonhoeffer Works, the English translation series of Bonhoeffer's complete works published by Fortress Press. Her books include *Bystanders: Conscience and Complicity during the Holocaust* (Praeger, 1999) and *For the Soul of the People: Protestant Protest against Hitler* (Oxford University Press, 1992).

**Thomas F. Torrance** (1913–2007), who studied with Karl Barth, was arguably the greatest twentieth-century dogmatic theologian in the English-speaking world. He served for twenty-seven years as Professor of Christian Dogmatics at New College in the University of Edinburgh. Among his numerous books are *Karl Barth: Biblical and Evangelical Theologian* (T. & T. Clark, 1990) and *The Trinitarian Faith: The Evangelical Theology of the Ancient Catholic Church* (T. & T. Clark, 1988).

**C. E. B. Cranfield** (1915–2015) taught New Testament for thirty years at the University of Durham. He is the author of several well-received commentaries, including his massive two-volume commentary on Romans for the International Critical Commentary series (T. & T. Clark, 2000).

**Hans Küng** is an internationally acclaimed Swiss Catholic priest, theologian, and author. Among his many honors, he received the international Karl Barth Prize in 1992. A prolific author, his first book rocked the ecumenical world by locating a number of areas of agreement in the doctrine of justification between Karl Barth and the Roman Catholic Church. He concluded that the differences were not fundamental and did not warrant a division in the church. *Justification: The Doctrine of Karl Barth and a Catholic Reflection* (New York: Nelson, 1964). The volume includes a letter from Barth saying that Küng has understood him correctly.

**Ellen T. Charry** is the Margaret W. Harmon Professor of Systematic Theology at Princeton Theological Seminary, emerita. Her current research undertakes a thorough reconstruction of the theological relationship between Judaism and Christianity, currently entitled *For God's Sake: The Wall of Hostility Has Come Down*. Among her many books is *Psalms 1–50: Sighs and Songs of Israel* (Brazos, 2015).

# Acknowledgments

Cranfield, C. E. B. "Light from St. Paul on Christian-Jewish Relations." In *The Witness of the Jews to God*, edited by David W. Torrance, 22–31. Edinburgh: Handsel Press, 1982.

Hunsinger, George. "After Barth: A Christian Appreciation of Jews and Judaism." *Pro Ecclesia* 24, no. 3 (2015): 390–402.

Küng, Hans. "From Anti-Semitism to Theological Dialogue." In *Christians and Jews*, edited by Hans Küng and Walter Kasper, 9–16. New York: Seabury Press, 1975.

Torrance, Thomas F. "The Divine Vocation and Destiny of Israel in World History." In *The Witness of the Jews to God*, edited by David W. Torrance, 85–104. Edinburgh: Handsel Press, 1982.

# Index

Aaron, 21, 39
Abraham, 25, 152, 153; and the imitation of God's justice, 11; sickness of, 12
*Adam* ("the man"), 6–7, 6n13
Adam-Christ dichotomy, 161
*Agape and Eros* (Nygren), 16n54
Althaus, Paul, 115
Amitiés judéo-chrétiennes, 106
Anderson, Raymond, 83, 90, 95n22
*Another Reformation: Postliberal Christianity and the Jews* (Ochs), 81
*Anselm: Fides Quaerens Intellectum; Anselm's Proof of the Existence of God in the Context of His Theological Scheme* (Barth), 95n22
*Answer to Faustus* (Augustine), 155–58
anti-evangelicalism, 66
anti-Judaism, 66
anti-Semitism, 27, 60, 63, 112, 113; Christian anti-Semitism, 61, 107, 114, 123, 141; in the Middle Ages, 157–58; Nazi anti-Semitism, 141; in postwar Europe, 101–3, 105; psychological motives operative in, 141–42; rise of in Germany, 104; as a sin against the Holy Spirit, 72; as treachery toward Jesus himself, 142
Aquinas. *See* Thomas Aquinas
Aristotle, 14; on God as the highest good, 20, 20n73
"Atheistic Theology" (Rosenzweig), 24

Augustine, 17n56, 66, 160, 164; comments on Psalm 59, 156; on the distinction between *signa data* and *signa naturalia*, 89; on the doctrine of election, 155, 158–59; proto-Israelology of, 154–59; on punishment as an act of caring or kindness, 158n6
Auschwitz Protocol, 109
*avodah zarah* ("strange worship"), 46

Baeck, Leo, 25, 105, 143
baptism, 36; Jewish baptism (*t'vilah*), 168; sacramental baptism, 169. *See also* Jesus Christ, baptism of
Barmen Declaration (1934), 27, 112–13, 115
Barth, Karl, 46; accusations against of being a warmonger, 108–9; on the "awakening from above," 15, 16; on baptism, 36; commentary on Job, 84–85; criticism of Augustine on the question of the God-human relationship, 17n56; criticism of the law being divorced from the gospel, 28; on "dead Israel," 161; and the doctrine of the one twofold people of God, 63, 97; on free grace, 34; on God as a necessary object of human speech, 88; the idea of "covenant" as a central feature of his theology, 26, 31, 32, 161; on the irrevocability of God's cov-

enant with Israel, 62, 63; on "Israel forgetfulness," 161; Israelology of, 160–64; on Jesus as both Lord and servant, 162; on Jews and Judaism as the object of his thought, 1–2; on knowing God, 91–92; on the location of both election and rejection within a covenant framework, 161–62; monetary support of the state of Israel by, 36; as neither anti-Jewish nor anti-Semitic, 2n2; opposition of to Nazi Germany, 108–9; rejection of "natural theology" by, 4n9, 49–50; rejection of the theory of "orders" (created orders of God) by, 29–30; reparative inquiry of, 82–83; retrieval of metaphysics from its abandonment by modern philosophers by, 22–23; saving of Jews during World War II by, 50–51; sermons of at the church in Bonn, 35; on supersessionism as a Christian form of anti-Semitism, 27; support of for rescue networks in Nazi Germany, 109; Tambach lecture of (1919), 25; on theory versus praxis, 10n28; on the Torah, 31. *See also* Barth, Karl, and the rabbinic tradition; Barth, Karl, postwar interfaith encounters of; Barth, Karl, relationship of with Jews; New Testament, Barth's view of

Barth, Karl, and the rabbinic tradition, 5–12; and the interpretation of Micah 6:8, 6–12, 14

Barth, Karl, postwar interfaith encounters of, 103–17 *passim*; attendance of at CIMADE (Comité inter-mouvements auprès des évacués) organization meeting, 110; attendance of at the Seelisberg meeting, 105, 108–9; discussions between Barth and the Emunah group, 111–12, 116; reasons for Barth's invitation to Seelisberg, 108, 115

Barth, Karl, relationship of with Jews, 1–2, 24–26, 81, 116, 117; on anti-Semitism as a sin against the Holy Spirit, 72; and assessment of the synagogue, 33–36; attitudes of Barth toward Judaism, 112–13; discouragement of Christian missions to Jews by, 64–65, 163–64; on Jesus as the bridge between Christians and Jews, 35; on the Jewish form of the covenant as "passing away," 161, 162; on Jews remaining elected by God, 34; and reflections on the law, 29–33; on the suffering of the Jews, 72

Barth, Markus, 51

Barthians, 80–81; ability of to say "no," 83–84; on the good news of Scripture, 90–91; postliberal Barthians, 81n6; virtues of, 83. *See also* Barthians, illustrations of Barthian "no-saying"

Barthians, illustrations of Barthian "no-saying": saying no to natural theology, 88–90; saying no to those treating all inquiry as reparative, 85–87; saying no to those treating all language and inquiry as conventional, 84–85; saying no to those treating one single method of reparative inquiry as if it applies to all conditions of disrepair (dogmatic dogmatism), 87–88

*Barth's Table Talk* (Barth and Godsey), 90

Beit Hillel, 92n20

Beit Shammai, 92n20

Ben-Chorin, Schalom, 145

Berkowitz, Eliezer, 88

Bethel Confession (1933), 29, 30

Bethge, Eberhard, 29

Bible, the, 45, 157; biblical scholarship, 124; polyvalence of biblical texts, 98

Bickel, Erich, 108

Bloch, Ernst, 143

Bonhoeffer, Dietrich, 28, 29, 114, 115–16

"border crossers," 107

# INDEX

British Council of Christians and Jews, 103
Brod, Max, 143
Brunner, Emil, 109
Buber, Martin, 16n54, 31, 32–33, 39, 127, 143, 144, 145; on "thinking with the eyes," 124
Busch, Eberhard, 111n30, 112; on Barth's double negative, 86; on Barth's interpretation of revelation, 87. *See also* Busch, Eberhard, dialogue with David Novak and George Hunsinger
Busch, Eberhard, dialogue with David Novak and George Hunsinger, 37–59 *passim*; appreciation of Barth, 53–54; debate concerning true religions, 40–43; on the gospel as divine revelation, 44–45; on the impact of the Holocaust, 57–58; on Jews as the chosen people of God, 37–40; on the uniqueness of the Holocaust, 56; view of natural theology, 48–49; on what Christians and Jews can learn from each other, 50–51

Caiaphas, 169
Cain, 152, 155, 157, 169
Calvin, John, 26, 44, 58, 160; on the need for the Holy Spirit, 45; on *sensus divinitatis*, 4
Calvinists, 58; Dutch Calvinists, 59
Canaanites, 32
Cartesianism, 84
Catalano, Rosann, 75
Catholicism: Eastern Catholics, 64; Nicene Catholics, 64; Reformational Catholics, 64; Roman Catholics, 64. *See also* Second Vatican Council
Chagall, Marc, 145
Chamberlain, Houston Stewart, 141
Charry, Ellen, 64n3
Christianity, 5, 26, 28, 42–43, 47, 68, 77, 78, 80, 96, 138, 142, 157; anti-Judaic Christianity, 60, 141; early Christianity, 66–67; eschatology of, 167n9; ethnocentric versions of, 115; in Europe, 48; gift of to Judaism, 167–68; Jewish converts to, 107, 175; Jewish perceptions of, 94; Jewish roots of, 106, 115; Nicene Christianity, 62, 64; relationship with Judaism, 110, 111–12, 116, 117, 122–23, 139, 151 (*see also* Paul, implications of his teachings for Christian-Jewish relations); solidarity with Jews, 61, 62, 65; as theological partners with Jews, 147–48
*Christianity in Jewish Terms* (Frymer-Kensky, Novak, Ochs, Sandmel, and Signer), 96, 97
Christians, 25, 70, 101; as "children of the living God," 35; enmity/schism between Christians and Jews, 119, 139, 143–44; factions among, 63–64; gentile Christians, 135, 139, 169; inseparable bond with Jews, 27, 35, 119; Jewish belief that Christians are guilty of idolatry, 47–48; "non-Aryan" Christians, 109; as not replacing Jews in God's covenant, 31; openness to the Old Testament's autonomy, 142–43; and the "teaching of contempt" for Jews, 106; and the threat of Marcionism, 5. *See also* Christians, lessons to be learned from Israel; Torah, the, studying of by Jews and Christians together
Christians, lessons to be learned from Israel: Israel can help us understand the atonement, 124–27; Israel can help us understand the interaction of God with the world, 127; Israel can help us understand Jesus, 123–24
Christology, and engagement with the Old Testament, 137
*Church Dogmatics* (Barth), 5, 14, 31, 83, 90; pattern of argumentation in, 99
"Church and the Jewish Question, The" (Barth), 28–29
Cicero, on friendship, 148, 149
CIMADE (Comité inter-mouvements auprès des évacués) organization, 110

## Index

Clinchy, Everett, and the organization of the Seelisberg meeting, 103–5
Coccejus, Johannes, 26
Cohen, Arthur, 114; on the de-Judaizing of Christian theology, 114
Cohen, Hermann, 6n11, 22, 143
Cohn, Emil, 28, 31
Council of Christians and Jews: British, 103; German, 106; Swiss, 105, 108

*Dabru Emet* (Novak, Ochs, Kensky, and Signer), 46–47, 94; arguments for reading of as reparative inquiry, 94–95, 101; Barthian readings of, 95; content of that is guided by the Word, 95–96; and the love of Torah / the Old Testament, 101–2; original statement of, 75–76; origins of and primary motivation for, 77–80; reaction to from churches in the United States, 79; as a response to crisis, 99–100; response to from the Jewish public in the United States, 79–10; scholarly attention given to, 79; on sharing the Word in Jewish-Christian dialogue, 97–98; text of the Jewish Statement on Christians and Christianity in, 173–76; worldly and religious issues addressed by, 96–97
Day of Atonement, 125, 169, 170
Declaration of the Rights of Man, 140
Demann, Paul, 106
*Der Vormarsch (The Forward Advance)*, 28
dialogue, as our common speaking of the *logos*, 2–3
Dietrich, Suzanne de, 110
*dinim* (the communal obligation to set up courts of law), 11n30
dogmatics, 54n6
dogmatism, 90; dogmatic dogmatism, 87–88
dualism, Hegelian, 160–61
duty, 7–8, 8n17

*ecclesia*: Christian *ecclesia*, 123, 126; Jewish *ecclesia*, 123, 126
Eckardt, Alice, 76
Ehrlich, Ernst Ludwig, 106
Einstein, Albert, 124, 143
election, doctrine of, 155, 158–59, 160, 162
Eliot, T. S., 11
Enlightenment, the, 140
Episcopalians, 52
*eros*, divine, 15–18, 15–16n53, 16n54
*Eros*, human, 16n54; and the difference between erotic desire and lustful desire, 16–17n55
Esau, 152, 158–59
Estonia, 113

faith, 33, 125; in Christ's atoning death, 169–70; framework of, 28
Faith and Order Commission of the National Council of Churches, 76–77
"First Commandment as a Theological Axiom" (Barth), 27
Flusser, David, 145
Ford, David, 81, 84
foundationalism, 84
freedom, divine, 37, 85
*Freedom and Law* (Rashkover), 85
Frei, Hans, 81
*Freiburger Rundbrief*, 106, 111
Freud, Sigmund, 143
Freudenberg, Adolf, 105, 108, 109
French Protestants, 58, 110
French Revolution, 140
friendship, 148–50, 166–67; Cicero's definition of, 148, 149; long-term friendship, 148–49
*From Enemy to Brother* (Connelly), 107
Frymer-Kensky, Tikva, 46, 75

*gemilut hasadim* ("acts of loving kindness"), 11–12
gentiles, 3, 25, 66, 70; gentile Christians, 135, 139, 169; need of for Jesus, 169–70; salvation of, 156, 159
German Protestants (*Deutsche Chris-*

183

INDEX

*ten*), 27, 28, 56, 114–15; identification of the law with the decrees of the German government, 30; root failure of German Protestant theology, 30
Germany, Nazi, 30, 83, 103, 108, 109, 114, 141
Gobineau, Arthur, 141
God, 8, 61, 65; claim of on humans, 14; as Creator God, 89; and the death of Jesus, 159–60; desire of for humans, 15–16; divine faithfulness of, 121; God's election of his people Israel, 10, 14; God's love, 10 (*see also* God, covenantal love of); grace of, 20, 34, 170; hiddenness of, 86, 88; imitation of, 11, 12; as limited, 165; mercy of, 158–59; partnering with God's name, 87–88; pleasure and displeasure of, 21, 21n76; recognition of the name "God," 4n9; redeeming work/purpose of, 88, 118; relationship with humanity, 49, 71, 118; as the same in the Old and New Testaments, 48; truthfulness of, 35; will of, 30, 92n20, 119, 159. *See also* God, acknowledging the commands of; God, covenantal love of
God, acknowledging the commands of: through the way of *haggadah*, 9–10; through the way of *halakha* (the commandments of God represented as law), 8–9
God, covenantal love of, 70–74; the inseparability of God's love for Israel and for Jesus, 71–72; and the universality of God's love, 70–71
*God in Search of Man* (Heschel), 15
"Gospel in the Present Time, The" (Barth), 34
Green, Garret, 81
Greene-McCreight, Kathryn, 98
Gregg, Tom, on Barth's "theology against religion," 85–86
"Guilt of the Others, The" (Thielicke and Diem), 56

Halivni, David Weiss, 91; on the difference between Beit Hillel and Beit Shammai, 92n20
Hardy, Daniel, 81
Harnack, Adolf von, 26
Hauerwas, Stanley, 81
Herrmann, Wilhelm, 6n11
Herzl, Theodor, 144
Heschel, Joshua, 15
Hildebrand, Dietrich von, 110
Hirsch, Emanuel, 115
Hitler, Adolf, 28, 55
Hobbes, Thomas, on the state of war (*bellum omnium contra omnes*), 8
Holocaust, the, 106; Christian complicity in, 112, 113; Christian enmity toward Jews leading to, 69; demographics of, 113; discussion concerning the uniqueness of, 55–57; impact of, 55–58
Holy Spirit, the, 45, 72, 128
Hromádka, Josef, 108
Humanism, 140; radical humanism, 84
Humility, 88, 131; divine humility, 12–13
Hunsinger, George, 81; on Barth's understanding of church doctrine, 98; on "grounding," 98–99; on Jews and Christians as one indivisible people of God, 97–98. *See also* Hunsinger, George, dialogue with David Novak and Eberhard Busch
Hunsinger, George, dialogue with David Novak and Eberhard Busch, 37–59 *passim*
Husserl, Edmund, 43
Hutchins, Robert, 51

iconography, Christian, 72
idolatry, 65; gentile idolatry, 45–46; Jewish belief that Christians are guilty of idolatry, 47–48. See also *abodah zarah* ("strange worship")
inquiry: conventional inquiry, 82, 83, 90–91; reparative inquiry, 82–83, 85–87, 90–91, 94

Institute of Christian and Jewish Studies (ICJS), 75, 77, 97
International Conference of Christians and Jews, 103
interreligious dialogue, process of, 116–17
Iron Guard, the, 113
Isaac, 25, 152
Isaac, Jules, 105, 106
Islam, 5, 41, 47, 139, 142, 166
Israel: creation of as a national unit because of the covenant with God, 32; hardening of, 66, 151; irrevocability of God's covenant with, 62, 63; the "Israel of God," 151–52, 151n3; the "New Israel," 141; response of to God's loving election, 11, 14, 34; revival of the state of, 141. *See also* Christians, lessons to be learned from Israel; Israel, divine vocation and destiny of; Thieme, Karl, on the old and the new Israel
Israel, divine vocation and destiny of, 118–19; Israel as the only people with messianic promise, 121–22; Israel as the unique partner of divine revelation, 120–21; Israel's place in salvation history, 119; Israel's place in the consummation of all things, 122–23
Israelology, Christian, 148, 150–51, 150n2; Augustine's proto-Israelology, 154–59; Paul's Israelology, 151–54

Jacob, 20, 25, 50, 152, 158–59, 173
Jenson, Robert, 81
*Jesus and Israel* (Isaac), 106
Jesus Christ, 27, 46, 66, 69, 98, 112, 131; Aryanization of, 161; atonement of sins through Jesus's death, 169–70; baptism of, 126; bond of with the Jews in covenantal love, 71–72, 72–73, 121, 132; as both Lord and servant, 162; as the bridge between Christians and Jews, 35; and the coming world community (*oikoumene*), 118; crucifixion of, 121, 127, 157; full participation of in the suffering of the Jews, 73–74; gospel of, 138; Jewish-Christian dialogue concerning, 144–46; Jewishness of, 110, 138–39, 142; love of, 60; love of and for, 62; parousia of, 135; reign of in peace, 127; relationship of with the Father and with God's children, 70–71; resurrection of, 100, 110; as the "Suffering Servant," 125–26; understanding of through lessons learned from Israel, 123–24
Jewish Christian community, possibility of, 68n9
Jewish diaspora, 169
*Jewish Faith in Our Time* (Schoeps), 31
"Jewish Question and Its Christian Answer, The" (Barth), 111, 111n30
"Jewish Statement on Christians and Christianity, A" (Novak et al.), 75–76; primary statements of, 76
Jews, 77–78, 109; as "children of the living God," 35; choosing of God by the Jews, 38; as the chosen people of God, 37–39; enmity/schism between Christians and Jews, 119, 139, 143–44; identification of the cross with marauding crusaders, 78n3; Jewish belief that Christians are guilty of idolatry, 47–48; Jewish-Christian relationship, 110, 111–12, 116, 117, 122–23, 139; and the mystery of the Jews' rejection of Jesus as the Messiah, 66; salvation of, 130, 132, 135, 141; as *Stamm Abrahams*, 111; sufferings of, 126–27, 140–41; as theological partners with Christians, 147–48; transfer of Jews from Hungary to concentration camps by the German army, 35–36; as witnesses to God's election, 34. *See also* Barth, Karl, relationship of with Jews
Job, 84–85
John the Baptist, Gruenewald painting of, 25

185

INDEX

Joseph, and Potiphar's wife, 17–18
*Joseph and His Brothers* (Mann), 17
Judaeophilia, 69, 71
Judaism, 5, 26, 65, 80; Christian polemics against, 154–55; eschatology of, 167n9; factions among, 63–64; gift of to Christianity, 168–70; medieval Judaism, 45, 46; messianic Judaism, 68, 68n8; relationship of with Christianity, 110, 111–12, 116, 117, 122–23, 139, 151 (*see also* Paul, implications of his teachings for Christian-Jewish relations); spiritual situation of, 143; teaching of concerning gentiles, 3. *See also* theology, Jewish theology of "the other"
Justice, 6, 8–9, 10, 76, 87, 88, 143, 158; commitment to, 61; divine justice, 11, 12–13, 19; pursuit of, 19

kabbalistic thought, and the "awakening from below," 15–16
Kafka, Franz, 143
Kaufmann, Franz, 110
Kaufmann group, 109–10
*Kingship of God* (Buber), 31, 32, 33
*Kirchenkampf* (church struggle), 114, 115
*Kirchtentag* meetings, 106
Klausner, Joseph, 144
Kurz, Gertrud, 108

Language: change in a society's language system, 82; "language use in times of nonpeace," 82; "language use in times of peace," 81–82
Latvia, 113
lawgiving, divine, 85
Le Chambon-sur-Lignon, 58, 62, 65
Leighton, Chris, 75
Lindbeck, George, 81, 98
Lindsay, Mark, 88
Lithuania, 113
love: elective love, 10; selective love, 10. *See also* God, covenantal love of
Luckner, Gertrud, 105, 106
Luther, Martin, 161

Macmurray, John, 127
Maimonides, Moses, 3, 3n8, 9; on the commandment "You shall love your neighbor as yourself," 11–12; on describing what God does compared to what God is, 20–21, 87; on human reason, 8; on Scripture-based "dialogue," 4
Manichaeism, 147, 148, 158, 159; Manichaean dualism, 160
Mann, Thomas, 17–18, 17n57
Mantello, George, 109
Marcionism, 5, 147–48, 148n1, 156
Maritain, Jacques, 105, 110
Marquardt, Friedrich-Wilhelm, 106
Marshall, Bruce, 65
McCormack, Bruce, 81, 97, 99–100
McKeon, Richard, 51
Merz, Georg, 28
Micah 6:8, interpretation of by Barth and in the rabbinic tradition, 6–12, 22
Middle Ages, 45, 140, 141, 155, 157–58
midrashim, 9
monotheism, 46, 47, 139
Montefiore, Claude G., 144
Moses, 13, 20, 21, 25, 32, 39, 44, 163

Nahmanides, 13
National Conference of Christians and Jews (NCCJ), 77, 103, 105, 107; primary methodology of, 104
National Religious Campaign Against Torture, 61
National Socialism, 30
Nature, 22, 32, 49–50, 89–90; as the creation of God, 48–49; the "state of nature" (*status naturalis*), 4n9
*New Encounter, The* (Oesterreicher), 110–11
New Testament, 25–26, 112, 120, 141, 142, 143, 146; Barth's view of, 25, 31, 32, 34
Nicene-Constantinopolitan Creed, 64n3
Noachian covenant, 166
*Nostra Aetate*, 106, 110, 111

Novak, David, 61, 75, 80, 90; on partnering with God's name, 87–88. *See also* Novak, David, dialogue of with George Hunsinger and Eberhard Busch

Novak, David, dialogue with George Hunsinger and Eberhard Busch, 37–59 *passim*; appreciation of Barth, 52–53, 54–55; on Christian and Jewish belief in the same God, 45–47; connection of to Barth, 51; debate concerning true religions, 40–43; on Jews as the chosen people of God, 37–40; on the Torah as divine revelation, 43–44; on the uniqueness of the Holocaust, 55–56; view of natural theology, 49–50; on what Christians and Jews can learn from each other, 50–51

Nygren, Anders, 16

Obrecht, Charlie, 75
Ochs, Peter, 46, 75
"Ode to Joy" (Schiller), 49
Oesterreicher, John, 106, 110, 114
Old Testament, 33, 76, 112, 118–19, 136–37, 138, 143, 163, 173–74; Christ and the Old Testament, 132, 134–35; Christology and engagement with the Old Testament, 137; as the First Testament, 38, 57; *leitmotif* of, 37; openness of Christianity to the Old Testament's autonomy, 142–43
"One-Way Bridge, The" (A. Cohen), 114
*On Spiritual Friendship* (Cicero), 149
"Orders." *See* Barth, Karl, rejection of the theory of "orders" (created orders of God) by
Ornstein, Hans, 105, 108
*Our Brother Jesus: The Nazarene from a Jewish Viewpoint* (Ben-Chorin), 145

Palestinians, Arab, 142
partnership, divine, 19–22; "the good" the divine-human partnership is to accomplish, 19–20
*pathos*, divine, 15–16n53
Patmos Circle, 24, 25; and the theology of Barth, 26
Paul, 34, 61, 111, 139, 167n9, 170; on Christ's sacrifice on the cross, 121; and early Christianity, 66–67; on gentiles, 121–22; on the hardening of Israel, 66, 151; Israelology of, 151–54; on "the righteousness of the law" (*dikaiosyne ek nomou*), 28. *See also* Paul, implications of his teachings for Christian-Jewish relations
Paul, implications of his teachings for Christian-Jewish relations: that the belief in Jesus is to believe according to the fullness of the Old Testaments attestation of Christ, 132–33; Christians and Jews are bound together in hope, 134–35; duty of the Christian church to pray for the Jews' salvation, 129–30; failure of the Jews to attain the law of righteousness, 131; failure of the Jews to recognize God's righteousness, 130–31; recognition of the chasm that separates Jews and Christians, 128; recognition of the Jews' zeal for God, 130; recognition that Jews are still Paul's brethren, 128–29; that the salvation of the Jews is a sheer matter of God's mercy, 131–32; self-righteousness and elf-complacency of both Jews and Christians, 134; on the services of Jewish and Christian communities, 135–37; the special guilt of the Jews, 133–34
Philo-Semitism, 60, 69, 71, 72; grounding of in covenantal love, 73
"Philosophical Responses to the Holocaust" (Novak), 57
philosophy, modern, 22–23
Pietism, 140
Pius XII (pope), 104

INDEX

Plato, 14; on God's relationship to the good, 20, 20n73
pluralism, democratic, 103, 104
Poland, 113
punishment, as an act of caring or kindness, 158, 158n6

quantum physics, 124

rabbis, and the reading of Scripture, 5–6
Rabbis for Human Rights, 61
racism, 38, 120
Rashkover, Randi, 80–81, 85; on revelation, 100
reason, 8, 22, 100
Rebecca, 152
Reformation, the, 44, 140, 141
religion, 22; debate concerning true religions, 40–43
*Religion of Reason* (Cohen), 22
*Representative, The* (Hochhuth), 140
revelation, divine, 7, 24, 32–33, 62, 88, 100, 120; Barth's interpretation of, 87; the church's understanding of mediated through Israel, 123; the gospel as divine revelation, 44–45; the Torah as divine revelation, 43–44
Riegner, Gerhard, 105
Romania, 113
Rosenstock, Eugen, 25
Rosenzweig, Franz, 13, 16n54, 24, 143, 160; on the church and the synagogue, 33–34; gift to Barth of a prayer book, 25–26; on Judaism having "no dogmatic structure," 44

Sabbath day, sanctification of (*qiddush*), 8
salvation, 24–26, 120, 122, 123; of gentiles, 156, 159; of Jews, 130, 132, 135, 141; salvation history, 84, 141, 162; subjective experience of, 84; universal salvation, 126, 131, 166
Sandmel, David, 75
Sauvage, Pierre, 59

Schiller, Friedrich, 49
Schleiermacher, Friedrich, 26, 34, 35
Schoeps, Hans-Joachim, 27–28, 31, 143
Scripture (the Word), 119, 134, 167n9. *See also* Scripture (the Word), reception of
Scripture (the Word), reception of; and the commitment to combat Christian anti-Semitism, 107; and the rabbinic distinction between the plain sense (*peshat*) of and the interpreted sense (*derash*) of Scripture, 91–92; the reparative Word and plain sense (*peshat*) reception of, 98; is the Word received when human language is at peace with itself or not at peace? 99–100
Second Temple, destruction of (*Chorban*), 93
Second Vatican Council, 106, 140, 141, 142. See also *Nostra Aetate*
Seelisberg meeting, 103–8; as laying the foundation for post-Holocaust theology and post-Holocaust Christian-Jewish dialogue, 106, 107, 113–14; prominent participants in, 104–5; report of ("The Task of the Churches"), 105; and the "Ten Points of Seelisberg" (Isaac), 105–6
Sherman, Franklin, 76
Signer, Michael, 46–47, 75
Simeon, 169
sin, 133; atonement for through Jesus, 169; confession of, 169
skepticism, radical, 90
Society for Scriptural Reasoning, 97
Song of Songs, as an allegory comparing God's love to the love between a man and woman, 18
Soulen, Kendall, 147
Soviet Union, 113
Spinoza, Baruch, 38, 43
Staewen, Gertrud, 109
Stein, Edith, 143
Strasbourg Cathedral, 34

Study Group on Christian-Jewish Relations, 77
supersessionism: the case for soft supersessionism, 60–70; as a Christian form of anti-Semitism, 27; soft-supersessionism, 68n10, 73; "structural supersessionism," 147
Swiss Reformed Church, 35

Talmud, the, 3, 4, 9
Taubes, Zwi, 108
theology, 79, 80, 116, 155; "crusade theology," 108; de-Judaizing of Christian theology, 114; Jewish theology of "the other," 165–66, 170; postliberal Christian theology, 79. *See also* theology, natural
theology, natural, 4n9, 81; Busch's view of, 48–49; Novak's view of, 49–50; Ochs's view of, 88–90
Thieme, Karl, 106, 110; on the old and the new Israel, 111
Thomas Aquinas, 8; on the Jews, 159–60
Thurneysen, Eduard, 108
"Time of Expectation" (Barth), 31
"Time of Recollection" (Barth), 31
Tito, Josef, 113
Torah, the, 1, 2, 4–5, 31, 39, 80, 88, 125, 138; as divine revelation, 43–44; God's giving of the Torah (*mattan torah*), 14; Israel's reception of the Torah (*qabbalat ha-torah*), 14–15; revelation of on Sinai (*mattan torah*), 92; studying of by Jews and Christians together, 3n8; Torah observance, 67, 68; the written Torah (Hebrew Scriptures, the Old Testament), 3, 4n10

Torah Min-Hashamayim, 44
*torah qua* "teaching," 9, 9n25
*To Simplician* (Augustine), 158
*Tractatus adversus Judaeos* (Augustine), 154–55
Trocmé, André, 58, 62

UNESCO (United Nations Educational, Scientific and Cultural Organization), 103

Vatican II. *See* Second Vatican Council
Visser 't Hooft, Wilhelm, 108, 109
Visseur, Pierre, 108
Vogt, Paul, 50–51, 105, 109
*Volk*, the, 29; secular orders of, 27

Weapons of the Spirit (1987), 58–59
Weil, Simone, 143
Weiße Rose, 55
Wellhausen, Julius, 43
Westminster Shorter Catechism, 162
"what is good" (*mah tov*), 13–15
Whitehead, Alfred North, 50
Wittgenstein, Ludwig, 68n10
World Council of Churches, 140
Wyschogrod, Michael, 52, 80

xenophobia, 165n8, 170

Yohanan bar Nappaha, 88
Yom Kippur, 125; liturgies of, 170
Yugoslavia, 113

Zaiman, Joel, 75
*Zohar*, the, 15n50
Zophar, 84

www.ingramcontent.com/pod-product-compliance
Lightning Source LLC
Chambersburg PA
CBHW030112010526
44116CB00005B/208